AFTER ...
Joan's Story

Leslie Johnson

AFTER … Joan’s Story

AFTER … Joan’s Story

PUBLISHED BY:

Leslie Johnson

Ebook ISBN 978-1-9685630-0-4
Paperback ISBN 978-1-0693588-8-2
Hardcover ISBN 978-1-0693588-9-9

AFTER … Joan's Story

This book is a work of fiction. Names, characters, organizations and events portrayed in this novel are either products of the author's imagination or are used fictitiously. References to real people, events, establishments, organizations or locations are intended only to provide a sense of authenticity and are used fictitiously. Any resemblance to actual events, places and organizations or persons, living or dead, is entirely coincidental.

The publisher does not have any control over or any responsibility for any author or third-party websites referred to in or on this book.

DEDICATION

This book is dedicated to my mom.

AFTER … Joan's Story

ACKNOWLEDGMENTS

The writing of AFTER … Joan’s Story has been a long journey. It has been grueling and time consuming, inspiring and gratifying all at the same time. Written words are such brilliant ways to express one’s thoughts and feelings and to learn to understand what goes on inside.

I want to thank my original writing pals who joined me on weekend mornings to work on their projects, while I wrote this book. Brock and Shannon, I still miss those days. They were adventures into storytelling, laughter and troubleshooting the issues that slowed the writing process.

Here’s a shout out to my writing group, The River Bottom Writers. You listened to my chapters and provided valuable feedback. I will always be indebted to all of you. Ken, thanks for being the first to read the entire manuscript and for telling me that I had created something worthy of publication.

I also send much gratitude to Shirley Fleming for reading the book and for providing valuable insight into relationships. Your wisdom was needed to make this book more solid and more believable. Thanks to Jacquie Van Waardhuizen for beta reading and giving me valuable feedback.

Finally, I would like to thank my editor, Jonas Saul for reading and editing my words to make them stronger and more powerful. You came into my life at exactly the right moment, and you have been encouraging and helpful with your insight into the writing process and your feedback. Thank you, thank you, thank you.

CHAPTER ONE

Leah rushed ahead of me through the back door of the house, swinging a paper bag from Classy Miss. Jonathon and Debbie's wedding was only two weeks away. My daughter and I had been shopping for a month, and now she finally had what she wanted. A perky little pink dress that I thought was a little too revealing, but she insisted it was what all the girls her age were wearing. The saleslady assured me Leah was right. Reluctantly, I paid for the dress.

Joe came in on our heels. It was nearing suppertime, so I stashed my purse and prepared the meal. Leah excitedly told her father about her find. Looking over at Joe seated at the table, I saw he had no clue about flounces, fringes, and ruffles, but he was smiling knowingly.

"I'll try it on so you can see, okay Daddy?"

He nodded, and she sprang up the stairs with youthful exuberance. Her door slammed, and Joe turned his attention to me.

"Did it cost a lot?"

"No, it was actually on sale." That was true. I paid more than we agreed, but Leah was insistent. After the saleslady's comments, I found no reason not to get her the dress. We could well afford it. "Supper in twenty minutes."

Joe grunted, standing up. He moved to the living room, where he relaxed before dinner. I shoved the frozen fries into the oven. Then, I dropped the burgers I had formed before we left for the city on the grill. The meat sizzled, making me smile. There was something so fulfilling about cooking for your family. Tonight's meal was more casual than normal. I reserved it for days when I wasn't home in time to make a proper meal. Burgers and fries were not on Joe's list of established farm fare.

Frozen peas and carrots from my garden would round out our supper. I set the table and added pickles and condiments to the lazy Susan.

I heard Leah coming down the stairs, guessing she was wearing her dress shoes as she usually skipped down. "Dad is in the living room."

Moving into the hall, I watched as Leah swirled around in front of her father. She had taken the time to put her hair up, making her look older than her fifteen years.

"What do you think, Daddy?"

"I think it's lovely."

Leah curtsied, beaming from ear to ear. Then she turned on her heels and headed to the front door. "I am going to go show Jon and Debbie," she called over her shoulder as the screen door hissed closed.

"Tell them supper is ready," I called after her, turning to go back to the kitchen.

"Wait one minute, Joan," Joe said in a voice demanding obedience. I walked into the living room to stand in front of his chair. "So, you think that dress is appropriate for our daughter?"

I pushed my hands behind my back to prevent Joe from seeing my fear at his question. I had learned to keep my expression lax, but there didn't seem to be anything I could do about shaking hands. "It has a little jacket. I don't know why she didn't put that on."

"It has no back, thin straps, and it's obvious she's not wearing her um … undergarments."

"It's the style, Joe. Most young girls are wearing strapless gowns nowadays."

"I don't care what other parents are letting their children wear. I do not want our daughter to look like a whore on the day of her brother's wedding."

My heart pounded. I did my best to control my voice. "With the jacket on, she will look very proper. That's how she looked to me in the store. I will make sure she wears the jacket."

"You'd better. It's your job to keep our children in line."

Holding my breath, I returned to the kitchen in time to rescue the burgers from incineration. Within moments, Jon and Debbie came in with Leah. She ran upstairs to change, and I called Caleb to come down for dinner. We sat together as a family, with Jonathon and Debbie discussing the work they had finished in the house that day.

Their home had lots of character. It was a used house Joe had picked up in Stavely and moved onto a new basement he and Jonathon had dug on the property. As a journeyman electrician, Jonathon had rewired the home to modern standards, and now he and Debbie were working on a few minor renovations, including paint choices.

I caught Caleb's eye across the table. He smirked and ducked his head—grateful no one was asking questions about his day. He'd won an award for his poetry, but he hadn't shared that with anyone else in the family.

When Jonathon stopped talking, Leah took over, bubbling about her day, which was the normal course of our meals. No one seemed to keep up with her, and somehow, we all indulged in her behavior. Today's stories were about where we had lunch, where she found her dress, and how she couldn't wait for the wedding.

Joe smiled at her adoringly, unwilling to acknowledge that his baby girl was growing up.

CHAPTER TWO

May twenty-second dawned with the promise to be a glorious day. There were no clouds in the sky. I hoped the small breeze brushing the new leaves wouldn't change to a blustery wind before we took the pictures. Getting the flowers from the florist was the only thing left on my list of preparations for the day.

I made breakfast for the crew: Jonathon, his best man, Thad, Leah, Caleb, and, of course, Joe. The conversation was vibrant. Everyone seemed jubilant, including Joe. Caleb even volunteered to help with the morning chores. Afterward, he and Joe came together, smiling as if all had gone well. I was elated that there was finally hope for the two of them.

Caleb seemed to come into his own in many ways in the past year. His daydreaming and losing track of what he was doing had fallen away. He focused on the tasks at hand. Joe considered him some help, though he'd never be a "Jonathon." Caleb rarely helped his dad. He still recognized his place in the family, but at least there was a softening of the tensions between them, and I no longer needed to mediate all the time.

Caleb had good marks in school. He was in line for a scholarship, which made me proud. I think Joe was proud, too. He would never compliment Caleb for anything he considered sissified—like book learning. If Caleb had made the football team and excelled at sports, Joe would have shouted from the rooftops. Being clever and smart didn't measure up to the prowess of physical strength in Joe's mind, anyway.

Caleb's lack of coordination is not apparent when you look at him. He certainly appears to be athletic. In my mind, I believe he didn't try because he wanted his dad to accept him for the person he was, not just for his ability to catch and throw a ball.

I smiled as Joe stepped into the kitchen, followed by Caleb. This new camaraderie set the mood for our family for the duration of the wedding. Caleb joined in the conversation around the breakfast table. With my whole heart, I believed our family had turned a corner—that this wedding would draw us together and keep us together as we marched into the new decade.

Looking around the crowded table and listening as the chatter filled the room, life couldn't get much better.

A flurry of activities filled the morning. Leah

helped me with the dishes, and then we dashed off to the hairdresser. Caleb offered to pick up the flowers and deliver the corsages to the bride and her entourage. The boutonnieres and the flowers for Leah and me were sitting on the kitchen table when we returned. Caleb and his friend, Paul, were lounging in the living room, playing one of the many video games they enjoyed. I never knew what they were. They all seemed too complicated for me. I watched momentarily as a vehicle sped down a road, taking the corner with such speed that it tipped onto two wheels.

"Time to get ready, fellas. Have you showered?"

"Yeah. Dad is in there now. Jonathon and Thad are done. They're downstairs playing ping pong, working off the nerves." Caleb smiled. "We just need to put on our duds, and then we're ready. We have … what … an hour."

"Just about, I guess."

I left them to their devices and climbed the stairs. Joe was in our room, his hair dripping, a towel tied loosely around his waist. My heart caught in my throat as I glimpsed the man he was nearly thirty years ago, the man who stood at the end of that long aisle in the church, the man I loved with all my heart and whom I married for better or worse. Today was one of those better days. Love washed over me. I beamed.

Joe turned to the door as I entered. He smiled back. "I love what they did with your hair, Joan."

I reached up self-consciously and patted the side of

my head. The hairdresser had created a French roll by sweeping back my hair. I was not up on hairstyles, so I was only guessing. The stylist used a rather large comb with zircon studs to hold the roll in place. A drizzle of loose curls hung in front of my ears. Looking in the mirror, I hardly recognized myself.

I stripped off my old navy blouse and jeans and slipped into the pink and black dress I purchased for the occasion.

Joe dressed in his navy suit. He looked so handsome, freshly shaved, and smelling of English Leather.

It crossed my mind to ravage him, but I never initiated physical contact between us. Joe was the man in our relationship, as he had reminded me, the only time I had tried. I smiled brightly at him as I knotted his tie. I was a little out of practice, but I got it done. Smoothing his lapels across his broad chest—he caught my right hand, brought it to his lips, and kissed the back of it. He smiled, keeping my hand there for a moment before releasing it.

"Well, Joan, we've done it. Our baby, our firstborn, is starting his own family today. I'm proud of him. Debbie is a nice girl. In a year, we'll hear the pitter-patter of tiny feet—grandkids. The circle of life."

I smiled back. It was going to be a good day if Joe was philosophizing.

He gestured toward the door. "Shall we?"

We left the room, heading back to the main floor.

Joe went first, and I hung back to knock at Leah's door. She opened it immediately, and my breath caught at the sight of her. At fifteen, she was all grown up. Her lovely pink dress with the short jacket magnified the brilliance of her big blue-green eyes. She'd also applied a touch of makeup, and I silently hoped her father wouldn't cause a scene over it. Her long ginger-blond tresses draped softly from the knot atop her head. She looked much older than her years and very much a young woman.

Heading downstairs together, I grabbed her hand and squeezed it. She was my baby, and I was so proud of her. I wanted her to know. She smiled and squeezed back.

We met up with the men standing in the living room—they were a handsome group in suits and tuxedos, all tall and lean. Jonathon oozed confidence on the surface, but his smile quivered ever so slightly. He was nervous. I wouldn't have expected anything else. Getting married is an enormous step in anyone's life. There are no guarantees, even if you know the person well. It was always a gamble. Marriage didn't solve all the issues or promise a happily ever after. Life wasn't like that.

Joe looked over his shoulder, his eyebrows raised ever so slightly at Leah's appearance. The group stilled, waiting. I held my breath in anticipation.

Jonathon broke the tension. "Wow, sis! You look great."

Caleb simply nodded. Paul's eyes widened, and he

grinned.

Joe's smile took a second. Then he reached for Leah's hand. "My baby girl is all grown up. When did that happen?"

I exhaled.

"Let's get a move on," I said brightly.

We headed out to the vehicles. Caleb agreed to drive the family truck to the wedding. He and Paul climbed in and headed out before us. Thad and the handsome groom took Jonathon's brand new Ford, a wedding present from his dad and me. I noticed Jonathon let Thad drive. I smiled.

Joe, Leah, and I took my Jeep. Although it was fairly new, it was not fancy. It served its purpose as a vehicle to get me around. It was cost-effective and paid for. We followed the other two vehicles, staying back as the dust from the gravel road spewed out behind those traveling before us.

Once we hit the pavement, we were quite far behind the other two.

We couldn't even see Caleb.

Not that it mattered—we were all headed in the same direction.

CHAPTER THREE

There were already many vehicles in the parking lot of the church. We parked close to Jonathon's truck and entered the building. Someone was playing hymns, the sound waving over the soft murmur of hushed voices. Everyone was waiting in anticipation of the blessed event. Jonathon and Thad were nowhere in sight, but Caleb and Paul stood waiting in the foyer.

Debbie's cousins were beside the open doors on the left side of the church. Two of Jonathon's football team members stood at the other set of doors on the right. We headed toward those doors. One of the young men escorted Joe and me to the front, and the other took Leah's arm and walked behind. Many faces turned to smile at us—we smiled back. Joe walked stiffly at being the center of attention. He needn't have worried. When people spotted Leah, they forgot Joe was even there.

Seated in the front pew, Joe shifted uncomfortably as we waited for the ceremony to begin. It wasn't long before the boys came out of the choir room and took their places at the front of the church, with the minister standing behind them. The organ stopped playing, and the church grew silent. A few seconds later, the opening chords of the wedding march filled the room, and the congregation stood to face the back of the church.

Debbie's cousin's children started down the aisle together, looking like cherubs, adorable in their little outfits. Behind them, Debbie's maid of honor entered wearing her royal blue taffeta knee-length gown. Cameras flashed as the trio passed. The doors at the back of the church were closed momentarily. When the small group reached the front of the church, the doors flew open again to reveal a stunning bride standing proudly by her father's side. A snowy white veil hid her face. She moved forward with grace and beauty. With a nervous hint of a smile on his slightly flushed face, her father appeared to be dragged unwillingly to the front of the church. He looked straight ahead, his eyes on where he would turn his daughter over to our son.

At the front of the church, the minister asked his question, and Mr. Somerville nodded his response while placing Debbie's hand into Jonathon's. He then stepped back and slipped into the front pew opposite ours. His sister and her family shuffled slightly to give him room. I wondered how he would make out now that Debbie was getting married. It had been the two of them for more than a few years. He'd be alone now. That thought made me sad. I shook off my reverie and focused on the proceedings at the front of the church.

Jonathon tucked Debbie's veil back, smiling as he took her hand once more and stepped back to face the minister. There were readings and blessings. I watched intently as the ceremony took them through their vows. Then it was over. The minister pronounced them married, and after a brief kiss, they moved off to a corner to sign the register while a soloist stepped into place. The smile on my face didn't fade as the beautiful voice serenaded us. Tears welled up as I fervently wished, not for the first time, that Jonathon and Debbie would receive a blessing of enduring love. Joe squeezed my hand gently.

Minutes later, the minister presented them to the congregation as Mr. and Mrs. Jonathon Bradshaw. The couple skipped down the aisle, smiling for pictures occasionally. We followed not far behind, taking our place on the steps outside the church, grateful for the congratulatory words as the congregation spilled onto the street.

When the last of the well-wishers had offered their pearls of wisdom, we headed to the park in the center of town for more pictures. There was a lot of waiting around, as most of the photos were of the bride and groom. I was glad to be part of it, although Joe was getting restless. He had never been a man who enjoyed waiting—it seemed to him a waste of time—time, he said, was better spent on something constructive, not wasted by waiting.

Eventually, the photos were done, and we headed for the community hall. We found our table, where we greeted the newlyweds. As they entered, the crowd let out a roar.

The festivities were well underway.

Joe, who didn't drink, was unhappy about alcohol being served at the reception. He had no control over that, however. Mr. Somerville was paying, and he wanted it available, so it was. Most of those gathered had a form of it at their table. Joe kept a watchful eye on Caleb to ensure he didn't partake.

The supper was delicious, and the caterers were top-notch. The master of ceremonies was humorous and lively. He kept things moving. Leah gave such a touching welcome to the bride from our family, which had me in tears. She expressed exactly how I felt about Debbie. Joe smiled at his daughter. He was smiling a lot that night, and I was glad.

CHAPTER FOUR

The reception wound down, and the speeches and toasts were over. The master of ceremonies turned the festivities over to the band. While the trend for weddings was to hire a DJ, Debbie's father insisted on having a proper band. I agreed with him. Nothing was finer than a good dance band, and the one on stage was one of the best in the county.

The bride and groom swept onto the floor for the first dance, and then Jonathon collected me for the second. After that, they opened the dance floor for everyone. Jonathon handed me over to Joe, and we danced for one song. Joe had never been much of a dancer, so the night passed with many people popping by the table to offer congratulations and talk. I found myself lost when men outnumbered me. I sat quietly for a spell, watching the dancers and occasionally catching glimpses of my children.

Leah was the life of the party—as usual. There was a group of young men and women always surrounding her. I noticed she danced several times with Ryan James. He looked like a nice boy, although I knew little about him. Eventually, the wives came to rescue me from their husbands, and the night passed quickly. I lost track of Caleb and Leah about that time. Jonathon and Debbie were easy to spot, but the others seemed to fade into the crowd. I wasn't worried, as I had raised them well, and they knew better than to be missing when it was time to go home.

On my trip to the washroom near the end of the night, I saw Caleb hunkered near the back with a gang of kids his age. They were lounging around, chatting. I motioned him over.

"Have you seen Leah?" Because I wasn't looking for deception, I didn't see any. Later, as I relived the night over and over and over in my head in the wee hours of the mornings when sleep eluded me, I recalled the subtle shift in his expression.

"She's around here somewhere, Mom. I just saw her a few minutes ago with Amanda and Ryan. Maybe they're upstairs."

"We're not supposed to be using the upstairs, so get up there, find her, and tell her we're leaving in half an hour." I smiled at him, patted his cheek, and went on my way.

The bride and groom gathered on stage as I exited the washroom. They thanked us all for coming, and then we had the traditional tossing of the garter and the bouquet. I noticed Caleb didn't get into the mix of bachelors eager to catch the garter. He stood well back against the wall and laughed at all the others scrambling to own the prized piece of elastic, lace, and ribbon. Then it was the girls' turn, and I was certain Leah would be in the middle, hoping Debbie would single her out and throw the bouquet in her direction. She didn't take part, either. I couldn't even see her in the group gathered around the perimeter. The tiniest niggling of fear crept across the base of my hairline. Where was she?

Then I told myself I was being silly. Maybe my kids didn't like this marital superstition. Maybe she was still upstairs. It wouldn't be the first time she disobeyed instructions from her brother. I guess I'd have to get her myself. As I walked across the floor, Jonathon and Debbie swept up to me. There were hugs and wishes for a wonderful honeymoon. I assured them I would take care of the last inspection of their new house before their return.

I watched the two circle the room, saying their goodbyes to key people, and then they slipped out the front door into the night. A few characters followed them out, but not many. As I stood there, I nearly forgot my mission. Then I spotted Caleb again and headed toward him.

I saw he was trying desperately to avoid me. When

he spotted me coming, he backed up and turned slightly, pretending he hadn't. I called his name. His shoulders sagged slightly as he turned back to me.

This time, I was ready when I asked him. "Where's Leah? Is she still upstairs?"

Caleb sighed. "No, Mom. She's not upstairs."

"Where is she?"

"She left at about ten-thirty, promising she'd be right back. She was just going for a drive with Ryan. But they haven't come back yet. I don't know where she is."

The color drained from my face. I was instantly concerned about Joe's reaction but also angry at Leah's lack of respect for us and her reputation. Driving with a boy—being gone for hours—only meant less driving and more parking was going on. I may have been a virgin when I married, but I wasn't naïve about what went on between the sexes before marriage.

"Why didn't you tell me when I asked earlier?"

"I thought she'd be back before you found out she was gone. I'm sorry! I tried to stop her, just so you know."

That's my girl, I thought. She had a mind of her own. Now, to tell Joe. Immediately, Joe's temper sparked, and he snapped angrily at Caleb.

"Why didn't you stop her?"

"I tried, but she wouldn't listen to me. She said she wouldn't be gone long, but she never returned. I don't know where they went."

Caleb was defiant, but not so forcibly that he pushed

Joe further.

Joe gathered his wits and made plans to search for Leah. He interrogated Caleb, Paul, and Steve to find out where young people park nowadays. Then Joe and I took my vehicle and drove to the south and east of the town, searching for Leah. On our way, I phoned Ryan's parents, hoping they would have news.

The couple was in bed when I called, and they seemed unconcerned about the kids. "Ryan is an excellent driver," Mrs. James assured me. "It's probably a flat tire or something like that. I'm sure they are both all right. I promise to call you if I hear from him."

Not satisfied with her answers, I suggested the kids had perhaps gone to park somewhere. She assured me that their son would not take advantage of my daughter. If any parking were being done, my daughter would have influenced that. Already on edge, I rolled my eyes, thanked them for their help, and ended the call.

Joe and I drove on.

Caleb and his friend Paul had taken the truck, driving roads north and west of the town. We rendezvoused back at the farm, but neither group was successful. Joe and I had driven slowly down several gravel roads, looking for signs that they might have hit the ditch, but in the darkness, we saw nothing. The boys reported the same findings when they arrived home.

At three in the morning, Caleb and Paul finally called it a night. Minutes later, with rounded shoulders, Joe mumbled that he had morning chores as he headed to bed. I thought about going with him, but I wouldn't sleep. I was so disappointed and angry with Leah. What was she thinking? What if she fell pregnant? Joe would have a coronary right after he killed her.

I sat in the rocking chair, fretting, stewing, thinking, and worrying as the rest of the house fell into slumber. The sun peaked over the horizon when I heard Joe come down the stairs. He looked like he hadn't slept as he stood in the doorway.

"Is she not home yet?"

I shook my head. He turned away, and I followed him into the kitchen. I made him an Ovaltine, but he refused breakfast, saying he only wanted a piece of toast. I buttered a couple of slices for him and set them on the table.

Holding his head in his hands, staring at his mug of Ovaltine, I saw he was in obvious anguish. "Where is she, Joan? Why didn't she come home? It can't be good. It just can't be."

He pushed the toast away and stood up. Brushing his hand across my shoulders as he passed me, he went out to the back porch, pulled on his boots, and headed out into the yard. I sat there, Joe's touch lingering hotly on my shoulders.

At six-thirty, I could no longer stand the nagging voice in my head. I called the police. They told me not to worry. She'd certainly come home on her own. There were no reported accidents. She was probably just embarrassed about being out with a boy overnight.

They'd call us if they had any news.

Joe returned a couple of hours later, his face deeply etched with worry. I simply shook my head at his silent question.

"We'll have to go out looking for her again. She can't have disappeared. What are her friends saying?"

"I called several of them, getting most of them out of bed. No one knows a thing."

We needed to go to church to pray for her, but we wouldn't. While Joe was out, I called the pastor and asked him to pray for us. He'd been sympathetic to our plight, offering assurances that God had us in his hands, and promised to offer us up to the congregation for prayer. Joe wouldn't be happy about that, and I had wrestled with myself all night, wondering if I would forever damage my daughter's reputation by talking to the pastor. I finally decided I needed help—but kept Joe in the dark.

Getting busy, I made sandwiches and hot drinks for Caleb and Paul. Once I was done, I would rouse them. There was no sense in sending them out searching on empty stomachs. This way, they could eat and search simultaneously. Four toasted bacon and tomato sandwiches wrapped in wax paper sat on the table. Two thermoses of a hot, iced tea mix sat beside them.

I headed upstairs to wake them.

A car pulled into the yard as I passed the living room.

I rushed to the window, thinking Leah had finally

come home.

CHAPTER FIVE

The police car came to a stop. A flurry of thoughts passed through my mind—visions of Leah sleeping in a jail cell, of an accident, visions of Leah and Ryan stuck in the mud on some back road and being rescued, cold and hungry but safe. Stories that could be true and some that I hoped weren't.

Gratefulness, anxiety, fear, and hope coursed through my veins as I watched two constables step out of the vehicle and walk up the front sidewalk. Leah wasn't with them. Was she still in jail? I looked around them to the back seat of the vehicle. Why hadn't they brought her home?

I ran to the door, calling for Joe as I went. Hearing the panic in my voice, he hurried down the stairs, meeting me at the door moments after I had pulled it open.

They introduced themselves, but to this day, I cannot remember their names. The moment I saw their faces, it was clear they weren't coming with the news I wanted to hear.

"Mrs. Bradshaw, Mr. Bradshaw. I'm sorry …"

"No!" I shouted, shaking my head and backing away from the door.

Joe grabbed me and steered me toward the living room and onto the couch. The officers followed. After Joe guided me to the sofa, they continued.

"They found your daughter, Leah, and Ryan James this morning in a vehicle. Both were dead at the scene. I'm so sorry."

Staring at the officer, I prayed his words were not true, but knowing they were. When Leah didn't come home, there really was only one outcome that made sense.

"Thank you for coming to tell us." Joe headed to the door.

"No, I need to know …" I jumped to my feet, crossing the space between us and grabbing the sleeve of the officer closest to me.

"Joan, please." Joe stared hard at me.

"No, Joe. I need to know. Are they sure it's her? There is no way she can be gone. I mean, she was here yesterday. She looked lovely, didn't she, Joe? Tell them. Tell them how pretty she looked yesterday." I was standing on the edge but didn't want to own this reality.

The men exchanged glances.

"I'm not crazy," I yelled. "She's only fifteen years old. Leah can't be dead. She has her whole life ahead of her."

Joe took hold of me and steered me back to the couch. I looked over at the officer. "Please, please tell me she isn't dead."

"I'm sorry, ma'am."

I gulped back tears. "What happened? Can you tell me that, at least?"

"Are you sure, ma'am?" He stared at me. In his eyes, I saw the sadness of his duty. What he had witnessed was not something I wanted to hear. Yet, I had to hear it.

"Please." I waited.

The older officer cleared his throat and then told the story. I would repeatedly hear these words in this man's voice for the rest of my life. He would become the link between Leah and me for as long as I lived, and I couldn't even remember his name.

"The investigation is incomplete, but I can tell you they were driving down Old Coach Road. They came around that wide corner before the bridge, heading back toward Freyden and probably going too fast for the road conditions. They just resurfaced the road, and there was a lot of loose gravel in that area. Ryan was not an experienced driver, having only received his license last month. It seems likely he was incapable of handling the vehicle when he lost control. It left the road, caught a boulder in the ditch, and flipped end over end, landing upside down in the creek. There were no signs of braking. Both your daughter and Ryan died instantly."

I looked into his face—his blue eyes glassy with unshed tears.

"I have a daughter of my own." He reached out and squeezed my shoulder. "She's fourteen, and I can't imagine how I'd manage with this news. If there's anything you need …" He looked at Joe.

Joe nodded and lumbered toward the door. The officers followed, and I wasn't far behind. I saw Joe was already beginning to carry the weight of this news on his broad shoulders. The officers shook Joe's hand, replaced their hats, and stepped out into the sunshine of the beautiful May morning. I shook my head, wondering how the sun would dare to shine if my baby was dead. It was unfathomable that I would never see her smiling eyes again or see her expressive face as she came home from school, excitedly sharing her news. How was it possible that I would not see her marry or see her children grow up and prosper?

I turned from the door, not sure where I was going. Not sure what I wanted to do. On the landing of the stairs, still in his pajamas, Caleb stood with an unrecognizable expression.

In a voice much calmer than I felt, I asked, "You heard?"

He nodded, turned on his heels, and went back up the stairs. I didn't follow.

I went into the kitchen and sat down heavily at the table. Joe came and sat down across from me. I looked at him, noticing for the first time the tears streaming down his handsome, weather-worn face. His dark hair appeared disheveled, as though he had been running his hand through it.

"Oh, Joe!"

He broke at my words. Sobs shook his body. Wracking, wet, angry sobs. He folded his arms onto the table, laid his head down, and wept. Getting to my feet, I leaned over him, holding him in my arms. My eyes were dry. Numbness infiltrated me. Inside, there was nothing, not even empathy, for Joe. I was simply going through the motions.

As Joe's sobs subsided, I made a pot of tea. Joe rarely drank coffee or tea. We needed something to carry us through. Caleb came down, grabbed two glasses of milk and a handful of cookies, and returned to his room. Normally, I would have protested and insisted he have something more substantial for breakfast. I just found all my fight was gone.

The sandwiches I'd made for him and Paul, and the two thermoses sat untouched on the counter.

CHAPTER SIX

The phone calls came later. The news of the accident traveled like wildfire in a sun-scorched stubble field. Neighbors, fellow church members, drifted into the yard, bringing food: casseroles, fresh bread, buns, and pies. It was nearly lunchtime when I finally remembered that I should call the bed-and-breakfast where Jonathon and Debbie would be that night. Hating to ruin their honeymoon, it was more monstrous that their wedding anniversary would also be the anniversary of the day we lost our little girl.

I had to call my family, too. My mother was still vacationing south of the border. For years, she left Canada for Arizona's warmer, sunnier climate a few weeks before Christmas. She stayed the allotted six months, never returning before the middle of June, even refusing to come home for Jonathon's wedding. We argued about her decision, but she told me they wouldn't be getting married before her intended return date if they had wanted her at the wedding. She was a stubborn old woman.

My sister, Susan, lived in Newfoundland. She'd met a man from there who'd come to Alberta to make his fortune. They were married, and when things slowed in the oil patch, they packed up and moved back to his home province. I hadn't seen Susan in years. She had no money for trips home, and I never felt the urge to visit her out there. Our relationship reflected the vast physical distance between us, as we were never close as girls growing up—we were miles apart.

I called my mother first, and her answering machine picked up. I left a message for her to call back, and Susan answered before the second ring.

"What do you want?" She sounded drunk and belligerent. "Called to gloat about your precious son's wedding, have you? Well, I don't want to hear it."

"Susan!" I shouted angrily. "Why are you being so snide?"

"No reason, Joan dear. No reason at all." The bitterness in her words dripped through the phone.

"I called with bad news, I'm afraid."

"What? Did Mom finally kick the bucket, leaving me the family jewels?" She guffawed, a hoarse, rasping laugh from smoking far too many cigarettes.

The venom spewing from my sister's soul shouldn't

have surprised me. She was not a cheerful person, and marrying Dick hadn't brought her the riches and lifestyle she coveted. Dick was a dreamer and a bit of a player. Handsome and fun-loving, it was easy to see what she saw in him, but his lack of vision and follow-through made it impossible for him to get ahead. He was one of those men who never truly grew up.

"Susan, please! I didn't call to get into a fight with you. I called because … we …" Not able to contain my grief, the tears welled up and raced down my cheeks. My throat closed, making it hard to talk. I finally spit the words out. "Leah's dead, Susan. She died in a car accident last night."

There was a long silence on the other end of the phone. It was so quiet I wondered if she had hung up on me.

"Hello?"

"I heard ya! Sorry about that. She's in a better place, though. Off this shithole of a rock. That's the silver lining, I guess." There was a moment of silence as I tried to process her words. "Not much I can do for ya. But I am sorry to hear about it."

"Thank you. I just thought you ought to know. I'll be in touch when we know the date of the funeral."

"Don't bother. I won't be able to come anyway." She hung up.

I sat there with the receiver in my hand for a minute, listening to the dial tone. Not wanting another load of family comfort, I hoped my mother would not call back.

Joe disappeared, heading to the barn for some peace. I heard the tractor start up and watched from the kitchen window as he drove out across the field. I didn't know where he was going. The seeding had been done, and the hay crop was not yet ready to be mowed. I think he just needed to be away with his feelings.

I hosted those coming to offer condolences, making excuses for Joe's absence. Caleb reappeared briefly, but he didn't stay. I hadn't spoken with him. I didn't know how he was feeling or what he was thinking. I wanted everyone to leave, to go away so I could be with my thoughts and emotions. Instead, diligent to the core, I made coffee and tea and let the people tell stories of Leah.

Finally, the last of them went out the door, hugging me tight and promising me support. I wished I had told them I wanted Leah to come back through the door—for this to be a nightmare I could wake from. Instead, I smiled and accepted the hugs, the pats on the back, the words of comfort, nodding like a bobblehead doll in the window of a car without shocks.

Closing the door after the last well-wisher, the weariness fell heavily on my shoulders. I hadn't drunk enough water, nor had I eaten much food. Too tired to do anything about that, I slowly climbed the stairs.

The back door slammed shut. Joe was home.

I trudged upward. Caleb's door was closed. I heard music playing softly through the panels. I knocked. The music stopped. The door opened. Caleb stood there—his expression unreadable. I remember wondering how he became so good at hiding his emotions. Had he always been like this?

I stood there, not sure how to proceed. "Are you okay?"

He hadn't stepped back to allow me into his room, leaving me awkwardly in the hallway. Caleb leaned against the doorjamb, his body language oozing a relaxed casualness that angered me. This family had just lost its sunshine, and this boy wasn't affected. Somewhere in the deep recesses of my heart, it was apparent I was misreading the situation. I was just too tired to find any compassion. I snapped.

"What is your problem?"

Based on his reaction, it was as if someone had slapped him across the face. He pushed himself off the doorjamb, stepping back into his room.

"Fuck you." He slammed the door in my face.

CHAPTER SEVEN

Caleb's venom sent a shock wave through my body. I had never heard such language spoken ever, let alone in my home. Even when Joe had lost his temper, he never used profanity. I stood there in the hallway, staring at Caleb's closed door, hardly daring to breathe. Then, the wave of regret and sorrow rolled across my shoulders, and I stumbled to my bedroom. I threw myself on my bed and let the waves roll over me.

Feeling like I carried the world today, I allowed self-pity to take hold. The storm settled behind my eyes as I howled like a wounded cat. I needed to get this out of me—it was too heavy, too dark, too much to bear.

In my anguish, I was aware of Joe coming into the room. He came to my side of the bed, gently helping me up. So torn with grief, I was of no help to him. My arms hung limp at my sides, my tears flowing like rivulets down my cheeks. Gently, he stripped off my blouse and bra before hoisting me off the bed. While holding me upright with one arm, he pulled off my slacks with the other. Then he slipped a nightgown over my head. Wobbling beside the bed, he steadied me as he pulled back the covers. After he helped me onto the bed, he pulled the covers up under my chin.

Looking into his drawn face, a flood of gratitude for his care swept over me. He leaned down and kissed my brow. As he moved away, I curled into myself, my stomach tight with knots.

How would I face another day without my lovely girl in my life? How could God be so cruel as to take her from me? For one brief second, I wondered, *Why Leah? Why not Caleb?*

I was immediately ashamed of that thought, regretting that I hadn't controlled my mind.

The tears subsided. I lay hiccoughing and sniffling, my back to Joe as he lay quietly beside me. Feeling the need to be held and comforted in Joe's strength, I thought about turning to him.

I didn't move.

Sleeping until this nightmare was over was compelling. It would be easier to get things sorted. It would be easier than living it. Maybe all I needed was the right bargaining chip with God to bring my darling girl back. Sleep seemed to be a safe alternative to living in a world without her.

I lay there, my breathing growing deeper and more relaxed as sleep tiptoed up behind me, finally catching up with me. Offering no resistance, I slept.

When the sun peeked over the horizon the next morning, I turned my back on the window, pulled up the covers, snuggling deeper into the dream world. The reality was too much to bear. I had no desire to spend another day out where the sun shone when it shouldn't, where the birds sang when they should be weeping. No longer centered. My world no longer spun on its axis.

Joe rose. He padded barefoot down the hallway to the bathroom. Minutes later, he was back, freshly shaved and ready for his day. I heard him pull on his clothes.

"Are you getting up?"

I lay there, not bothering to respond.

"Joan?"

"What?"

"Are you going to get up?"

"No, I don't want to."

"Well, neither do I, but life goes on, and you can't hide from it."

Angry, I sighed and rolled over, putting my back to him. Once again, I was facing the window. That annoyed me, too. Once I heard him leave the room, I turned my back to the window once more.

How could anyone understand my guilt and shame? Maybe Joe wished Caleb was gone instead of Leah, too. But if he were thinking such thoughts, he wouldn't share them with me. It seemed inconceivable that I had thought it myself, and it pained me as much as losing my precious girl.

Thinking of her brought joy, as it often did. But that passed quickly. I couldn't stop thinking about the expectation of laying her to rest with dignity and decorum in the next couple of days. How could I give her a last goodbye when she was such an integral part of my life? The depth of pain rocked me. Tears welled in my eyes. This was so hard. Why? What had I ever done to deserve this? I pummeled Joe's pillow in frustration.

Exhaustion crept up behind me and poked me between the shoulder blades. I collapsed, breathing hard. For several minutes, I lay there, my mind going through the events of the last two days. Recycling memories, refining them, and storing them for the future.

Much later, with regret, I threw back the covers. I couldn't be the weak link here—I needed to be strong. Leah would want me to be strong, I reasoned with myself as I lay debating whether I should stay in bed forever. Unaware of anyone in my circle who'd lost a child, I had no one from whom to draw inspiration. I was a reluctant pioneer who didn't want to make the journey but had no choice. That angered me more than anything. This was not my choice or my chosen path. I had to bear the burden of this accident. No parent should ever have to bear this. It wasn't fair. I didn't deserve it.

When I arrived in the kitchen, I found remnants of the toast and Ovaltine Joe had made for himself before leaving to do his chores. Caleb was sitting in the living room, staring out the front window. His hair looked messy, and he was wearing his pajamas for the second day.

I stood in the doorway, watching him. He didn't seem to notice me for a few minutes. When he looked at me, I observed that he still had a tight rein on his emotions.

"Morning," I said gently.

I wondered if he was thinking about our exchange last night. Ashamed that I lost my temper with him, I decided during my lay-in to forget those ugly words and try to go forward from there.

Caleb stared at me. I saw he was trying to work his thoughts into words but wasn't getting there. Love and compassion flooded my chest. I walked toward him.

Just then, the front door flew open, and Jonathon rushed inside, Debbie right behind him.

"Mom!" he called out before seeing me. I turned toward them, swept up in his embrace. "We drove all night. Oh, my God, I still can't believe it!"

He held me tightly against his body. Debbie stood awkwardly off to the side, unsure where she should be in this situation. I saw she was feeling like an outsider, and I didn't want that for her. She and Leah spent some time together, and over the years, they would become fast friends and allies. Someone had stolen that from both girls, adding another loss and burden for us to bear. I patted Jonathon's back, and he released me. I stepped away and gave Deb a quick hug.

When I turned back to the living room, it was empty. Caleb had made his escape. A twinge of regret swung in and out of my chest. I took a deep breath and headed back to the kitchen, Jonathon and Debbie trailing behind.

I filled the kettle and plugged it in before offering to make them some breakfast. Debbie sat like a lump beside Jonathon and, for the first time since I met her, a niggling of hatred for her tingled up my spine. She should make toast for me, I thought angrily. She should serve me. I've just lost my daughter, and I'm still looking after their needs. This tiny seed slipped inside my heart, unchallenged because grief and sorrow had temporarily overwhelmed my ability to censor such horrid thoughts. A weed of anger and malice would germinate toward my daughter-in-law, manifesting in snide comments and a total lack of support.

Caleb's emotional state went unchecked. Those hurtful and angry words still hung in the air between us. Jonathon's untimely arrival cut off my attempt to repair what should never be severed. Over the next few days, Caleb stayed out of sight in his room. He came down for meals and answered perfunctory questions but otherwise stayed silent and invisible. He'd always been like that, withdrawing into himself. The other two never hid their emotions.

Caleb was so different, and during this time of loss and grief, he removed himself from our lives while living under the same roof. I didn't know how to reach him, how to bring him back into the fold. The knowledge that it seemed I had also lost my second-born, as if someone had plucked him from this earth, compounded my grief over Leah, which was already too much to bear.

CHAPTER EIGHT

The minister arrived later that morning. Joe and I spoke with him at length, taking comfort from his words as we planned the funeral for our girl. Waves of anguish rolled up and over me like the sea. Thankfully, these feelings receded quickly, allowing me to complete mundane tasks and look after my family. These waves would stay with me for the rest of my life. They would grow intense if I heard the laughter of a teenage girl, heard one of Leah's favorite songs, or saw trinkets and knick-knacks she would want in the stores she loved to frequent.

I think the whole town turned out for Leah's funeral. I kept my emotions tight—Joe, too, was stoic. Jonathon had moist eyes, and Debbie sobbed like a little girl. I hated her for that, too. Caleb was there, sitting at the end of the row beside Debbie. I pictured him wearing the same outfit he wore at the wedding. Then, my mind would play tricks on me, and I wondered if I was only remembering him at the wedding and not at the funeral. It was so close to the nuptials that it seemed surreal. Even when I sat and concentrated and tried to bring him into proper focus on that day, his image escaped me.

In the months after her passing, Joe and I argued over Leah's room. He wanted to clear all her belongings out. I'd finally have a sewing room, he argued. He said it would be unhealthy to keep her belongings. He affiliated it with cancer. By cutting it out, you prevented the disease from spreading. I expressed shock and accused him of wanting to erase her memory.

"Her stuff is not her memory. She'll always live here." He pounded his chest with his fist. "I just think we ought to clear it out, help you get rid of the pain you're living in. You need to let her go, Joan. She is not coming back."

I couldn't, though. I just couldn't do it. We fought over this often in the early days after Leah's death. Eventually, Joe stopped bringing it up, but not before it drove a wedge between us. We drifted away from each other as Leah's ghost remained entrenched in the house.

When my grief threatened to consume me, I would open her closed door and imagine she was out with friends. She was just gone for a minute—she would be right back. Sometimes, I imagined her behind the closed door, listening to music. In this way, I thought I was coping better, never letting my grief consume me. I grew frustrated with Joe when he refused to talk about her. If I mentioned her name, Joe would shoot me a disgusted look and leave the room. I didn't understand how he shoved her out of our lives so quickly and completely.

Forgotten in all the fuss was Caleb. He finished high school and went to work for the summer, seldom coming home. Whenever he was home, he told me he was staying at Paul's. I couldn't blame him. We never talked about that night and those ugly words. I missed the opportunity, and then it was simply too late. I couldn't bridge the rift without putting in some serious effort. As I struggled with my loss, I just didn't have it in me.

We forgot about Caleb's graduation ceremony. It was a week after we laid our girl to rest. I didn't even remember it until much later in the summer, and Joe never once mentioned missing it out loud to me. When I realized how unworthy and unwanted my son must be feeling, with everything that happened that spring and summer, I sat down and sobbed. I cried for myself, for Caleb, for Leah. Moments like that were frequent. I cried at the drop of a hat most days unless Joe was home. Then, I pretended all was well.

Jonathon and Debbie didn't finish their honeymoon. Instead, they settled into their new home, and Jonathon went back to work. I don't know how Debbie spent her days. She stayed on her own, never coming over to visit me unless Jonathon brought her. I sometimes looked across the yard at the tidy little structure and thought angrily that she was probably watching soap operas and drinking iced tea—a kept woman. Turned out she was taking an online course, studying to be a geriatric recreational facilitator. I should have been proud of her.

But I didn't know, nor did I care.

As a daughter, Debbie was a poor replacement for my Leah.

CHAPTER NINE

Joe and I never resumed our relationship. After we ceased fighting about Leah's room, he stopped trying to reach me at all. He grew edgier, lashing out in anger whenever he thought I failed him. For several months, I stopped being particular about my appearance. He criticized me often for that. We stopped going to church, and the few friends I had—stopped calling.

Jonathon did his best to be a bridge, but it wasn't his job. Soon, he stopped coming for his morning break, and Joe followed suit. They went to Jonathon's house, and I spent more time on my own, alone with my thoughts and my insurmountable grief.

A shroud of loss settled down over the house. Joe and I passed each other most days without talking. There were no caresses, pats, hugs, or intimacies, including conversations. I cooked meals for him, did his laundry, and kept the house tidy, but all of it was done with a sense of duty, not love. I missed my family.

Loneliness became my constant companion. Joe left the house at seven and didn't come home until suppertime. I spent a lot of time reliving the past, remembering the days when this house had life in it. I was careful to keep my memories to myself. Joe lost his temper when I tried to bring up something that happened when the kids were young.

Caleb went on to university that fall. He came home for Thanksgiving and Christmas, but he wasn't present. His life in the city was an unknown, but the distance that bloomed at Leah's death had only grown. He didn't speak unless spoken to and spent most of his time upstairs in his room. He didn't stay for New Year's, claiming he had plans with friends. I didn't stop him. Pulling him out of himself took more effort than I had.

Knowing that I would have to be the one to reach out to bring Caleb back into my life, I drove to Crawford to have lunch with him for his birthday. Joe didn't come, claiming that calving season required him to stay at home.

We met at the restaurant of his choice and had a pleasant time. Caleb seemed more himself than he had for a long time, and I wondered at the change. Then, a pretty brunette stopped by the table, a server based on her attire. Clearly, this girl was responsible for the change in my son.

"Mom, I'd like you to meet Andrea Pritchard. Andrea, this is my mom."

The girl beamed at Caleb before turning to me and shaking my hand. "It's a real honor to meet you. You have a brilliant son here."

Caleb snaked a possessive arm around her waist. She let it stay for a moment before moving back out of reach. "I need to get back to work before Jared sees me." She smiled again. "This isn't my section, so I'd be in for one of his many lectures." She rolled her eyes and laughed as she walked away. Caleb watched her go with a look I knew only too well. It was the same gaze I'd seen when Jonathon looked at Debbie.

Months later, when Caleb brought Andrea to the farm for the first time, I saw why he liked her. She had a bubbly personality and a zest for life that was infectious. When she laughed, it sounded like music, inspiring the people around her to laugh along.

Even Joe liked her, though he wondered what she was doing with Caleb, suggesting she could do better. Although I didn't argue, I took offense on behalf of Caleb. Joe seldom had a good word for anyone anymore, and he hated Caleb's moodiness. He didn't see that he acted the same. Caleb hadn't fallen far from the tree after all.

I was happy my boy had found someone capable of reaching inside his pensiveness and dragging him to the surface. Caleb had changed again, this time for the better.

By late September, I was once again finding it hard to reach my son on the phone. Because the university was back in session, I blamed it on Caleb's busy schedule, even though I did not know if it was busy or not. It just seemed easier to accept he was engaged than to believe he had fallen back into his uncommunicative ways.

I left a message reminding him to come home for Thanksgiving and telling him Andrea was more than welcome to join us. He never called back, but with a hopeful heart, there were place settings for both of them at the table. They never showed up.

Inside, I was worried, but Joe was no help. When I mentioned my concern, he shrugged it off. "He's a young man, focusing on his own life. He'll be okay. I think we are his past, or at least that's how he acts. Just move on."

That was Joe's answer to everything. I was supposed to move on from Leah and now from Caleb. Not wanting to let go of either of them. I kept phoning Caleb and leaving messages. Finally, I couldn't stand it anymore. On the twenty-fifth of October, I left a message for Caleb.

"Hi Caleb, it's Mom. I've been missing you, and since you can't find the time to return my calls, this is your notice that your father and I will be coming into the city on October twenty-ninth. We will take you and Andrea for supper—you name the place. Since you missed Thanksgiving, I will not be taking no for an answer. Call me back to confirm, and I'll see you soon. Love you!"

Again, there was no response, and three days before we were to meet up in the city, it was time to tell Joe about my plans.

CHAPTER TEN

Wham! Joe's hand slammed onto the table. The dishes clattered, and my freshly poured cup of tea was sloshed over the lip of my mug and onto the table. I held myself stiff, not wanting to give him the satisfaction of cowering against his rage.

"I'm telling you for the last time, I am not going to the city to have supper with that boy," he yelled. "Caleb hasn't done a damn thing since he left for university to deserve it. He lives half an hour away, and yet I can count on one hand the number of times he's been home. We just had Thanksgiving, and that boy didn't bother to show up. If I remember correctly, you set a place for him—didn't you?" Joe stared hard at me, expecting an answer. "Well, didn't you?" he yelled when I failed to respond.

I nodded, stuffing back the tears.

"That's what I thought." Joe nodded. "The only time we hear from Caleb is when he needs money. That's all I'm good for! I won't have it. I am not giving up my night to go into the city just to have dinner with him. If Caleb wants to see us, he'll come home. Until then, this subject is closed."

Grabbing several napkins, I dabbed at the spilled tea, keeping my face averted to prevent Joe from seeing the tears I had unsuccessfully squelched. I stood, tossing the napkins into the trash before clearing the table. My heart ached—a yearning so intense it felt like spikes being driven through it.

Losing Leah rose anew, twisting my heart. Biting down on my fist to prevent a scream from escaping, I was overwhelmed by the longing to hear her laughter, her sweet, childlike voice, or one of her stories about life at school. I wanted to hear her storm down the stairs like she used to. The quiet was too hard to bear when my yearning was so deep.

It was more than the empty nest syndrome that people talk about on those afternoon television programs. This was different because she wasn't coming back. Caleb was missing most of the time, unconcerned with my needs, and Jonathon had moved on with his life. It was just Joe and me.

I heard Joe's chair scrape across the worn linoleum floor as he pushed back from the table. I didn't turn around. Holding onto the sink, I waited to exhale.

If only I could turn back the clock to the time when laughter and voices filled the house. But there are no second chances in life.

The squeak of Joe's recliner told me he was in the living room.

Alone in the kitchen, I sighed.

The sun had set while we were eating supper. Looking out the window behind the sink, I let the water run over the dirty dishes. My heart stirred again, aching anew for the rituals that were no longer part of my life. Washing the dishes had been a family affair for my children and me. The energy of their liveliness would dance around the kitchen as I washed and they rinsed, dried, and put away. It was togetherness and camaraderie that no longer existed. Oh, how I missed my kids.

I was lonely for them, for the laughter and stories they used to tell around the supper table. It had been a long time since joy had filled this room or enveloped me, and I was tired of the emptiness in my life.

Why couldn't Joe be reasonable about anything? He used to have a little give and take. Now, he was firm in his denial of frivolity and fun. Anger rose, and I wanted to throw something through the window just to hear the tinkle of the glass as it shattered. That level of recklessness was out of character. Instead, I grabbed hold of the sink once more and stood there, forcing the anger back. A sad lethargy filled the unbearable emptiness in its wake. Weariness draped itself across my shoulders, and the world settled back in place. Pushing away from the sink, I started back on my chores.

Joe's light snores traveled from the next room as I washed and rinsed the dishes. I could picture him in his recliner, the newspaper lying open on his chest. In twenty minutes, he would wake up, finish the paper, and then head out to check the cows one last time. A man of routine, he would come back in, watch the news, and then retire for the night.

The doorbell chimed. Startled, I dropped the cup I was drying. It fell back into the sink of soapy water and disappeared under the foam. I wiped my hands on the tea towel, tossed it onto the faded laminate countertop, and moved into the hallway. I caught my reflection in the mirror and took a second to push some stray strands of limp brown hair behind my ears.

"Stop fussing and get the door." Joe barked from his chair as the bell rang again. He hadn't moved from his reclined position. He folded the newspaper and set it on the side table before sitting up.

Another surge of anger reared up, and I tamped it down. Taking a deep breath, I pulled open the door and flipped on the outside light.

Two police officers stood there—one on the landing and the other behind him, on the second stair from the bottom. My heart stopped as my thoughts raced around all the "what ifs" I could think of. The blood in my veins went cold. I could feel it thickening and slowing—turning to jelly. An uncomfortable prickling in my hands made me grimace, and all I could hear was the sound of my heart trying to move the sluggish blood through my constricted veins.

Whatever was coming, I didn't want to hear it.

CHAPTER ELEVEN

The first officer pulled open the screen door, and I flinched as it removed the barrier between us. "Mrs. Bradshaw?" His voice was soft yet commanding. He stepped into the house.

My head emptied of all thought. Staring wide-eyed, my heart crashing against my ribs, I saw myself shrinking as the walls moved closer.

The police officer took my hands and looked deep into my eyes. "Breathe. Just breathe. You can do it."

A large concrete weight settled on my chest, but taking his advice, I took in some air. Adrenaline kicked in, causing my body to vibrate. My breath came in tiny gasps, and my legs wobbled as I tried to move away from him.

Joe came up behind me, pulling me back out of the

way. Then he took charge. "I'm Joe Bradshaw. What's this all about?"

"Mr. Bradshaw." The officer nodded. His tone carried more authority and less compassion. He held the door open for his partner. As the two of them moved into the entryway, their presence filled the small space, and Joe moved farther back, dragging me with him. I couldn't stop staring at the uniformed men. It was déjà vu of the morning when they came to tell us about Leah.

The cool night air seeped past them, wrapping me in its clutches. I trembled more violently. The screen door eased closed with a familiar hiss.

I saw the first officer nod toward the living room. Joe scowled, waiting for me to precede him, but my thoughts couldn't connect to my body through the thick paste of fear. Joe gripped my arm, ushering me into the room and onto the couch.

I sat hard, keeping myself on the edge of the sofa, ready to run. The room wavered as panic raced through my core. Noticing my hands were shaking, I clamped them together and tucked them into my lap, waiting. The longer these men stayed quiet, the more anxious I became. I wanted to scream at them to say something, and I wanted to shout for them to stay quiet.

The first officer cleared his throat. "I'm Constable Harrison, and this is Constable Morris." He gestured toward the man standing just inside the room. "I'm sorry to have to tell you this," he said. "Your son, Caleb Andrew Bradshaw, is deceased."

Caleb, dead? No, that's not right. This was supposed to be about my mother or my sister. Not my son. They had it wrong.

"Car accident?" Joe asked.

"No. He, um—it appears that he took his own life."

Took his own life. That was even more bizarre than him being dead. "I don't believe you," I whispered into my chest. "He wouldn't do that."

"Pardon me?" Constable Harrison leaned forward. "I didn't catch that."

Not willing to repeat my thoughts, I shook my head. He would just tell me I was wrong. Looking up, I caught compassion in his eyes. I longed to feel it, to let it soothe my festering wounds. Humiliation fell like a curtain between us as I dropped my eyes in shame. According to him, our son had killed himself. He must know—all about us. Children of good parents don't kill themselves.

Joe stood and moved toward the door. "Thank you for coming," he said, cutting off any opportunity to know more.

Looking at Constable Harrison, I could see by his expression that he had more to tell. He said nothing as he turned and walked toward the door.

I jumped to my feet, desperate for answers. "No. Stop," I called. "I need to know …"

"What do you need to know, Joan?" Joe snapped. "That he slit his wrists or that he swallowed his gun? What?"

My stomach lurched at the harshness of those

words. Bitterness gagged me, and I fell to my knees, barely keeping my supper down. White heat seared my resolve. I could hear feet shuffling as I fought my body. "Please?" I called, looking up.

Constable Harrison looked at Joe, then at me.

Coming back into the room, he gently lifted me back onto the couch. Then he kneeled beside me. In a soft voice filled with sorrow, he told me that Caleb had been found in his car at the bridge on Old Coach Road. Closing my eyes, I saw myself there. I had gone there a hundred times in the past year and a half. It was the place where Leah had lost her life.

"Go on," I mumbled.

"He wasn't alone. There was another person in the car with him."

"Did he …?"

He nodded. "From what we know so far, he killed her before killing himself."

"Andrea?" I asked.

"Andrea." He nodded.

"Did he leave a note?"

Constable Harrison shook his head slightly. We stayed like that for a minute, just the two of us. Alone. Together. Everything beyond him had fallen away. The bubble burst when Joe loudly cleared his throat.

Constable Harrison looked at him, then back at me, before rising. He nodded at me. "Are you going to be all right?"

I understood his meaning. For his sake, I swallowed

hard and nodded.

He turned and walked out of the room, his partner preceding him. Joe closed the door behind them and then returned to the room. His face was dark. I held my breath.

"Satisfied?" he finally asked as he paced back and forth in front of me. "You had to know that you raised a monster." He ran his hands through his curly, dark locks and down over his face. "A selfish …" He stopped, unable to find the words, and I wasn't ready to assist him or supply him with ammunition.

My heart was numb. Believing I lived in the pit of despair already, it surprised me how empty I felt—as if someone had hooked me up to a vacuum cleaner and sucked all the life out of me. I was aware of Joe pacing the floor and mumbling, but it was like I no longer existed. The walls faded into the background, and all I could hear was the refrigerator's hum—a soft, static sound that neither rose nor fell.

"I have decided," Joe shouted, bringing me back to the room with a gasp. He moved to stand directly in front of me. "Look at me when I'm talking to you!" he ordered.

I looked up at him. My heart skipped as I recognized the anger in his face.

"I have decided, from this moment on, you are not to mention that boy's name in this house. We no longer have a son by that name. There will be no funeral, no memorial, no nothing. He is dead and gone. Do you hear me?" He waited for me to respond. "Do you hear me?" he bellowed, forcing me to shrink back away from him.

Knowing that I had no choice, I nodded.

"Good. Don't disappoint me." He left the room. I heard soft rustling at the back door as he donned his coat and boots. Then he went out into the night, slamming the door behind him. The house relaxed with his departure. Or maybe that was just me.

CHAPTER TWELVE

The weight of having to bury another child washed over me as I lay in my bed hours later. Joe, thankfully, hadn't come back from wherever he'd gone. I was alone with my thoughts and my grief. Not that he would support my sorrow. He wasn't like that anymore.

My thoughts became consumed with the anticipation of the funeral service. Joe had ruled against it, but he would come around. He had to. We had to take care of Caleb. He was our son.

Rising in the morning, I slogged through my chores. The air seemed to have jelled overnight, and it took a herculean effort to move about. Every task I started remained unfinished—two slices of toast sat unbuttered in the toaster. The kettle had boiled half a dozen times, yet I hadn't made a cup of tea. Every time I opened the fridge door, I couldn't remember what I was looking for. I hadn't made my bed, and I hadn't dressed for the day. I was still wearing the clothes I'd worn yesterday—the ones I'd slept in.

Joe appeared at ten o'clock on his morning break. I wasn't expecting him. After Leah's death, he changed his routine and took his morning break at Jonathon's house.

Without preamble, he said, "I'm going upstairs to change. I will have some cocoa when I come back down." He left the room, then turned back. "Those the same clothes you wore yesterday?"

I looked down at my clothes and then back to Joe.

"You look like hell. Maybe you could take care of that by lunchtime."

Deflated, I allowed tears to roll down my cheeks. All morning, I waited for a sign that he was sorry. I wanted to rush into his arms and have him tell me everything would be okay—like he used to do when we were first married.

"Well, don't just stand there looking all weepy. Get my cocoa." He left the room.

For a minute, I couldn't move. Then, I forced myself to get started. Most of my baking went to Jonathon's. I scrounged in the freezer and found a bag of muffins and a dozen assorted cookies.

Joe returned to the kitchen—his hair still wet from his shower. I set his cup of cocoa in front of him. His face was stony with determination, and I hoped he was struggling with his grief. I watched his jaw work back and forth as he stirred a generous helping of heavy cream into his mug. The spoon clinking musically against the cup was the only sound in the house.

After he set his spoon on the table, he shoved the plate of muffins across the table. "Why do you insist on putting these damn things out? You know I hate blueberries and raisins."

"I thought Jonathon was coming, and besides, those bran muffins are raisin-free. I used dried cranberries."

"Dried cranberries, eh? Like that's better?"

I moved the plate of muffins to the counter. Joe pulled the plate of cookies closer to him. I watched as he chose a chocolate chip cookie, which he dipped into his hot chocolate. He shook it three times, sucked out the excess liquid before biting into it. He repeated the steps until the cookie was gone. Then he chose another.

"So, is Jonathon coming?" I asked, taking my seat at the table.

"Nope. He says he needs space."

"Space? What's that supposed to mean?"

"It means we're all sick of you moping around like the world has done you wrong. When you learn to smile again, he'll probably be back."

I was stunned. Had I been so miserable that Jonathon didn't want to be around me? Or was Joe twisting things to suit his own purpose? Whatever that may be. I hung my head and waited as the room fell into silence.

"What are we going to do about the funeral?" I finally blurted out. "I mean, do you think we should have it in the church or just something at the cemetery?"

Joe's head snapped back as he fixed a steely stare on me. Standing abruptly, he knocked his chair into the wall.

Needing answers, I jumped to my feet to intercept him before he went out the back door. "Please, Joe. We must talk about this. We need to provide for Caleb."

I never saw it coming. In all our years of marriage, I had ducked many verbal assaults, but not once had Joe ever struck me. My mind emptied with the force of his slap. Instinctively, I raised my hand to my cheek, placing my icy fingers on the crimson welt that bloomed there.

Without a word, Joe pushed me out of his way and moved into the entryway.

Standing there, tears flowing down my face, I waited for an apology. Hoping Joe would rush back and wrap his arms around me, I watched the door expectantly. He didn't come back.

When he spoke, he called to me from the back door. "I'm sorry I had to slap you, Joan. But I told you we weren't having a funeral. I also said never to mention his name again, and you did both. I hope you understand now that this subject is off-limits. If you don't want another, make sure you keep a civil tongue in your head when I come in for my lunch. Or else …"

The threat hung there as the back door slammed closed. I sank to my knees and let the sobs break free. I was living in a nightmare that I wished I could wake from. My husband had lost his mind. Joe proved to be strict and structured over the years, but he'd never been deliberately cruel.

He'd softened a lot when Leah came along. He doted on her, and she was the one who made him do things he didn't want to do. It was Leah who toned down the tension between Joe and Caleb. It never dissipated completely, but Joe made more of an effort when she was around. When she died, the whole family dynamic changed.

When I climbed off the floor using a chair, I cleared the table. I considered tossing the muffins into the trash, but I opted to put them into a freezer bag instead. I would send them across to Jonathon and Debbie. They would eat them.

I went through the rest of my morning on autopilot. I made hot soup and sandwiches for lunch. Jonathon came in with his dad. He offered no sympathy for the loss of his brother, and following his lead, I never mentioned it either. It was like every other day, except it wasn't. A dark cloud of sadness kept winding itself around my heart.

At about one o'clock, the first call came. I didn't recognize the phone number, and I was going to ignore it until I realized it could be one of Caleb's friends calling to pass on condolences. I answered the phone.

"Mother of Satan, are you proud of yourself? Did that boy fill you with pride?" asked the gravelly voice on the other end. I couldn't tell whether it was a man or a woman. There was a lot of distortion in the vocal patterns. "You sad he killed himself?"

It took me a minute to comprehend what was being said. "Who is this?" I asked. "What do you mean? Why are you calling me?"

"I'm calling to let you know your son will burn in hell and you and your husband, right along with him. You are evil, and I hope you rot …"

I hung up the phone. It rang again in just a few seconds. The same number. I let it ring, grateful for the first time that Joe never allowed us to have an answering machine. The phone rang and rang and rang until I couldn't stand it for another minute. I picked up the receiver and cut the connection.

Again, the phone rang within seconds. Staring at it momentarily, I lifted the receiver before disconnecting the call. Leaving the handset off the phone. I trembled, closing my eyes as the dial tone hummed, keeping me safe from the craziness that seemed intent on destroying my sanity.

It lasted only a short time. The happy dial tone changed to an annoying beep that grated on my nerves, making me edgy. Finally, I hung up the phone. I expected it to ring right away, but it stayed quiet. I went back to making supper.

The phone rang about three minutes later. I stared at it, letting it ring several times before I walked over close enough to see the call display. Another unknown number. This time, the call display showed a name, though I didn't recognize it either. I hesitated, my hand hovering over the handset. Finally, I took a deep breath and picked it up.

A series of expletives and abusive language pierced my ear. I pulled the phone back and stared at the handset like it was the problem. Anger burned, and I slammed the handset against the counter before hanging it up.

This time, I removed the phone from the wall and unplugged it. Then, I hung it back up and went back to work. The phone in the living room jingled. I ignored it for the first twenty rings, then stormed into the living room, grabbed the receiver, and yelled, "Why are you doing this? Just leave us alone!" I slammed the phone down and burst into tears.

The phone rang again, and I listened to it for a moment before reaching down and unplugging it as well. Then I went upstairs to the bedroom and unplugged that extension before returning to the kitchen to finish making supper.

When Joe came in, I told him about the calls.

He shrugged. "People have a right to their opinion." Then he plugged the phones back in. The first call came twenty minutes later. Joe answered it. He never said a word. He listened to the caller and then thanked him for taking the time to call.

"Was that someone we know or one of those prank calls?" I asked as I plugged the kettle in to boil.

"It was some poor stiff giving me an earful. He

won't be calling back. See how easy it is. They only want someone to listen."

"But they are saying such horrible things," I said, incredulous that he would think this was normal.

"Might do you some good to listen. These people are speaking the truth, and maybe if you listened, you'd get this dang foolish idea of having a funeral out of your system. He ain't worth it, I can assure you."

With that, Joe sat down at the table and finished his supper.

CHAPTER THIRTEEN

The next morning, after planning for Jonathon's wife, Debbie, to take care of lunch, I headed to town. Joe said nothing when I told him I was going shopping. I don't think he believed me, but he said nothing.

I pulled into the church parking lot and parked near the door. Taking a deep breath, I grabbed my purse and headed to the door. Showtime.

Inside, Terry Preston, the church secretary, sat at her computer. She looked up as I came into the room. A flash of pity crossed her round face before being replaced by a mask of bland disinterest.

After exchanging banal pleasantries, she showed me into the pastor's office.

He was just hanging up the phone when I walked in. He smiled at me without warmth or compassion. Pastor

Mark was new to our church. He'd only been in the pulpit since late summer. I heard he preached well enough, but we hadn't met. I wasn't sure he even knew who I was.

"Pastor Mark, this is Joan Bradshaw," Terry said before she closed the door.

I stood there, unsure of what to do.

Pastor Mark stood up and gestured toward the chairs in front of his desk. "Please take a seat," he said before sitting again.

I sat down in the nearest chair and set my purse on the chair beside me.

Folding his hands on the desk in front of him, Pastor Mark asked, "What can I do for you today, Mrs. Bradshaw?"

Remembering how Pastor John came to our house when Leah died—how he stayed long into the night talking and praying with us—this felt wrong. I wasn't naïve enough to think that the news of Caleb's death hadn't been circulating around town. I was sure everyone knew what he had done in explicit detail.

"We need to bury our son."

"I see." He leaned back in his chair, folding his arms across his chest.

"I know you've never met him, and I'm sure you've heard the stories. But he was a good boy, and yes, he did a bad thing, but he was our son, and we need to honor his life, you know?"

Pastor Mark stared at me.

I shifted in my chair before continuing. "When he was small, he used to be part of this church. He even led a Sunday school class when he was in high school. He's a good boy. I mean, he was a good boy. And I don't know what happened to him, and I don't know why he did the things they say he did, but he wasn't a bad person."

Leaning forward, Pastor Mark said, "I'm sorry, Mrs. Bradshaw, but I've spoken with your husband, and I cannot bury your son."

It was like he'd slapped me. I sat back in shock. What did he mean by that? Did he mean couldn't or wouldn't? Then it hit me. He'd admitted to speaking to Joe.

Jumping to my feet, I knocked over the chair. "I thought this was a house of God!" I shouted. "I thought if I needed compassion, this is where I would find it."

"Calm down, Mrs. Bradshaw," Pastor Mark said. "And please sit down."

But I wasn't staying. The room was closing in on me, and I needed air. I turned to leave, then remembered my purse. I leaned back to pick it up. As I swung it into my arms, I accidentally knocked over the framed photograph of the pastor's family. For a brief second, I was going to apologize, but something else came over me. I reached over and swept all the stuff off his desk and onto the floor. The trays of files and papers and his Bible hit the floor. That photograph of the perfect family flew across the small expanse before crashing into the filing cabinet. The glass shattered with a satisfying tinkle.

I raced for the door and pulled it open. Terry was standing in the doorway, reaching for the doorknob. I bowled her over as I rushed from the room. Outside, I ran to my Jeep, chirping the tires as I sped away from the church. Unsure where to go, I needed to get away. I drove up and down the streets, trying to think of anyone who might help me, someone who would listen and sympathize with my situation.

As I drove past the police station, I remembered Constable Harrison's face. On impulse, I pulled into the small parking lot and parked. I turned off the ignition, grabbed my purse, and prepared to exit the vehicle. Overwhelming fear stopped me. Would I find help inside? Would I find compassion? Or would I simply be told to go home and talk to my husband?

I closed the door and leaned back in my seat. Tears flooded down my cheeks. This was insane. My son was dead, and no one seemed to care. Not about him, not about me.

What was I going to do?

CHAPTER FOURTEEN

I sat in my vehicle for a few minutes, trying to control my emotions. I was in no fit state to drive, and I didn't think being parked at the police station was an issue. When I had myself under control, I put the key in the ignition and started the engine.

Before I could put the vehicle in gear, someone tapped on my window. I shrieked, my heart leaping into my throat. Turning to the window, I saw Constable Harrison's concerned face. The compassion I saw there broke my resolve, and a flood of new tears spilled out. I turned the engine off as he pulled the door open.

It took me a second to realize I hadn't released my seatbelt. When I was free, Constable Harrison helped me to the ground. Neither of us spoke as he took my arm and escorted me into the building. We walked past a few desks, some occupied, others empty. Curious looks followed us as we passed. He stopped in front of a gun-metal gray door. Opening it, he gestured for me to proceed.

I stepped into the bleak room. The air was stale, with a hint of antiseptic. A lone table sat on one side. The walls were concrete and painted the same drab color as the door. I sat in one of the three orange plastic chairs. Eyebolts embedded in the concrete under the long table, which was also attached to the floor, caused me to shudder.

Exhausted and embarrassed, I lay my head in my arms and cried again.

"I'll get us some coffee," Constable Harrison said as he walked back to the door.

"No coffee for me, thanks," I said through tears.

"Tea?"

I nodded, and he left the room. When he returned, I felt silly for taking up his time. He set down two Styrofoam cups and a box of tissues. I grabbed several, wiped my eyes, and blew my nose. The normalcy of that helped me feel a little stronger.

"I should go," I said, pushing back my chair.

Constable Harrison didn't move. He just looked at me, and I stopped trying to run.

"I don't know where to start," I confessed.

Neither of us moved or spoke for another minute. He seemed to savor his coffee, even though it smelled slightly burned. I looked at my tea. A filmy residue on the surface made it unappealing, so I moved the cup to my left.

Finally, he broke the silence. "So, Mrs. Bradshaw, do you have some information regarding your son's case?"

I shook my head sadly, looking down at the table.

"Okay," he drawled. "I have something to tell you, and it's not pretty. There was another victim of your son's apparent rampage. Her name is Brenda Taylor. She was Andrea's best friend."

"Oh no." I groaned, my stomach clenching. I rocked back and forth in my chair, trying to accept this latest news. I didn't want to believe that Caleb could have done what he did to Andrea. Now, there was an innocent victim in this catastrophe. The news seemed too heavy to bear, though I didn't have a choice.

"I'm sorry, Mrs. Bradshaw. I wasn't sure I should come out to the farm to give you this news, and then I saw you in the parking lot … It seemed like providence."

Silence filled the space between us as he waited for me to compose myself.

Finally, he asked, "Is there something I can do for you? You must have come for a reason?"

I looked up at him, tears forming in my eyes. "I just didn't know where to turn."

He waited for me to expound on my statement, and when I didn't, he said, "Tell me what's going on then."

The dam burst. I spilled out Joe's anger at the situation and his refusal to help organize or pay for a funeral.

"Did Joe do this?" he asked as he gently stroked my cheek, where some light bruising remained from Joe's slap.

I pulled away from his touch, my face flushing scarlet. Dropping my eyes away from his, I stared at the table. I didn't confirm his suspicions, but I didn't deny them, either.

"I can't help you if you don't talk to me," he continued. "Do you want to register a complaint?"

"Oh no. I mean … it's not … I'm not here about that, so … no … no way. I don't want to do that." I stammered in embarrassment.

Constable Harrison leaned back. "So, what can I help you with then?"

Taking a deep breath, I said, "I didn't know where to turn. I wasn't even sure there was help for me here. That's why I was going to leave when you knocked on my window. I felt foolish." Looking up to make sure he was paying attention, I continued. "I went to the church today, and Pastor Mark refused to help me do a funeral for my son, Caleb. I mean … he's a pastor, for crying out loud. It's his job to help people." I spat out those last words like they were distasteful.

Constable Harrison didn't reply. He sat there looking at me, waiting.

I dropped my eyes again. "Am I supposed to just leave Caleb to rot somewhere? He was my son …" I choked as a sob cut off my words. I grabbed more tissues and held them against my face while I rallied to control my runaway emotions.

"You didn't know Caleb. Beyond being a murderer who took his own life to escape his punishment, he was once a little boy who wanted nothing more than to be loved by his father. He was sweet-natured and kind. And could he write! He won awards for his writing. Did you know that?"

Constable Harrison shook his head. Encouraged to go on, I told him how Caleb would sit in the kitchen and tell me stories of magical kingdoms filled with magnificent creatures. And there was always a hero—the small but fearless boy who would save the day by slaying the evil warlords, who were usually hornets or wasps. I laughed. "A hornet stung him once, and they became the villains of many stories after that. He had a brilliant imagination, and his eyes would sparkle when he would share them with me." I smiled at the memories.

"But Joe couldn't or wouldn't see how clever Caleb was. He wasn't into book learning. He valued physical prowess, and Caleb didn't measure up." My tears returned as I humbled myself to the truth. "I wasn't a very good champion for him, I guess. I tried, but in the end, I valued peace more. My son grew up never knowing he had value. And that's why I can't let Joe do this to him again. He deserved more when he was alive, and there is nothing I can do to make amends for that. But I cannot permit him to be dumped in some pauper's grave."

When I had finished, Constable Harrison spoke. "Have you heard of Serenity Funeral Chapel?"

"In Crawford?" I asked as I visualized the large stucco building on the major thoroughfare of the nearby city.

"That's the one. I think you'd find someone there to help. Would you like me to call them?"

"You'd do that for me?"

"Well, it's not part of my regular duties, but I can't resist a damsel in distress."

More tears flooded my eyes. Constable Harrison left the room and was gone for several minutes. When he returned, he handed me a piece of paper with a name, address, and phone number on it.

"I've spoken to Mr. Jorgenson. He is aware of your situation and is expecting you. I didn't want to confirm that you would be there today, but he'll be there until five. Otherwise, just call him to set up a meeting."

I stuffed the paper into my purse, gratitude flooding my soul. Tears threatened to flow again, so I took a deep breath and stuffed them back. I had done enough crying in front of this man.

"Thank you, Constable Harrison. I really appreciate this …"

"All in a day's work." He smiled as he stepped over to open the door for me.

"No, it's not, so thank you. I wish I could repay you somehow."

"Um. Well, there is one thing, and this may be presumptuous of me, but here's a card for a counselor in Crawford. Should you ever need to talk, this person is a superb listener. There's a lot on your plate and …" He handed me the business card without finishing his thoughts.

I took it without looking at it, then tucked it in the outside pocket of my purse. I stepped through the door and walked back the way I'd come. Constable Harrison followed until we arrived at the main entry. Then he stepped in front of me to hold open both the inner and the outer foyer doors for me. I crossed the parking lot, aware that he was watching. I glanced back as I came to my vehicle. With a tiny wave, I hurried into the driver's seat.

Pulling out of the parking lot, I drove with decorum in case he was still watching. Staying on Main Street, I came to the highway. Thirty minutes later, I was pulling into the Serenity Funeral Chapel parking lot.

CHAPTER FIFTEEN

Inside the funeral home, it took a minute for my eyes to adjust as the door closed quietly behind me. I stood in a pale foyer, the colors calming and peaceful. Ahead of me was a coat rack, the silver hangers empty. I moved toward them.

On my left was a long hallway, and on my right was a closed door. A burnished wood sign told me this was the "Wedgewood Room." Wondering if this was the office, I knocked. When no one answered, I turned and wandered slowly down the wide hallway.

At the end, just as the hallway opened to a large spacious room, I paused at a closed door on my left that bore another burnished wooden plaque showing I had reached the office. I heard voices on the other side, so I knocked and waited. No one came, and guessing they were busy, I moved toward the room ahead.

The space was immense, with walls retreating twenty feet on either side of the hallway opening. The ceiling also went four feet higher, lending to the feeling of vastness. A semicircle of soft blue chairs awaited, with the rows wider at the back and narrowing toward the front where a short, raised platform stood. The room could easily hold two hundred people.

A podium was just offside the middle aisle, leaving a wide area large enough for a casket to sit to the right. The room featured soft blue paint, which gave it a tranquil atmosphere. As I made my way down the aisle, the soft carpeting absorbed the sound of my footsteps while the tranquil decor surrounded me, creating a comfortable and peaceful ambiance.

There was only one thing wrong with this place. The room was too big. I wasn't foolish enough to think there would be a large turnout for Caleb's funeral. He hadn't died a hero. To many people, he was a monster who deserved nothing. Would any of his friends even come? I didn't expect anyone from Freyden to be willing to go against the church directive. This place wouldn't do. It was too big.

Overwhelmed with despair, I sat in a nearby chair. How was this going to work? I did not know how to honor my son or celebrate his brief life in a space this large. It would feel barren to see a multitude of empty chairs with a few people scattered among them. Caleb would get lost in the silence.

I felt, rather than heard, someone approaching. Turning, I saw a tall, handsome man step toward me. He smiled warmly and extended his hand.

"I'm Frank Jorgenson. You must be Mrs. Bradshaw."

I nodded.

"Ben Harrison told me a bit about your situation. From what I understand, this room will be too large for your needs. I have another room I think you should see. It's quite nice. Please, come this way."

I followed him back down the hallway to the door I had first knocked on. Mr. Jorgenson opened the door, stepping into the room ahead of me. Pointing to the two overstuffed loveseats and three chairs, he explained, "For small gatherings, we use this room, or for a large funeral, this room is where the family waits in private. A small kitchen is also behind that folding panel if you intend to serve refreshments."

I nodded, taking in the ambiance as I circled the room. It was intimate and warm, large enough for twenty chairs and a casket. Mr. Jorgenson watched me closely as I assessed the room, feeling it would suit my needs perfectly.

I nodded. "This room is ideal."

"Good, now if you come into the office, we can discuss the service.

As we exited the room, a striking woman breezed in the door carrying a grocery bag. Mr. Jorgenson introduced me. "This is my wife, Gwen. Gwen, this is

Mrs. Bradshaw. I'm sorry …" he said, looking at me. "I don't know your first name."

"Joan. It's Joan."

"Hello, Joan." Gwen shifted her purse to her shoulder before extending her hand toward me. Her hands were icy from being outside, and her grip was firm but easy.

"This way, then, Joan." Mr. Jorgenson pointed with his head toward another white door just beyond. "Would you like something to drink? Coffee? Tea? Water?"

I thought of the unappealing cup of tea that I left untouched at the police station. I shook my head but then changed my mind. "A glass of water would be nice, thank you."

"Be right back," Gwen said as she hurried past us toward the office.

Entering the room ahead of Mr. Jorgenson, I perched on the edge of the couch while he took one of the two chairs opposite. With shaking hands, I lifted a shiny brochure off the coffee table between us. Neither of us spoke until Gwen walked into the room carrying a tray of beverages. She set this on the table and then sat down next to me.

Mr. Jorgenson cleared his throat. "Now, Mrs. Bradshaw, Joan, I don't mean to seem tactless, but am I to understand that financial hardship is involved?"

I tried to speak but could not find the words. How do you tell a perfect stranger that a father would not pay for his son's funeral? It was probably audacious of me to even suggest they wait for payment.

"It's okay," he assured me. "This happens more often than you might believe. No one is ever ready for this. Very few people plan for this eventuality, and, in this case, it was far too soon."

Tears sprang to my eyes. "No, this wasn't … um—" I stopped, unable to continue.

"Okay, then let's talk about fundamentals first. Are you thinking of burial or cremation?"

The question caught me off guard. We'd buried Leah, and I hadn't thought about cremation as an option. I hesitated. "I think burial?" Burial was traditional, after all—it was what we had always done. Cremations have become more popular since the turn of the century.

A glance passed between the Jorgensons, and a spark of anger flared. I was outside their nonverbal communication, making me unsure and uncomfortable about continuing.

Leaning forward, Mr. Jorgenson said soothingly, "I was going to suggest that you consider cremation." His words clarified the look that passed between them. "I say this because it is a little less costly, but mostly because, with your son, vandalism of a grave site is common. It could be quite distressing, not to mention financially cumbersome, to be forced to do ongoing repairs."

"Oh, my God!" It horrified me that people, strangers with malice in their hearts, would destroy a monument that had nothing to do with them. I sat there feeling angry again. Angry, I would not have a place to go to, a gravesite to tend, or a way to memorialize my son. I would be left with an urn—one that would not be welcome at home.

Finally, knowing I had no choice, I answered quietly, nodding as I spoke. "I see … okay."

One hurdle behind us, I saw them make quick eye contact with each other again. I was being managed, but I also didn't think I had much choice in the matter.

"Okay, now let's talk about costs."

The expensive cost of a funeral shocked me. Looking at the information, I tried to tally in my head how much we'd spent on Leah's funeral. I could not fathom it. How had Joe never told me what he'd paid?

I sighed. If I stuck to the basics, the service wouldn't bankrupt me. We discussed music, refreshments, and the service itself. Because I didn't expect many people—in fact, it might be me alone. I could manage the sandwiches and a few cakes if they could supply the coffee and tea. Other than the actual cremation, the most expensive part of the service was the newspapers' notices. These were expensive. I was looking at those costs and wondering what to do. Picture, no picture. The thought of writing an obituary was overwhelming. I noticed, of course, that they could do that, too, for a price.

Mr. Jorgenson was jotting reminders in his notebook. When he'd finished writing, he looked at me and addressed the newspaper issue.

"I would advise against putting anything in the

newspaper. Those who want to attend will attempt to contact you to find out when the funeral will be. Putting this information in the public realm would invite ghouls and sensation seekers and maybe even protesters and other sorts of onlookers."

Aghast at the levels people would sink to, I shook my head. I hated the world, realizing even as that idea came to me how insane I was being. Sure, there were people out there who lived on the edge of humanity, but I hoped he was wrong and that most people wouldn't give this much attention. I entertained the thought that some might feel compassion for us, for me, and for what we were going through.

I left them shortly after, having kept the costs manageable. Frank and I agreed on a payment plan where I could make monthly installments. We didn't qualify for government help since we weren't destitute. Well, "we" may not be, but I certainly had no income. I didn't know how I would pay, but I would find a way.

CHAPTER SIXTEEN

I drove home, thinking about my choices. Mr. Jorgenson said they would cremate Caleb's body as soon as the police released it. When I asked about a viewing, he told me that there was too much damage for him to be recognizable. This was just one more fact that threatened to crush me. I would never hug my boy—to tell him I loved him one last time. I tried to think back to the last time I said those words and couldn't recall.

Not remembering proved I was a horrible mother. I had failed Caleb, and now there was nothing I could do to make that right, ever. Any chance of rectifying this was gone.

As I passed through Freyden, I saw smoke billowing in the distance. It looked like it might be near our place. A random thought flashed into my mind.

Don't bad things come in three? I lost Leah two years ago, now Caleb. Was my home now in danger? The tires slipped and spun as I hit the gravel road, going too fast. Trying to gain traction, I eased off the gas and slowed my pace. It wouldn't help if I didn't get home at all.

Rolling up and down the hills leading toward our farm, I kept hoping to see the fire was at a neighbor's house. Every time I reached the top of a hill in anticipation, my disappointment grew as I saw that the fire was indeed over the next rise. I drove on faster than I normally would have but slow enough to keep control of my vehicle.

I turned into our farmyard, parked hastily at the side of the house, and leaped out, leaving the door open, the keys hanging from the ignition. Racing across the yard, I found Joe and Jonathon tossing things into a huge bonfire they'd built in the middle of the road leading to the barn. It took me a moment to understand what I saw.

Joe was flipping through photo albums, tossing pictures into the fire. The headboard and the footboard of the single bed that once sat in Caleb's room were both chopped in half. They formed a high pyramid. The flames licked happily at the feast they provided. The ground held a few coils from the mattress, which served as the base for the fire.

A scrap of denim and a flash of red from Caleb's old shirt left behind when he moved to Crawford for university were curled helplessly against the flames' hunger. Jonathon had some books, which he was tearing at, throwing bundles of pages into the fire, slowly feeding the flames with things Caleb treasured. I stopped momentarily, unable to process the scene as it lay before me.

With my heart pounding double time in my chest, I closed the distance between me and the men in my life. "Stop, Joe! What are you doing?"

Trying to grab the album from his hands, I was no match for Joe. He was taller than me, so he simply lifted the book out of reach. I tried again and missed. He turned his back to me as I pummeled his chest with my fists. I grabbed onto his arm and hung there, trying to reach for the album. Joe continued his mission, undeterred. He simply twisted and turned easily, keeping my clawing hands at bay. Jonathon tossed the rest of the books into the flames, sending sparks upward into the sky. He came around and dragged me off his father, allowing Joe the freedom to complete his task.

As I lay in the dust where Jonathon had dropped me, it was clear I had lost the battle. Sobs wracked my body as I watched the remnants of my son's life disappear in the flames. The pages of his books curled as they caught fire. Jonathon stayed on watch, poking the blaze from time to time with a pitchfork. Joe retreated to the house briefly and then came out to stand and watch with Jonathon.

Looking through puffy red eyes, my emotions spent, I saw so many similarities. They were images of one another—both faces I loved and cherished for as long as I could remember. I looked from one to the other and, for the first time, I didn't know who they were. It was like looking at strangers. In defeat, I struggled to stand.

I walked to my jeep, retrieved my purse and keys, then went to the house. I sat in the living room with a cold, wet facecloth across my tired eyes—waiting for Joe to come in with the next ultimatum. It never came.

Dusk cast its shadows into the room, causing them to lengthen and grow deeper until they enveloped the house in the dark stillness of the night. I finally stood up from my perch, looking out into the yard. The fire was done. The lights in Jonathon's place blazed brightly across the wide expanse of green grass that separated our houses. I pondered whether Joe was in the barn, waiting for me to retire, or if he was enjoying a cozy time with his son.

Suddenly, I realized I didn't care.

I closed the door and went to bed.

CHAPTER SEVENTEEN

I awoke the next day to an empty house. Tears rose afresh as I wandered from room to room, looking at the space where Caleb had once slept. His closet door stood open, exposing naked hangers. Stepping into the room, the bareness of despair overwhelmed me. There was nothing left, not even a tiny scrap of paper.

Moving farther down the hallway to Leah's room, I opened the closed door. The sting of her loss hit me anew. The room looked like it always had—a room filled with youthful exuberance tinted with a smattering of the woman she would have become had she not made one foolish choice.

Is that the same thing with Caleb? Had he made one foolish choice, or were there several leading to the tragic disaster? The burden of wishing I had known what was going on in my boy's head, wanting desperately to understand what was in his heart at the fateful moment, threatened to sink me. How would I ever know? He was gone.

Closing the door to Leah's room, I headed into the kitchen. I wasn't hungry, but lightheadedness drove me to eat something. Standing at the window, looking out into the yard, I ate a piece of dry toast. Joe and Jonathon shoveled the debris from yesterday's fire into the wheelbarrow. In a few weeks, there would be little evidence that something horrible happened on that spot.

Joe came in a short time later. I was sitting in the living room, quietly wondering what to do with the rest of my life, trying to reconcile myself to living with a man who could be so thoughtless and cruel. He didn't speak to me, even though part of me really wanted him to. I wanted the fantasy of his regret not only at the madness of yesterday but for the hatred he held in his heart. I wanted warmth, compassion, and understanding. He was silent as he went up the stairs.

I heard him rustling around up there and wondered what he was doing. I didn't go up to check as I was fearful of another confrontation. Jonathon came in a few minutes later. He nodded at me but also remained silent. He went up the stairs, too. I heard more noise, and curiosity overcame my reservations. I slipped quietly up the stairs to see what was going on.

Joe had taken my clothes and moved them into Caleb's empty room. He had tossed the contents of my dresser drawers onto the floor. Jonathon wrestled the mattress from the bed in his old room across the hallway into Caleb's. His small dresser was already standing against the left wall beside the open closet door. My jewelry box and other belongings sat carelessly in the corner next to it.

Down the hallway, my husband was changing the knob on our bedroom door. He'd removed the original handle and replaced it with one I noticed needed a key. The last vestiges of my marriage crumbled into a million pieces as my heart exploded in rage, fear, and insurmountable grief.

I turned and ran down the stairs, grabbing my keys and purse as I raced out of the house. When I left the yard in my shiny red Jeep, gravel flew as I urged the vehicle forward at an outrageous pace. It fishtailed but stayed on the road, a dust cloud billowing behind me.

I had nowhere to go but needed to put some space between Joe and his feelings. Confused and hurt, I wondered what I had done to deserve such treatment. Seeing Joe twist the screws into a lock to keep me out of our marital bedroom completely severed our relationship. We could never bridge the distance that had been creeping between us since Leah's death. I was struggling with the misery that our marriage had become, unsure if I wanted to put it back together. Did I have a choice? I had nowhere to go, no money of my own, no job, no experience. I felt trapped.

My thoughts were all muddled up as I drove into

Crawford. Getting nowhere. I noticed a large coffee cup sign on my right. Deciding a nice cup of tea and some time to think would help put my feelings in black and white, I parked. If I could simplify my thoughts, it would help me know what I needed to do.

The name on the window was Jack's Diner. I noticed a red and black Help Wanted sign in the window by the door—but I paid little heed. I found a table at the back, admiring the artwork as I walked through. The place was busy with lots of laughter and chatter. It immediately made me feel better to hear life going on, even as mine crumbled to dust around me.

I ordered a cup of tea and a cinnamon bun. The server brought me a little Brown Betty teapot, a cup and saucer, and the biggest bun I'd seen in a while. It looked gooey and sweet—the cream cheese icing drizzled decadently over the top. I sank my teeth into it—the flavors exploding on my tongue. The bun contained perfectly balanced flavors. Just enough sticky, gooey caramel dripping from the bottom, just enough cinnamon to make it spicy, the icing balancing the sweetness of the caramelized brown sugar with the fleshy sweet bread. If I hadn't known better, I would have sworn I was in my kitchen, enjoying my baking. When I took the last bite, I closed my eyes in satisfaction.

Feeling fortified, I took an old grocery list out of my purse, found a pen, and made notes. It was clear I wasn't wanted at home. I violated Joe's delicate sense of propriety by trying to arrange a funeral for our son. I searched my heart and couldn't find remorse for that. Joe was wrong, and I would not obey him on that point. Could I stay with the tensions that existed in that house? Did I want to stay? If I were to leave, where would I go? Would my mother help me if I needed a place to stay? I would need money, and I would need a job.

I needed a job! At forty-six, I'd never had a job of my own. Unless you counted the summer I helped my great aunt by cleaning her house and cooking her meals. The old dear had passed on years ago, so she couldn't even give me a reference. Not that I imagined jobs of that sort were readily available. Could I be a nanny? Did I want to be a nanny? What else could I do? I did the books for the farm, tracking the bills and income. It was basic stuff. The books went to an accountant once a year for the income tax. He never complained about what I did, though I didn't think that qualified me to work in an office.

I could cook, of course, but most restaurants had chefs, people who went to school and studied culinary arts or something like that. Caleb and I had laughed that people went to college to learn how to cook as we perused his college calendar in the months before Leah died. I learned how to do that at home under my mother's tutelage, and my kids could at least do the basics. Now, I wondered if that avenue of employment was also closed because I didn't have a certificate.

I sighed just as the server came over with a pot of

hot water.

"That's a deep sigh." She smiled warmly at me. "Want some more hot water, hon?"

I nodded as tears sprang to my eyes at the sincere compassion I heard in her voice. I ducked my head, not wanting her to see, ashamed that such a simple thing would spark such emotion in me.

She saw, though.

With tenderness, she squeezed my shoulder as she refilled my little brown pot with hot water. I sat sniffling for a few minutes. If the dam burst, it would engulf me right here in this public place. I needed to be strong. I needed to get through this.

Shortly thereafter, the bustling restaurant calmed, and the server returned to ask if I needed anything else. I shook my head and thanked her.

"Do you want to talk about it?"

I blinked back more tears and, without understanding why, I poured out my heart to this total stranger.

"My life is falling apart." I looked up, expecting to find judgment, but she looked soft and inviting. I hung my head as if speaking to the table and continued. "You see, my son just died …"

CHAPTER EIGHTEEN

Thinking of my losses, a sob caught in my throat. The server patted my hand twice before excusing herself. She returned promptly with a box of tissues. I grabbed a few, holding them in my palm as I twisted my empty cup back and forth, working up the nerve to get my story out coherently. I wondered if I should tell her about Leah or if that would divert my pain from the truth of what was really going on. But Leah was part of the truth, and it was easy to talk about her.

"It was only a year and a half ago that I buried my daughter. Leah's death changed everything. She was spontaneous and enthusiastic and always seemed to exude an energy that infused the people around her. As a family, we had our share of difficult moments—times when we didn't see eye to eye. There were tensions between my husband Joe and my son, the one who just died. But Leah's presence was an antidote to all that. When she died, the light went out in our world. We became lost in our grief and our guilt …"

I stopped speaking as I stumbled on that word. Guilt. It was uncomfortable to acknowledge in those early days when my heart was raw. I asked God, *Why Leah? Why not Caleb?* It would have been easier for all of us had it been him. Leah would have helped us through, but Caleb was hard work and even harder following Leah's death. After failing to bridge the chasm between us since the day of those ugly words, I decided there was no reaching him, no getting through the walls he built up when she died.

These private thoughts had added shame to my relationship with Caleb. How could I love him properly when I wished he'd died and not Leah?

I sighed before continuing. "And now Caleb's dead and things at home …" I paused, thinking about Joe. Could I tell her what he had done? "Things at home are unbearable, and I don't know if I can stay, but I don't know if leaving is the answer either. Joe, that's my husband. He hasn't healed from Leah's death. He's still wounded, and now Caleb has gone and embarrassed him by taking his own life. He has refused to pay for a funeral, and he's angry with me because I can't let it go. How can I just let the government or whoever—bury him somewhere without a ceremony? He may not have been our easiest child, but he was ours."

I glanced up at the server, not sure what I'd find. There was only compassion, and as I faced her, my shame multiplied. If she knew the truth, would she feel the same way? But she didn't know about the murders, and I would tell no one that when Leah died, I had longed for a different outcome.

"So, what are you going to do now?"

"That's the million-dollar question, isn't it? I don't know. I am lost. Can I stay with Joe? He's so angry, and he's decided that it's my fault. His behavior was brutal when I needed his comfort, as he needed mine. He's so stubborn. I can't see that changing soon. I came here today to figure out what to do. If I stay, I'll be an unpaid slave, cooking his meals, cleaning his house, doing his laundry. There will be no support inside that house. He's turned my other son against me. I get heart palpitations just thinking about it."

She turned my list so she could read it. "It says here that if you leave, you need a job. What kind of job would you be looking for?"

"I don't know. You're going to laugh, but I'm forty-six years old, and I've never worked outside my home. I married right out of high school. I'm not qualified to do anything."

"Well, I think you must have some skills. You've raised your children. Put nutritious food on the table." She paused for a moment. I could see an idea sparked in her mind. "Say, can you bake?"

"You mean pies and cakes and that? Of course." I

blushed, not used to boasting. "I was actually thinking earlier that the cinnamon bun you served me might have come from my kitchen. It was so similar to the ones I bake."

She raised her eyebrows and smiled. "Well, then, I think I might be able to help you out."

"Really?"

"Did you notice the Help Wanted sign in the window?"

I nodded, suddenly unsure of where she was going. I didn't want to be a server. No offense to her, of course. Then, I scolded myself for being such a snob. If that was the job going and I needed a job, then perhaps I ought not to look a gift horse in the mouth.

"Well," she continued, "it just so happens that our baker is retiring. She's been with us for twenty years, and our customers are quite accustomed to her baking. In fact, that's one reason we've kept going when times have been tough. It's our loyal customers who come back day after day, week after week, for a coffee and a cinnamon bun, or a piece of carrot cake, or banana cream pie. You get my drift."

I nodded again.

"Of course, our soups and sandwiches are popular, too, but it's the baking that gets them. So, maybe you could try it and see if the job is for you? Then we can see if you're as good as you say you are." She smiled broadly now.

"Do you have to check it out with the boss first or

anything?" I wasn't sure a server could offer me a job.

"No need, I am the boss. I'm Rebecca Driscoll, but everybody calls me Beckie."

Surprised, I blurted out before I caught myself. "Isn't this place called Jack's Diner? Who's Jack?"

She laughed. I liked her laugh. It was deep and throaty and full of joy. "Jack is my father. He still comes in to make the daily soups. He can't quite retire. God knows he should learn to take it easy, but he's never been one to be idle. When I bought him out a few years ago, I kept the name. Although it was to honor him, I kept it because people know this place. A change in the name seemed unimportant."

Then I laughed. It felt good. Then I wondered, when was the last time I laughed? Certainly, before Leah died, maybe at the wedding, before my world went upside down. Because of that, I shoved my reservations aside and decided to try the job on for size.

Now, all I needed was a place to stay and a new home, and I could start over.

CHAPTER NINETEEN

Driving home, my emotions flipped between the anticipation of a fresh start and sorrow for deliberately breaking my marriage vows. For better or worse, the minister had said all those years ago. People get divorced all the time. I just never thought it would happen to me. The guilt I carried about Caleb's death amplified my conflict, as it seemed to have irreparably broken our family and left no other options for the future.

As I drove, my mind whirling in all directions, I would withdraw some money from our joint bank account to give me a start in my new life. I only needed a little. I only wanted a little. Although I didn't feel like Joe owed me, I could justify that a little of our money was mine for all the work I'd done over the years. I decided on ten thousand dollars. That would give me enough money to pay for Caleb's funeral, with some leftovers to help me set up a new apartment.

That night, while Joe slept behind his locked bedroom door, I worked feverishly to pack a few of my belongings. At the time he put that lock on, it was devastating, but now it worked to my advantage to be in a separate room. I packed clothes, a few mementos, and my cookbooks.

With each box and bag I filled, I quietly moved them to the back porch. When I had finished packing most of my meager belongings, I moved each piece to the Jeep, shifting and arranging things to make sure everything was out of sight at a casual glance.

My task completed, I returned to the house on tiptoe. Wandering through each room, I took mental notes. Every stick of furniture held a story, a memory. I had no choice but to leave it all behind. I had neither the room nor the workforce to move it out of the house.

In the dining room, I stood staring at our wedding china, which was displayed nicely in the beveled glass of the antique china cabinet. I turned and looked at the matching table and six chairs. These were the pieces I was going to regret leaving. Looking around the room, I thought back to that last family meal around this table when we were all still here. Easter—a year and a half ago.

It was a month before the wedding. Leah and Caleb on the one side, Jonathon and Debbie sat across, and Joe and I took up the ends. There was laughter and good-natured ribbing.

I strained to remember conversations, trying to capture each person around the table in my mind, but the words eluded me. Tears rolled down my cheeks as I walked around the table, lovingly stroking the backs of each chair. I stood a moment behind the one Caleb sat in, trying to revive him into my world. I did the same with Leah. It was hopeless. I couldn't raise them to save my soul.

I wandered through each room of the house, taking in the sounds and the memories, soaking in as much of it as I could. Then, I climbed the stairs and slipped under the covers of the single mattress on the floor. Jonathon hadn't moved the bedframe from his room, and I understood that being put into Caleb's old room was a direct message to the position Joe had delegated me to.

After my failure in the dining room, it surprised me how easily I could conjure up images of Caleb here. I could see him reading a book as he lay on his bed or studying the stars through the cheap telescope he received for Christmas when he was thirteen. I could almost hear his voice as he positioned the scope so I could see Venus that night so long ago.

"It's hard to tell it's a planet with the naked eye, and it's pretty boring. But it's now at inferior conjunction—that's when it's closest to being directly between us and the sun. It looks like a long, thin crescent. Here, look."

I did. It was amazing. I was glad I had climbed out

of bed in the wee hours of the morning to share this moment with my son. His passion was clear as he whispered information.

"Jupiter is on the opposite side from Venus. We're nearly in a parallel line. The sun—Venus—Earth and Jupiter. That's fascinating. Isn't it, Mom?"

"Yes. It is, Caleb."

As I thought about Joe's lack of enthusiasm for anything Caleb loved, I set aside that precious moment. Joe never saw Caleb's passionate side. Now, he never would.

I sighed—my loss, our loss—was palpable.

Snuggling deeper under the covers, I was thankful that Caleb had taken his telescope with him so it survived the fire. I hoped that one day I could retrieve it.

These thoughts lulled me deeper, and I fell into a dreamless sleep.

CHAPTER TWENTY

When I woke, the sun was shining through the curtain-less window. I looked at my watch. It was nearly eight a.m. I stumbled down the hall to the bathroom, where I relieved my bladder, brushed my teeth, and splashed cold water on my face. I had to think positively about my decision to leave. Today, I would find an apartment, and even if I had to sleep on the floor, I would not come home again.

I would find either some used furniture or maybe a furnished place to rent. If unsuccessful, I'd rent a storage locker for the belongings. It was not a good plan to carry the stuff around in my vehicle for days when I would park on the city streets.

Back in Caleb's room, I ran a brush through my hair, slipped into my clothes, and gathered the rest of my belongings into a bag. My jewelry box, alarm clock, Bible, and the novel I had started but hadn't turned a page since the news of Caleb's death. I wondered as I stuffed them into the plastic grocery bag if I would ever read again. I dropped my hairbrush into my purse and headed toward the door. Looking back, I saw the bareness of the room. There was nothing left for me here.

Downstairs in the kitchen, I found remnants of Joe's breakfast. A bowl, a pot with some oatmeal residue, a small sweaty plate with toast crumbs, and a mug with a little Ovaltine languishing in the bottom. I popped two slices of bread into the toaster, made a fresh pot of tea, and sat quietly, eating my breakfast and looking out the window. I saw the tractor leave the yard but couldn't tell if it was Joe or Jonathon behind the wheel. It didn't matter. I would not say goodbye, anyway. I needed to get my hands on the money before I uttered a word, or I would be homeless.

Having finished my breakfast, I ran to Leah's room and grabbed her jewelry box—the one with the ceramic mice on the top. I gave her that for her tenth birthday, and she still treasured it until she passed. Back downstairs, I gathered up the photo albums that lay on the living room floor. Joe had eradicated all traces of Caleb, but I treasured the rest as mementos from a life I no longer lived. I took the bags out to the car, along with my food processor, which was sitting on the counter.

I did one more rushed walk-through before I left the

house, knowing I was leaving for the last time. Fresh tears streamed down my face. I looked at the old white cabinets, scarred from age and use. I loved this kitchen. It held most of my cherished memories—the ones where the kids and I enjoyed time together after school.

More tears flowed, tears of regret and those for the deaths of so many things in life I'd taken for granted. I never imagined my life would turn out this way. It was incomprehensible that in two years—I had lost two of my children in tragic circumstances.

I also never expected to face the cruelty and malice I had experienced at the hands of the man I had given my life to. He had no regrets from my viewpoint. It was like he had the right to treat me with disdain for having a different opinion.

Although Jonathon had acted with his father, I still held onto the hope that one day, when this tragedy was behind us, he would reach out to me. Debbie, his wife, who'd been absent in all this family strife, was the unknown. She could steer Jonathon as much as his father did. From what I knew of her, I thought she was fair and just, and I could only hope she would have compassion for me. It was possible to interpret her silence as indicating complicity with Joe, difficulty in managing her emotions, or a reluctance to oppose her husband. I just didn't know.

I flashed forward to grandbabies, and my heart burst in two again. Could I be a part of their lives if I left? I couldn't bear the thought of being lost to them, so I forcefully pushed it out of my mind.

I had enough troubles to bear without borrowing more.

CHAPTER TWENTY-ONE

The bank manager eyed me suspiciously when I requested to cash in a few bonds before they were due. I silently prayed he wouldn't call Joe before I received the money.

"I need this money to pay for my son's funeral."

My statement seemed to ease his concerns. He relaxed. He knew the story. It had been in the newspapers—naming names and pointing fingers. With no further arguments, he moved the money into our joint account.

At the wicket, the teller, a member of our church, tried to get me to take a draft when I asked for my withdrawal in cash. I agreed to take half in a cashier's check, insisting I wanted the rest in bank notes. She finally counted out the funds in one-hundred-dollar bills, frowning slightly as she counted. I stuffed the bundles into my oversized purse, smiled politely, and thanked her.

Driving down Main Street, I went past the post office, past the café and the newspaper office, feeling numb. This town had been so crucial to me at one time. As a young bride and mother, I found these streets to be the roads to activities, play dates with the kids, coffee klatches, and quilting bees with friends. This town was my hometown. I wondered whether I'd ever be back, if I'd ever drive down these streets again.

I saw the police station just ahead. Constable Harrison sprang to my mind, and I smiled. He was the only person who showed me kindness during this whole mess. I was about to drive by when I stopped to thank him for his help and let him know what I was doing. A part of me still hoped the investigation would reveal some sign of exactly what happened on the night my son took his life. I hoped for a clue that would exonerate him, even though deep down, there was a fear there would be nothing to find.

He didn't seem surprised to see me as he ushered me down the hallway to the same interrogation room. We sat on opposite sides of the table.

"Thank you for helping me the other day. The Jorgensons were invaluable, and just like you said, they were compassionate and understanding. They are assisting me with the funeral. It will be on Saturday.

Tears flooded my eyes again. I wiped them away angrily, tired of feeling vulnerable to the pain. I took a deep breath. "Joe still isn't supportive of a funeral. He won't even come. He burned all of Caleb's stuff, too!"

Constable Harrison nodded. "I know. There is a video on YouTube."

I wasn't sure I heard him. I knew what YouTube was. Most parents these days are aware of the multitude of social media platforms out there.

"What video on YouTube?"

"You don't know about it? Well, we've been monitoring the internet, watching for comments about your son and what happened. It is part of investigations these days, monitoring social media sites to see what people are feeling and thinking. Sometimes people give themselves away—sometimes we see emotions running amok and can step in and prevent vigilantism and retaliations from happening." He glanced at me to be sure I was following and understanding.

I nodded.

"Anyway, this morning, this video appeared. It shows you running across the yard. You can't make out what is being said, just that the tone of your voice seems frantic. It shows the fire, you can see it's a bed frame …" He stopped. He didn't have to describe it any further. I was there. I experienced it. "We've contacted YouTube to request the removal of the video, but unfortunately, it has already garnered a lot of views. By the time they remove it, if they do, thousands will have already seen it and shared it. I'm sorry."

He left the room for a moment and came back with a laptop. A few seconds later, after tapping the keys, he turned the screen toward me.

"There's a blog, too, and we can't do much about that. The author is careful with her wording. Unfortunately, she is responsible for uploading the video as an attachment to her blog. I don't think you want to watch it, but if you do, just click on this right here." He pointed to the screen with his finger. I nodded and then took a deep breath. With my stomach rolling, I leaned forward and read the words of a blog post entitled "Burning in Hell …"

> "Following a speeding Joan Bradshaw from town yesterday, I witnessed a scene unlike any I'd ever experienced in my life. Joe Bradshaw and his son, Jonathon, were burning something. Watching the attached video, you will see a very distraught Joan trying to stop her husband, whose height and stature were to his advantage against her attempts. I can't be certain, but it looked like Joe was perhaps purging the belongings of his son, Caleb. The video will show clothes and books being tossed into a makeshift bonfire. Caleb Bradshaw, aged 20, is the "alleged" shooter in the brutal slaying of Andrea Pritchard, 19, and Brenda Taylor, 20. Caleb Bradshaw then took his own life. Hank Mackenzie, a local farmer, discovered two of the

> bodies early on the morning of October 28th. The authorities found the other body in her home during a welfare check. Freyden, a small town in the south, has never experienced such heinous and insidious violence in its 100-year history. The funerals for the deceased have yet to be completed."

I sat stunned. Who would have done such a vile thing? Then I remembered … It wasn't even a conscious memory, really. I saw Marlene Penner on the sidewalk in front of her house as I sped out of town the day before yesterday. Marlene Penner was a notorious town gossip. She must have followed me. I wasn't paying attention to what or who was behind me. I was so intent on the smoke billowing into the sky ahead of me. She must have smelled a good story, a tidbit, a morsel for her evil little gossiping world. Flames of anger and rage burst out of my chest, and I wanted to find her, grab her by the hair, and smash her face into the wall, the floor, and the ground. The passion for destruction terrified me for a moment. Then I burst into tears again.

I wasn't crying because of what happened to me or my family. I was crying because, at that moment, I understood what Caleb felt. Where those feelings came from or why he couldn't back away from them was the part I didn't understand. Those feelings of rage drove my son to do something unspeakable. I longed to know when they started. How long had he lived with them before allowing himself to act? I might never know.

When my sobbing subsided, my tears finally ended. Constable Harrison passed me a handful of tissues. I wiped my eyes and blew my nose, feeling self-conscious again.

"Thank you for always being so kind to me. I know you probably see me as the mother of a monster, maybe even a pathetic excuse for a parent …"

"Don't talk like that. I am aware of your daughter's death, and I know sometimes kids go off the rails for many reasons. Caleb had a choice that night. He didn't have to do what he did. We can only guess why he chose that path. So please don't put yourself down. You're strong and will make it through this tragedy, too."

Tears welled up again. Hearing kind words was foreign to me. I wanted to be that person, the one Constable Harrison saw, even as I worried he wasn't right. Looking at his kind face, I blurted out, "I am leaving Joe." My hasty disclosure shocked me. "I'm moving to Crawford, where I have a job at Jack's Diner on Fifth Street. I still need to find a place to live, but I can't stay here anymore." This time, no tears came. I sighed.

Constable Harrison patted my hand. "Good for you. I wish you luck with everything."

"You'll keep me posted, won't you?"

"The investigation is nearly complete, but I don't suppose we'll find out much more. Once the investigation is done, we can release some belongings from his apartment to you. Caleb's laptop, his phone.

There are some journals, too, if you want them."

His journals. Caleb's journals. I had completely forgotten about them. He has been writing since he was little, using a journal since grade eight when his creative writing teacher encouraged her students to keep one to exercise their writing muscles and organize thoughts and ideas. His journals would be the closest thing to having a conversation with him.

"Yes, please, I'd love to have those things back—when you're done with them, of course. And his telescope?"

"I believe that is still in the apartment. Once the investigation is complete, we will inform you, and the landlord will request that you clean out the place so he can rent it again. I will warn you, though. There is some damage to the place. It was a mess. You and Joe will likely have to pay for the repairs that the damage deposit won't cover."

I took my cue and trailed behind him to the door. He held it open, then followed me back down the hallway to the front door.

He reached out and took my hand. "I'll be in touch then." He smiled. "Good luck."

Releasing his hand, I left the building, feeling somewhat buoyed by his wishes.

I was starting a new life—wasn't I? Things were changing. In the past few days, huge decisions appeared before me—my choices pushing me in a new direction. I had lived a sheltered life until now. I'd worked hard, but I'd never been alone. How was that going to look or feel? I did not know. I couldn't muster more than a small sliver of hope among the numbness of grief and the sadness of loss.

CHAPTER TWENTY-TWO

The first stop I made in Crawford was at Serenity Funeral Chapel. I surprised the Jorgensons when I showed up and counted out the funds to pay for the funeral. Gwen suggested I stay for a cup of tea, but I declined. I needed to find a place to live.

Mr. Jorgenson squeezed my arm as he escorted me out of the office after telling them I had a job. "Well, I think someone is looking out for you, Joan. Jack's Diner is a landmark in this city, and Beckie is a lovely person. Gwen and I stop in there occasionally for coffee and one of those decadent sticky buns. We'd go daily if we didn't care about our waistlines." He chuckled, patting his firm midsection. "When we pop in, we will say hi."

"That would be lovely," I said sincerely. At that

moment, I realized how isolated I let my life become over these past few years. I used to have friends when the kids were young, but with Joe, it was hard. He demanded so much that I didn't give those friendships much consideration, to the point they were more like friendly acquaintances.

When Leah died, I found it impossible to turn to any of them for comfort. I was grateful for the help with the mundane things like meals, but I kept my grief and my thoughts to myself. After her funeral, I just couldn't bring myself to keep in touch with anyone. It all seemed like more work than I could manage. After a few months, it seemed impossible to even start again.

As I left, Gwen reached over to hug me before I went out the door. "We'll see you tomorrow at two o'clock," she whispered.

I nodded, my stomach flipping as I thought about the lonely send-off that I would give my son.

After leaving the funeral chapel, I drove several blocks and pulled into a gas station. I went inside to purchase a newspaper. I picked up the daily edition and saw Andrea and another girl smiling on the front page. My stomach lurched as I lifted the paper and read the caption.

Andrea Pritchard and Brenda Taylor died Sunday in what police are calling a case of domestic violence. For details on this and their upcoming funerals, see page A2.

My hands shook as I dug for the sixty cents to pay for the paper. In my vehicle, I opened the paper and read the column. On page two, there were a few more pictures, including pictures of Caleb from his social media account. The column recapitulated the story as I understood it and included details about burying both girls at different times on the same day.

For the first time since I heard the news, the full impact of what my son had done hit me. I had only focused on the loss of him in my life. The night I received the news, I briefly cast a sorrowful thought on Andrea, and I am not sure I even had one for Brenda when I heard about her death. It seemed like an afterthought in my world. The guilt of that weighed heavily.

The names of their parents and siblings were black and white, and each one became real to me at that moment. These people and many others would stand and face the fullness of their loss tomorrow.

The weight of all that guilt crushed me, and for a moment, I couldn't breathe. How would I ever be able to make this up to them? There was a deep need to make this right, and even as I scrambled to think of something, I realized it was futile. There was nothing I could do. Their daughters were never coming home again, and my son was responsible for that. It was a travesty, one that I longed to be free of. Yet, this devastating incident would never leave me.

It took several minutes before I could focus on why I bought the paper. I pulled out the classifieds, circled ads, and made calls. I set up three apartment viewings. I had a little time to waste before my first appointment, so I pulled into the Wright's Furniture store parking lot.

Inside, I walked through the groupings of furniture, trying a few couches and chairs along the way. I noted the costs of the pieces that appealed to me, knowing I couldn't afford to buy new ones.

A salesperson came along, offering to assist. I let her take down my information, even though I was only wasting her time.

CHAPTER TWENTY-THREE

The first two apartments I looked at were horrid. There was no other way to say that politely. Between small rooms, worn flooring, chipping paint, bathrooms that I was sure were not sanitary, and nefarious odors that I could not locate the source of, I was feeling completely discouraged. I prayed as I pulled into the parking lot of the last place on my list that Sam Goddard Towers would have a home for me.

The impressive eighteen-story building was a mere four blocks from Jack's Diner, which was perfect for me because downtown parking was expensive. I pulled into a visitor stall and hurried across the asphalt to the front door. Inside, a short, chubby man sporting a mop of grizzled gray hair springing madly in all directions stood wiping the buttons on the intercom system.

He wore a crisp white T-shirt with rainbow suspenders holding up his baggy, bright blue denim jeans. I pulled open the door and stood waiting for him to move so I could press the button for the building manager.

The man turned to me. "You Joan Bradshaw?"

"Yes. Are you Mr. Reimer?"

"Yep, call me Ted." Holding a large ring of keys on a retractable chain attached to his belt, he turned to insert one into the lock and pulled the door open, bracing it with his body. Then he turned back to me. "Bradshaw? Are you any relation to that monster that killed those girls, then killed himself?"

I looked at him, dumbstruck and unsure of how to answer. If I said yes, would I be turned down as a tenant? If I said no, what would that say about me? Was I being a coward?

Before I could answer, a small woman with tightly wound curls came around the corner. Something about how she held herself caused me to hold my breath as if expecting a storm.

"There you are, Ted. I've been trying to find you for hours." Without taking a breath, she continued. "There's something wrong with my garburator. You need to come right now."

Ted shook his head. "I'm Sorry, Mrs. Richards. I am showing this lady an apartment right now. I'll be there as soon as I'm done."

Mrs. Richards leveled a steely stare at me. It was so

intense I almost backed up. "No, it is not okay, but what can I do about it? You need to show an apartment!" Her head rocked side to side as she spat out the last word. Then she spun on her heel and disappeared the way she had come. The walls sighed.

Ted turned to me. "Sorry about that. Some people, eh?" He led the way through a spacious lobby, where three groups of oversized chairs sat together under the high ceiling. Fake trees and flowers sat in large pots beside these groupings, making the space feel warm and welcoming. The plush, dark green and burgundy rug made me feel like I stepped into a posh hotel.

I glanced around, amazed at how spacious and open the place felt. Ted walked purposefully down a short hallway behind the chairs. There stood two stainless steel elevator doors gleaming as if recently polished. He pushed the button to call the elevator. The doors to the left opened immediately. He stepped in, placed a hand against the doors to keep them from closing, and waited for me to follow. I stepped in, moved to the back, and turned to face the doors.

We rode up to the twelfth floor in silence, staring at the digital box announcing each floor as we passed. With a hitch and a lurch, the elevator stopped at twelve. When the doors opened, he stepped out ahead of me, and I followed. We turned left and headed down a wide, bright hallway.

I hadn't much experience with apartment buildings—I didn't really know what to expect. The walls had a soft, warm peach paint, and the carpet had a sturdy multi-colored Berber design. Everything was clean, polished, and quiet.

He led me down a maze of hallways to a light honey-colored door with 1234 displayed across it in five-inch black iron characters. He searched for a key on the large ring, found the right one, and opened the door. Again, he stepped into the apartment ahead of me. I followed.

Leaving the door open, he led me through the suite. I fell in love with it. The three main rooms had an open concept. A compact kitchen opened into an extremely spacious dining room, which spilled into another large space—bright with sunshine from the wide patio doors. A short hallway led to a large, spacious bedroom, a small storage room complete with laundry hookups, and a functional bathroom. This place seemed perfect.

The walls were a basic off-white color, but you could see that someone had freshly painted them. The dark tan carpets appeared clean and were obviously new since I couldn't see any visible traffic patterns. The drapes looked heavy—they were still sporting the plastic covering from the dry cleaners.

There was a French door in the bedroom leading out onto the patio that ran the length of the apartment. I walked through the door, admiring the several tones of brown brick on the outside of the building. I pulled open the door at the other end and stepped into the living room. This place was fantastic.

I turned back again to take another look. The patio was bookended with brown bricks on either end for privacy. Four rows of bricks framed the outside edge below the black wrought-iron railing and banister, making the space seem less exposed than if they had put the railing right into the floor. The solid floor had a vinyl covering, with drains in both corners. I stood in the late fall sunshine, visualizing the space alive with flowers in large pots and a cozy bistro table where I could sit, drinking tea and watching the city come to life on a sunny morning.

This was the place for me.

I'd known it the moment I stepped into the lobby.

CHAPTER TWENTY-FOUR

Following a quick tour of the building, Ted left to look after Mrs. Richards. Borrowing Ted's tape measure, I made a list for the secondhand store. When I returned the tool to Ted, he recommended I try the Thrift Store on Second Avenue.

It was a whirlwind of shopping, and I chose items based on function rather than beauty. I even bargained with the store to agree to deliver the furniture to the apartment in the morning after paying a hefty emergency delivery fee.

As I was about to head next door for dishes and cutlery, I noticed a striking painting of a bearded iris. I stood for a moment, staring at it while I debated buying it. Shaking my head, I walked out without it. What did I need with a painting when there was so much more I needed to buy?

After picking out a set of dishes, I realized that the used cutlery and other utensils were unappealing. I would pick up those items from a dollar store.

Still thinking of that picture, I backed out of my parking stall. I almost left the parking lot before I doubled back, parked my vehicle, and ran inside to purchase it. Using my credit card, I promised myself that this was a one-off. I would only use my credit card for emergencies in the future.

At the dollar store, I chose a variety of spatulas and baking utensils before finally returning to Wright's Furniture to get a new bed. Having seen what was on offer at the secondhand store, buying a used one was not an option.

The sales lady said she would try to arrange my delivery for the following morning but didn't think it would happen. It was more likely that they would deliver it on Sunday, the day after Caleb's funeral. Realizing that without a bed, I would have to sleep on the floor made me think about how haphazard my plan was. Going back to the farm, however, was not an option.

Should I get a hotel? I wouldn't be able to bake, but I would have a bed for the night. I wondered if my mom was home. Maybe I could sleep at her place. I couldn't decide if I was ready to call her, so I put off the decision.

My last stop was Walmart. There, I picked up the few small appliances I needed. Swinging down the bathroom aisle, I grabbed linens for the kitchen, bedroom, and bathroom before heading to the other side of the store.

I picked up some kitchen staples and groceries, things I would need to make lunch for the funeral. The more things I put into the cart, the more tired I became. When fatigue caught up with me, my cart was fairly overflowing. I pressed on to get the job done, and then I could rest.

Grabbing a jar of raspberry jam, I settled it carefully among the other items when it hit me. I didn't like raspberry jam—Joe liked raspberry jam. I preferred marmalade but seldom bought it because Joe thought it was a horrible condiment. Why was I buying raspberry jam?

I searched through my cart, then automatically pulled out items I had dropped in there, things I had bought just for Joe. I stacked them on the shelf beside me. My emotions rocked out of control. I looked around, fearful of what I was feeling and unsure of where to go. Should I go to the bathrooms and try to gather myself? They were a long way off. What if I just walked away from my cart?

Don't be silly, I thought. You'd just have to start all over again. I pushed the cart down the aisle and avoided eye contact with other shoppers. I didn't want anyone to notice my tears. My breath was coming in pants, though I tried hard to breathe deeply. I wasn't making any headway in getting the upper hand on my panic attack.

"Breathe, breathe, breathe," I muttered. I pushed the

cart forward, crossing the aisle. The need to walk away from items I had shed and all they represented—pushed me forward, though I didn't know where I was going. The counter in front of me appeared out of nowhere. I was in the pharmacy. Why was I in the pharmacy?

I saw the pharmacist behind the counter. He seemed to talk to me, but I couldn't hear him. I could see his mouth moving, but all I could hear was the ocean and my heart's loud, frantic beating. Darkness reached out and tugged me downward, and I fell into it. My fear dissipated as I surrounded myself with the black stillness.

When I opened my eyes, I saw a pair of unfamiliar deep brown eyes staring at me with concern on his handsome brown face.

"Where am I?" I looked around. My surroundings were clinical and unfamiliar. "What happened?" I uttered those words even as I remembered the strange need to walk, breathe, and get away. The cold floor offered little comfort against the embarrassment that infiltrated my being as I remembered.

"You fainted." His voice was kind. "How are you feeling?"

I lay there for a moment longer, assessing my situation. My heart rate returned to normal, but the dizziness remained. "Better." I smiled as I sat up.

"When was the last time you ate?"

I tried to remember. Had I eaten this morning? I thought back to my day. Yes, I ate breakfast for the last time in my kitchen at the farm. It wasn't hunger that caused me to faint. Panic had overcome me, causing me to hyperventilate, and I collapsed.

"I'm okay," I replied, avoiding his question. "There has been too much to deal with lately."

Another person wearing a white lab coat appeared and handed me a bottle of water. I noticed that people were milling about, pretending not to care but watching intently. I climbed to my feet.

The pharmacist, V. Sukhadya, by his nametag, assisted me. I wobbled a little, then straightened my shoulders, taking a deep breath in.

"Thank you for your kindness," I said. Then, I grabbed my cart and walked away. Those still looking on watched me leave, none of them hiding their curiosity as I passed.

I didn't know what else I needed. Shattered—all I wanted to do was go home. A deep longing consumed me. Even though the last time I experienced this feeling was at summer camp when I was ten, I recognized it as homesickness. I didn't know what to do. I longed for the familiar, the comfortable, but the farm was no longer home to me. It was a standoff—a war zone. The new apartment was empty and strange.

The deep longing intensified, and I wondered again where my mom was. Her place in one of those senior-only complexes didn't feel like home, and she hadn't for years.

Mom detested Joe. She was tactless with her

animosity, and Joe would get all riled up after one of her visits. Caleb was only a baby when Joe banned her from our home permanently. He demanded an apology for something she said, and she refused. He grabbed her by her arm and dragged her out of the house, throwing her purse and coat after her.

I was mortified, but crossing Joe was not the answer, so I kept quiet. Following that, I met her in the city for lunch occasionally. Joe did his best to make me uncomfortable about having her in my life. Her banishment hurt Mom, and even more so, I hadn't stood up to him. I tried to explain why. She didn't want to hear it. She filled her life with people her own age and soon had little time for me. Our relationship fell to a few calls a year.

As I thought of that day, my shame at what I'd allowed overwhelmed me. No wonder she avoided me. Even as I thought—my heart swelled with love for her. Being ostracized was undeserved, and shame fell on my shoulders for my cowardice to allow it to happen. Thinking back to my childhood, I recalled times when being with her was all the comfort I needed. That's what I wanted now. I wanted to roll back the clock, let go of all my fears and insecurities about the future, and let someone else look after me.

I paid cash at the till, counting only a single one-hundred-dollar bill left among a few other smaller bills still in my wallet. On my first day, I had spent all the cash I took from the account. It was closing in on suppertime. I headed back to the apartment.

As he had done earlier, Ted offered me the use of the apartment trolley to move in my purchases. If I stayed, I could bake the desserts for the funeral. A hotel was costly, and I had used up most of the cash. I would need to get a bank account and deposit the other half of what I took. But until then, I didn't have the funds for a hotel, and I was fearful of the greeting I would get from my mother.

CHAPTER TWENTY-FIVE

Even though the most pressing thing was getting the food ready for the next day, I took the time to pull the brown paper off the picture. I leaned it against the longest wall in the living room and stepped back to admire it. The artist captured the vibrant beauty of the Bearded Iris. It wasn't a scented flower, but they were majestic and showy. Looking at this picture was like going back in time. It settled my raging homesickness to a low burn.

With a sigh, I returned to the kitchen and unloaded the bags. I pulled out the ingredients I would need for baking, stacking them on the countertop between the fridge and the stove—the fresh vegetables and perishables I loaded into the fridge.

Wanting to clean the cabinets and line them with

some gingham shelf paper I purchased, I left the rest of the grocery items inside the bags. I set them on the dining room floor next to the end cabinet.

My food processor took up a lot of space in this tiny kitchen. I moved it to a less intrusive space before unpacking all the cooking utensils and new pots. Everything washable went into the sink filled with hot, soapy water.

My tummy grumbled loudly. Why hadn't I thought to grab a burger or something on the way here? Deciding a cup of tea might help, I found the kettle. As it rumbled to life, I looked at the clock on the stove. It was only six thirty, past Joe's suppertime. I hadn't called him. Was he worried? Was he angry? Did he even care? I searched through my purse and found my cell phone. No missed calls. That solved that mystery. He hadn't even bothered to call to see where I was, to find out if I was okay. What a jerk! I dropped the phone into my purse and stormed into the living room.

I stopped. The Bearded Iris picture was the only thing here that felt like home. The otherwise empty room shouted at me, making me feel like an interloper. I wandered through the rest of the rooms. My clothes were still in boxes in the bedroom. I had no bed to sleep on. Maybe I should go to a hotel. Maybe I should call my mom.

Then what about my baking? If I stayed, I could bake that night. If I went anywhere, I'd have to return early to get a start on things. That would mean baking while the delivery people were unloading my furniture. The feelings of abandonment rose over me again. Why am I even bothering? Who did I need to bring food for, anyway? No one was going to come. Nobody cared about Caleb, not after what he did. Nobody except me. I leaned back against the wall and sank to the floor in despair. Hugging my knees to my chest, I lay my head down and let the weariness take over. I thought back over the few calls I made to advise people of Caleb's funeral.

My sister did nothing more than grunt—my mother was a bit more sympathetic. Susan wasn't coming to the funeral. Her husband, Dick, suffered a heart attack during the summer, so money was tighter than normal without his income. My mother. I wasn't sure. She didn't commit to coming.

Most of the other calls I made received crisp politeness. Steve Haman's mom refused to give me Steve's number, so I left word with her. She was abrupt, which wasn't a surprise. She wasn't the warmest person by nature.

Paul's mother was more sympathetic but cool. She promised to tell Paul, who I was certain would tell Steve, even if his mother did not. I didn't know who else would show up. I didn't even know for certain that Paul would. My weariness intensified. It became more entrenched as I sat on the floor, allowing my thoughts to wander. My hunger, so defined a short time ago, disappeared into the background as my body succumbed to the weight of my life.

I steered my thoughts, wandering back to happier times, to days when life was simpler, and I was at peace. My breathing slowed, and my thoughts turned to dreams as sleep found me and swept me along without an argument.

A short time later, I woke up with my body stiff and my muscles screaming for release from the uncomfortable position. My legs wobbled under me as I stood. In the bathroom, I took a long look at myself in the mirror as I washed my hands. Again, I noticed my hair, vowing to do something about it soon.

The bone-weary expression on my face made my heart sink deeper. I was just so tired—I didn't know how much longer I could stay strong. Who did I need to stay strong for? Jonathon didn't need me. Joe certainly didn't want me. I had no one.

"Stop!" I shouted aloud. I was sick of thinking that same self-defeating thought over and over. Being alone was a momentary issue. Yes, things look bleak now. But that's what it was. A moment because I would make new friends. I had a job where I would be among new people. Everything would work out. And as I thought that—Constable Harrison's face swam into my thoughts. The caring and concern I saw in those blue eyes brought me to tears again.

I shook my head in disgust. Why was I thinking about him? He was just doing his job, not showing interest in me—for me. He was just performing his civic duty, which they paid him to do.

I wandered into the kitchen. The clock showed that it was after ten, which meant it was time to bake. My body still ached from my short stint on the floor. I really wanted a comfortable bed.

I walked down to the bedroom and took the comforter out of the package. Folding it up, I laid it on the floor. I gathered the top sheet from the bedding set I'd picked up and lay down on the comforter, pulling the sheet over me. Remembering all I had to do in the morning, I climbed out of bed and plugged in my alarm clock. I set the alarm and then slipped back onto my makeshift bed. It wasn't too comfortable, but it didn't take long before my weary body succumbed to the pull of sleep.

CHAPTER TWENTY-SIX

The next morning, I woke up with a start. There was too much light. I was late. I glanced at my alarm clock. It was eight-thirty. I had set the alarm for six. What happened? I grabbed the clock. In my tiredness last night, I hadn't realized that I had set the clock to six in the evening, not six in the morning. The alarm would go off at six that night.

Immediately after I washed my face, I rushed to the kitchen and stirred ingredients in a bowl. I slid some squares into the oven when the buzzer went. The brownies were already cooling on the counter. I picked up the phone on the wall by the door.

"We're here with a delivery for …" There was a pause, and I heard paper rustling. "A Mrs. Bradshaw. Is that you?"

"Yes." Then I stood there, not sure what to do next.

"Can you let us in?"

"How do I do that?"

"There's a button …" I looked at the button and clicked it. It disconnected the call. I placed the receiver back in the cradle and hurried down to the elevator.

In the foyer, I found two burly men: one leaning against the mailboxes and the other standing near the intercom system.

As I pulled open the door, the leaning man stood straight. "Doesn't look like she's going to let us in, Earl."

"Sorry!" I was breathless, not because of the race from my apartment but because of my anxiety at not knowing what to do.

"Um, Mrs. Bradshaw?"

"Yes, I'm Mrs. Bradshaw." I smiled, weak with relief.

"Oh great, I was waiting for you to buzz us in." He smiled a toothless grin.

"I'm sorry. This is all new to me. I didn't know how to do that."

"No worries." With that, the two men went to work.

Back in my kitchen, I put the eggs in a pot to boil before taking the squares out of the oven to cool. Whipping together a couple of cans of tuna with mayonnaise, mustard, and finely chopped dill pickles, I made the first batch of sandwiches. Then, I constructed some roast beef on a bun and a few with cold cuts, laying them out on a reusable aluminum serving platter. When the egg salads were complete, I covered the plate with cellophane.

As I whirled around the small kitchen, I took time to direct the two men to place my new furniture where I wanted it. My heart skipped a beat when the buzzer rang again. The stress of the day was wearing on my last nerve. As I reached for the intercom, I wondered if Joe would show up before I remembered he didn't know about this place.

I answered the call, and a man identified himself, saying he had a delivery from Wright's Furniture. When I complained I wasn't aware it was coming, he informed me that the saleslady had pulled a few strings to get my bed delivered early, and she had left several messages for me. When I checked my phone later, I realized I had put it on silent last night and forgot in the morning's madness to turn the ringer back on.

I looked around helplessly. I still didn't know how to let someone into the building. The two men were just coming in with another load of furniture. Intuitively, Earl understood what I needed. With another toothless grin, he showed me what to do. A wave of shame washed over me. When I met these fellows, I judged them as backwoods simpletons, all brawn and no brains. Yet here they were, showing me I wasn't as clever as I thought I was.

Not much later, the deliveries were complete, and I was signing papers. As a group, we shuffled toward the door. I thanked them profusely. I wondered if I should tip them for their hard work, but I didn't know the protocol for such a thing. They didn't hesitate, as if expecting something, so I dismissed my fretting.

With that done and behind me, I finished cleaning the kitchen from my sandwich preparations and then iced the squares. Feeling good about my work, I showered and changed into my black dress. I wore a little makeup but paid attention to my hair, dabbed on lipstick, and assessed myself in the bathroom mirror. Freshly shampooed, my hair didn't look as tired as it had yesterday, but I still thought a change would do me good. I had to stand on tiptoes to see below my waist. Perhaps I should have picked up a full-length mirror. Had I even seen one? I couldn't remember, but it might be worth a look. Not that I ever gaze much at myself in a mirror, but occasionally, it seemed important to have an overall view of how one appeared.

My tummy grumbled loudly. I realized I had eaten nothing since noon the day before. A wave of grief passed over me, and I wandered through the rooms of my new home. Each room held some furniture, but it did not have personal effects, as I had packed anything I brought from the farm into a cluster of boxes and bags sitting in the bedroom. I wondered if I would ever truly call this place home since the furniture filling it were things someone had discarded. Would I always refer to the farm as home? The thought made me sad. Sad, too, because I had another large goodbye standing before me—a final one.

My hunger was forgotten, and my heart burst as I realized that in the past few days, Caleb had once again taken a back seat to all that was going on in my world. Even in his death, he couldn't seem to be first. I wandered back and forth through the living room and dining room, crying more tears for Caleb. My poor lost boy.

CHAPTER TWENTY-SEVEN

Because of his injuries, I hadn't seen Caleb before cremation. There was something wrong with that. Since I hadn't witnessed the finality of death, I didn't know if the wound would ever be closed. An urn was cold and impersonal. I thought back to my father's funeral, to his body in the casket. It was cold and impersonal, too, his body lifeless and unreal in death. His shape was familiar, but without his spirit beneath the flesh, he looked like a stranger. I wouldn't see Caleb in this way, and I didn't know if that would be a good thing or not in the end.

Down front was a low table covered with a white cloth decorated with artistic imprints of angels. Atop the table was a large blue urn. Caleb.

I walked down the center aisle and placed my hand on the urn. It was cold—reflective of how it was being here. This was all I had left: a cold ceramic jar. No flesh and blood, no life. Nothing to hold tight, and to kiss and to tell …

I straightened my shoulders. If Joe and Jonathon didn't appear, I would need to be strong, and maybe even stronger if they did.

Frank Jorgenson stepped up behind me and put a kind hand on the back of my arm. Allowing him to guide me to a seat in the front row, I sat, feeling the loss of my world—losing all that had been important to me.

There was work yet to do, so I rallied my emotions. Frank helped me bring in the sandwiches and the squares. We put them in the small kitchen area, off the chapel. An urn of coffee was perking. The smell of the freshly brewed beverage was tantalizing to me. Maybe I'll take up drinking coffee. I've often wanted to, but Joe had been adamant we keep our bodies free of things that could be addictive. No alcohol, coffee, or tea, though he allowed me the herbal kind since it wasn't caffeinated.

I stepped back into the chapel to wait. It wasn't long before I heard someone coming down the little hall. Taking a deep breath, I readied myself to greet them. The first person through the door was Paul. He looked terrible, his unruly black curls framing his unusually pasty white face. Sad blue eyes peered at me, filled with dark emotions. He wasn't coping well.

He tried to smile, but his face crumpled, and tears raced down his cheeks. I took him instinctively into my arms. He sobbed, muttering how sorry he was. I patted and rubbed his back, shushing him, telling him all would be okay. He was a good foot taller than I was—his slight frame leaning over me, making it impossible to see around him. I was aware of other people coming in, but I didn't move. My attention was on this broken young man, this loyal friend to my son. Our embrace lasted a couple of minutes. He struggled to gain the upper hand on his profound grief. When we separated, I noticed Stephen standing off to the side, looking much like Paul.

Stephen looked as rumpled as usual despite having his sandy hair brushed smooth. His shirt was partially untucked, and his loose pants hung low on his round hips. At my glance, he stepped forward and embraced me briefly, his sorrow pulsing ominously, though he was not allowed to release it.

There were more people in the room now. I noticed a few college-aged kids sitting together in the last row on the right and another couple on the left. Stephen moved off to join Paul in the front row on the right side of the room. Paul's mother stepped forward, surprising me. She'd been off-putting when I called about the funeral. She swept me into a brief hug, whispered short words of condolence, and then moved off to sit beside her son. Constable Harrison stood at the back of the room next to Frank. He looked uncomfortable. I smiled at him. He nodded—but didn't move toward me.

I looked around the room. There were eleven people so far. Far better than I expected. A few more young people came in, three boys from Freyden. They were peripheral people in my son's life. Their appearance brought the number to fourteen. Now, if Joe, Jonathon, and Debbie would come. I wished with all my heart again. They needed to be there. I needed them to be here.

My mother wobbled into the room. I hadn't seen her in months. She seemed frail and much older than the last time I'd seen her. I stepped forward to greet her. She stiffened. She wouldn't accept a hug. I reached out and touched her arm, squeezing it gently.

"Thank you for coming."

Her gray eyes looked moist, but her demeanor was as cool as ever. "Had little choice. He was your son."

Her choice of words left me flat. My son, not your grandson.

"Not a big room. These chairs will not be comfortable. I hope it will not be a long service. Not if I must sit on one of those things."

"I've reserved the front row for the family." I pointed to the chairs on the left side of the room.

"No husband? No Jonathon?" she commented. Not waiting for a reply, she shuffled off toward the chairs. She sat in the second row, in the middle. Maybe she was leaving the room for my husband and son, though there were enough chairs for all of us.

CHAPTER TWENTY-EIGHT

I smiled wistfully at Gwen, who was sitting at the small portable keyboard off to the right, playing softly as the mourners found chairs. I stared at the picture of Caleb. In it, he was laughing. It was a beautiful picture, one of the few I had framed. It would have burned with all the other items that proved my son's existence if I had not taken it with me the morning I arranged the funeral.

My mind wandered back to the day that I took that picture—July. Caleb and Andrea had come out for a Sunday supper. They were already living together, and I had met Andrea once before, but this was her first visit to the farm. Caleb had taken her on a brief tour earlier, and then he disappeared up to his room while Andrea helped me set the table for supper.

Losing our Leah a year before had eased, although her absence from family gatherings like this was always poignant. I missed her. I noticed similarities between Leah and Andrea—her bubbly nature, for one. She also displayed mannerisms that were so delicately feminine that I wondered if there was a "girlie" sequence missing from my genetic makeup. Graceful. That's what she was! Graceful and fluid. They both moved effortlessly. Not that I wasn't feminine. It was that I wasn't elegant. I was in a gingham dress. They were in the evening gowns.

Caleb came downstairs then, carrying several journals. He set them on the table, picked up the top one, opened it to a marked page, and handed it to Andrea.

She took the book and read it. When she was done, she closed the book tenderly, handing the book back to Caleb as if she were holding a treasure.

"That is beautiful, Caleb."

She spontaneously leaned into him and kissed him on the lips. He blushed, smiling shyly at me. I grabbed the camera and snapped a picture of him, then another one of the two of them. I couldn't quite describe how that afternoon felt. Looking back, there was hope for our family for the first time since Leah's death. Caleb and this bouncy, beautiful girl gave me back just a taste of what our future could be. What had gone so wrong? Here we were, a few short months later, both gone forever. Both are at the hands of my son.

Jostling myself back from my reverie, I looked at

Frank. He raised his eyebrows slightly—I nodded to him and took my seat. Constable Harrison took the outside aisle and sat at the end of the first row, a few chairs away from me. Frank walked to the front. All the attendees sat up straight and faced forward expectantly. Frank cleared his throat, and the piano's musical tones ceased as he spoke.

Being a retired minister, Frank performed the ceremony like a pro. We started with Caleb's favorite hymn. Back in our seats, he regaled us with stories of Caleb and his faith in God in a solid, soothing voice.

Of course, he hadn't known him, but he created a generous depiction of who my son was by weaving the stories I told him on my first visit. Tears welled up and flowed, but I kept my deep sorrow under control. I didn't feel I needed to show the world how devastated I really was.

"Caleb Andrew Bradshaw was the second son of Joseph and Joan Bradshaw. He was born on a wintry day in March. He was an excellent student in school and a faithful child of God. When he was nine, he wanted to learn to play the saxophone. He didn't do very well."

There were a few chuckles.

"But there must have been a reason for his choice, and God works in mysterious ways. During that semester, he and his teacher, Henry Archibald, spent a lot of time together. Alice Archibald said at her husband's funeral the following spring that Caleb gave her husband a reason to live. Just as school started, he found out he had inoperable cancer. She wanted him to resign, and he might have if not for Caleb.

"The music lessons became a mission for the older man. He was determined to help Caleb learn to play. But as their friendship grew, it was a mutual passion for astronomy that kept them together. The two of them would spend hours in the attic of Mr. Archibald's house with a telescope staring at the heavens, the saxophone forgotten by the front door. Henry saw Caleb as the grandson he never had—he only had granddaughters. Caleb adored the older man.

"After Mr. Archibald passed, Caleb continued to look at the stars. He kept his saxophone for a few years as a reminder of his friend, but he never played it again. The next semester, he took up creative writing.

"It was here that his talents lay. He was a superb storyteller, and he excelled at writing. His teacher sent one of his poems to a competition. The poems were to be about spring, and I found a copy in the library archives. Here is "Spring" by Caleb Bradshaw.

Spring comes with joy
Sweeping away old winter chills
And the sunshine's warm embrace
Pulls flowers from the depths of loamy soil
The world shakes off its slumber
Color bursts from the grayness
Of old, forgotten snow and barren ground

Reborn for another day, another season
The sun grows stronger as it rises high
The bees hover above the flowers
For a gentle kiss, they lower themselves
To take and to give so that life may unfold
Anew
In this ritual, I find hope that one day soon
The sun will shine with favor upon my face
And I will find the warmth of that embrace
To take at first a gentle kiss
Then, let it grow until I'm consumed
And like the flowers of the field
I'll stand against the colorless world
Remembered for eternity."

I didn't know that Frank had found a copy. I had promised him on the day we had talked about the service. Unfortunately, the bonfire had changed that. It had been years since I heard that poem, and I was once again surprised that Caleb was so eloquent.

I left the service then, my mind going back to that day when Caleb came through the door after school like he was flying on a magic carpet. He was so thrilled, and I don't recall another time when I saw him this excited—before or since. It was magical to see him so happy.

There was that light in his eyes whenever he spoke of things he had a passion for.

He prattled on for twenty minutes, his brother and sister giving him time without interruption. Joe wasn't enthusiastic, but for once, he didn't cut the boy down. I couldn't recall a time when Caleb was as happy sitting down to eat as he was when he finished. More often, someone said or did something that cut him off and shut him down. That poem was a symbol of doing it right.

I came back from my reverie as the service was wrapping up.

"… Caleb left us too soon. We will cherish his memory for the young man he was and for what he brought to our lives."

I heard sniffles around the room. The stories shared moved people. When Frank finished, he opened the microphone for people to share personal stories. No one moved except to squiggle uncomfortably in their chairs. There was a strained cough or two. It was obvious no one wanted to come forward.

Frank stepped back and asked us to stand. We sang another hymn. When this was over, we remained standing as Frank poured out a verbal blessing of benediction. He mentioned people were welcome to stay for refreshments.

He stepped away from the podium and walked down the aisle, out of sight.

It was over.

CHAPTER TWENTY-NINE

I took a deep breath and closed my eyes, not ready for this to be over. I took another deep breath and another as hysteria threatened to overwhelm me. A warm hand settled on my shoulder. The connection to another human being calmed me. Putting a smile on my face, I looked back to see who had come along to help me. It was Constable Harrison. He removed his hand as I stood up.

"That was a nice service. I'm glad I came."

"Thank you for that. I appreciate the support. Oh, I see my mother has gone." I felt a stab of anger and sorrow together.

"I think she just went to the washroom—her coat is still hanging by the door," Constable Harrison replied. "But speaking of leaving, I'm on shift soon, so I should go. If you need me, though, please call. You still have my card, right?"

I nodded. He squeezed my arm and then left without looking back.

Glancing around the room, I noticed people sitting in groups of three or more—most of them had taken advantage of the small offering, tiny Styrofoam cups being held, or sitting on tables that had appeared as if by magic. Sandwiches and squares sat on small plates. I made the rounds, thanking people for coming. People told me their names, but I would never remember them. All were Caleb's friends from college. Each had a kind word or a short story to share. It pleased me they didn't hold Caleb's actions against him and came to pay their respects regardless of the heinous way his life ended.

As people filed out in small groups, moving off to their own lives, I noticed my mom's coat was now missing. Tossing off my anger, I moved to Paul's table. Life was too short to worry about my mother's lack of compassion.

I was making small talk with his mother as Paul and Stephen sat solemnly across the table from us. "Paul, how are you doing?" I reached over and touched his hand.

He blushed deeply, pulling his hands away as if burned with a hot poker. Tears welled up again.

"Paul?"

He looked at me, tears swimming in his grief-stricken blue eyes. He blinked, wiping angrily at his tears. Stephen elbowed him gently. Paul cleared his throat.

"I feel so bad, Mrs. Bradshaw. I was with Caleb that night, and I didn't stop him." He choked, coughed, and gathered his emotions.

Joyce pushed her chair back. "Paul, please, this is not the place." She heard it before.

I gave her a hard stare. "No, it is okay, Paul. Please continue."

Paul looked sideways at his mother before clearing his throat. He fidgeted with his cup, twisting it around and around, bouncing it noisily on the bottom rim as he told his story. "Caleb was really upset that day. He was worse than I'd ever seen him before." He glanced at me, making sure I was listening. "Andrea had moved out, you know …"

I didn't know that … I shook my head.

"Yes, he was sure she was seeing someone else for weeks. She wasn't in college this term. She was taking a semester off to earn money, so they weren't together too much. When he was in school, she was at home. When he was at home, she was working. She worked every weekend, too."

Why hadn't Caleb told me any of this?

"Well, Caleb came home that Friday. He'd been up in Calgary doing something with that Observatory. Anyway, he arrived home to find her stuff was gone. He called me, but I didn't know anything. We went looking for her on Saturday morning, but we couldn't even find her car. She wasn't working, either. It was like she'd disappeared off the face of the earth."

CHAPTER THIRTY

Paul's confession was heartbreaking. I could feel his guilt radiating from him, and I wanted more than anything to tell him to stop. Did I need to know all of this? Instead, I smiled and nodded, encouraging him to keep going.

"Well, we went to Brenda's place, Andrea's best friend. She wasn't home, either, but Caleb figured they were together somewhere. No one was talking. We ended up going to the bar, and Caleb just got wasted. I'd never seen him like that before." He glanced up again, his face crimson.

"The weekend was a blowout. Caleb just kept drinking. He drank all day Saturday at his place. Steve and I went over later in the afternoon and found him plastered. He was doing stupid party tricks, sitting in his underwear, totally sloshed. It wasn't good."

"We slept on the couch that night. Caleb was crying and screaming sometimes, laughing hysterically at others. We were real worried about him—not sure what to do." He looked at Stephen for confirmation. Stephen nodded in agreement but said nothing.

"Anyway, he seemed calmer on Sunday, like he'd got it out of his system. But he was real hung over. We went for a late breakfast at Smitty's. Caleb didn't eat, he looked real bad, and he was real quiet."

"We hung out at the apartment all afternoon, watching movies and playing video games. Caleb slept for a while, too. Then we grabbed some burgers for supper, and afterward, when we were driving home, he saw Brenda's car in the parking lot of The Edge—you know … that bar on the main drag?"

I didn't know it, really, but I nodded, showing he could continue.

"Well, he yelled we should go there, and I was trying to calm him down, you know, he kind of went from zero to sixty." Again, he looked at Stephen, and again, Stephen nodded as he sat there tearing chunks out of his Styrofoam cup.

"When I kept driving past, he threatened to jump out of the car. He even opened the door. Freaked me right out. So, I told him we'd go, and I went around the block. I hadn't even parked the car, and Caleb was out the door, walking fast toward the bar. We had to hustle to catch up to him." He stopped, looking around as if he needed something. Then he rubbed his hands over his face, tears flowing again. His eyes darted left and right, then he closed them and took a deep breath. He exhaled, gathered his thoughts, and finally continued.

"We get into the bar, and it's dark, so it takes a moment for our eyes to adjust. I spotted Andrea right off, but Caleb was looking in the wrong direction, so he didn't. She was sitting with Brenda and a couple of guys close to where the bar curved back toward the bathrooms. When Caleb saw her, he stopped, and, man, oh man, his face! He went pale like he was going to faint or something. Then, he, like, turned red, and his eyes went like slits. His whole body stiffened. I could tell he was angry—angrier than I'd ever seen him. He marched toward her table. Steve and I kind of hung back, not wanting to be part of whatever would go down. It wouldn't be good, but we were there for Caleb, you know."

Steve was nodding—but remained quiet.

"Caleb got to the table and stood there, his hands balled into fists. Man, he was tense. Andrea was laughing at something. She was kind of turned a little, so she didn't see him right away. Brenda saw him, and you could see the look of surprise cross her face, and everyone turned. He never said a word, you know. He just belted Andrea right across the face. It was so hard …" Paul choked on the words, tears flowing as he lived that night again. "It was so hard, it knocked her right over, chair and all."

My heart, already twisting as I listened to Paul retell the story of his last night with my son, wrenched painfully at his words. Oh, my God! Caleb! What were you thinking? The rage in his actions scared me. It was like I didn't know who he had become and when he changed. Paul lay his head down on his arms, clearly exhausted. However, the story wasn't done, so I waited. Joyce moved around the table. She pulled up a chair on the other side of her son and rubbed his back in large, swirling circles.

It took him a minute to gather himself. "Sorry," Paul said, lifting his head and sniffling loudly.

I shook my head at him. "You have nothing to be sorry for. I can't imagine how hard this is for you. It's hard for me to hear, so …"

He nodded. "Well, when Andrea hit the floor, all hell broke loose." He looked sideways at his mother. "Sorry." She patted his back. "The guy who was sitting beside Andrea got to his feet, his chair crashing to the floor behind him. He took a step toward Caleb, but Brenda got there first. She screamed at Caleb. Man, she has a filthy mouth." He blanched, "Um, *had* … a filthy mouth."

Steve just nodded. "She swung, Brenda, I mean, she swung at Caleb, and in one move, he took her by the hair and threw her onto the floor like she was a rag doll. It happened so fast—I don't even really know what I saw." He took a breath. "Did you know Brenda?" He looked at me, his question a diversion from the story.

I shook my head.

"Well, she wasn't a skinny chick like Andrea, but he tossed her to the floor like she was nothing. That's when the other guys got into his face, shouting and gesturing, and I thought, I mean, we thought …" He glanced at Stephen. "We'd better get Caleb out of there before he got his ass kicked."

"Other people were getting out of their chairs, too. Some were moving back, moving away from what was going down. Some of the bigger guys were standing their ground. The music was playing, and Brenda was yelling, but a hush fell over the room, sweeping across the crowd, and people became aware that something was happening. Then I saw the bouncers coming, so Steve and I grabbed hold of Caleb and tried pulling him out of there. He was pulling back, cursing at Andrea, spit flying. I've never seen him like that, man, oh man."

He squirmed in his chair. "One guy was helping Andrea up, and the other was helping Brenda. Andrea wasn't crying or anything. She looked sad-like, defeated. Her hair was hanging over her face, and I could see some blood. Brenda was making up for both of them—she hadn't stopped screaming at Caleb. Everybody all around the bar was staring at us. I told Caleb we had to get out of there, but he was still resisting. Then he said something to Andrea that chilled me … and it's even scarier now because … because of what …" He cleared his throat. "He said …" He gulped, drew in a breath, and gulped again.

CHAPTER THIRTY-ONE

I was on pins and needles, expectant and terrified.

"He said, 'This night won't end well for you.' Then he stopped pulling against us, so Steve and I got him the heck out of there. A couple of bouncers got there by then, and they pushed us out the door."

"When we got to the car, Caleb looked shrunken, like he'd lost weight. His face was blank and soft like he let go of everything. I don't know how to describe it. It was totally weird. He asked me to take him home. So, I did. When I got to the apartment, Steve and I got out, like we were going to go in with him, you know. But he stopped us and told us he would pack a bag and go home, that he needed to be home with his folks. So, we left him there. I remember looking in the rearview mirror, and he waved to us as we left. I drove out of the parking lot, then I turned around and went back, but he was gone. The light in the apartment was on, so I waited for a while, just sitting there. I don't know why. We were there for maybe fifteen or twenty minutes, and nothing changed. I was going to ring the bell, but then the lights in the apartment went out.

"I couldn't decide whether to leave before he got down to that parking lot. I was pretty sure he'd see us when he came out. I didn't want him to think we didn't trust him or something. But we stayed, and I turned off the car instead. We sat there in the cold, waiting for him to come down." He paused, tipped his empty cup up, and looked inside. "But Caleb never came down. We waited five, maybe ten minutes, and he never showed up, so we thought he must have changed his mind and gone to bed. So, we left."

"The next day, though, Caleb didn't show up for school. I tried calling his cell, but he wasn't picking up. I left messages, but he never called me back." Tears were flowing again. "I went by the apartment at lunch, and his car was gone, so I figured he must have gone home and that maybe he took a day off to clear his head, you know. It wasn't until later that I realized I hadn't seen Brenda—not that we were close, but I'd see her around sometimes. It just never occurred to me to think something like that would ever happen."

He looked at me then, guilt etched in his deep blue eyes. "I shouldn't have left Caleb that night. I should have listened to my gut and stayed whether or not he wanted us to. It wouldn't have happened, and he would still be here if only I stayed." His voice broke again, but he cleared his throat and squared his shoulders. He seemed ready to take his punishment like a man.

He would not get that from me.

CHAPTER THIRTY-TWO

The story that Paul shared shattered me to my core. The brutality my son manifested that night shocked me. It was barbaric and sordid. Inside, my heart beat double time. My stomach rolled like a ship in a tempest. I wished with all my heart I had heard none of it, but I did. It hurts to think I raised someone who had so much anger in his being that he could do such unthinkable things.

I was unsure how to settle my equilibrium and restore some semblance of peace. Who was this boy? I realized my son was someone I didn't know, yet I had raised him. The longing to talk to him, to find out what had gone so wrong—where it had gone wrong—flooded my senses. I needed to fix it, even if it was too late. The desire to set things right was paramount in my mind.

I didn't know where to start, though. Caleb was

gone, and I couldn't talk to him. Anger percolated, but I quickly shut it down. I couldn't do anything to help Caleb now—it was too late for him. My guilt could also wait. For the moment, I needed to take care of the boy across the table from me. I needed to make him a priority, to keep him from crashing his life upon the rocky shore of guilt and shame. If I didn't, he would become another casualty of Caleb's actions.

"Paul, you had no way of knowing this would happen. No one could. What happened that night was unthinkable. None of us in the same place would have thought that Caleb could do what he did. You cannot, Paul—" I took his hands again. This time, he didn't pull away. He just looked at me with teary blue eyes. "You cannot blame yourself for not doing something because no one could have guessed what was happening inside Caleb's head. You did all you could. You are not to blame for this. Do you understand me?" I squeezed his hand, and he gently reciprocated.

Then he nodded and pulled his hands away. I couldn't tell if he agreed with me or was just placating me.

"Maybe you should see someone, talk to someone. I don't want you carrying this burden—it's not yours to carry. Please, for my sake …"

Joyce nodded at me. "He'll be fine. I'll make sure of that. Thank you."

"No, thank you, and Paul—thank you for telling me—I'm so glad you did. I'm sorry you had to go through it again." When I stood up, he did too. I hugged him, trying to take all his guilt upon my shoulders where it belonged. Released from my embrace, he turned and left, his mother following.

Steve stood awkwardly for a moment as if waiting to say something, but he stayed silent. I smiled at him.

"Thank you for coming."

He nodded, turned away, and slumped out of the room. I watched him go, shaking my head at his rumpled shirt, which had come untucked at the back. A rush of affection for him washed over me. He always looked so disheveled, and it was hard not to want to fix him up. It was a motherly instinct. I sighed as he disappeared.

I looked around. The room was empty, and I was alone. I sat at the table, exhausted. Paul's story whirled images of a demented soul through my mind. My stomach lurched and clenched, and my heart, already sorely bruised, was being crushed beyond repair.

I took notice of the debris left behind. Styrofoam plates and cups sat on tables or on the floor beside chairs. Going into the kitchen area, I found a trash bin. Bringing it back to the room, I cleaned up, glad to have something to occupy my mind. I needed to run the story through my head again, but not here—in my bed, alone. My bed! I wouldn't ever be in my bed again—not that one. I had a new bed, a new home.

Anger at Joe and the situation he forced me into rose like a rocket ship on the launching pad. I could feel my face burning as it roared through my body. Intent on cleansing my rage, I ferociously tossed the cups and plates into the garbage. I didn't hear Frank enter the room.

"You don't need to clean up."

I jumped, nearly dropping the garbage can I held in my left hand.

"Yikes, you scared me." I laughed then, a little of the tension leaving my shoulders.

"Didn't mean to do that." He chuckled, too, reaching for a few cups and putting them in the bin before he took the can from me. "You okay?"

"Yeah, I guess. It's been a long day … a long week, no, I lie …" I paused. "It's been a long life. I am so tired and don't know how I will cope."

Frank patted me on the shoulder. "You'll cope," he assured me. "You're made of sturdy stuff, and you'll make it through." He slipped me a business card. I took it without thinking. "But if you need to talk to someone, this woman is a good listener."

I looked at the card. It was for a therapist.

I nodded and went into the kitchen to gather the remaining food.

CHAPTER THIRTY-THREE

The platters were much easier to carry empty. I stacked them together, pulled on my jacket, and hoisted my purse to my shoulder before picking them up and heading out the door. It was a delicate maneuver to open the door, but I managed. I had years of practice juggling groceries and other assorted parcels and keys. Heading back to the apartment, I was only a few blocks away when I realized I needed to go to Caleb's apartment. I didn't understand why. He wasn't there, but Paul's story fueled a need in me I couldn't put to rest. I turned back the way I came.

Minutes later, as I pulled into the parking lot, I remembered the only time I had visited him there—just after he moved in. I was in Crawford to pick up the new light fixture for the bathroom. The old one was burning bulbs faster than I could change them, and the last time, I thought I smelled something burning. He helped me by picking up some catalogs from the wholesalers. It took some time, and there were so many choices.

I finally settled on the wrought iron pieces with white globes. It looked rather old-fashioned—country-styled. It's not modern and compact. It would fit nicely with the décor of the house.

I was hoping to take Caleb to lunch that day and see his new apartment, but he seemed reluctant, insisting he'd meet me at the restaurant. I persisted, and he relented.

His apartment was the typical square block, three stories with an off-white stucco façade. The architect tried to give it a Spanish feel by adding arches between the pillars that held up the red-tiled roof covering the door to protect tenants and visitors from the weather as they rang buzzers or inserted keys in locks. The building's back and front mirrored one another, the front facing the street and the back facing the parking lot.

Coming from the east, I unknowingly drove past the entry to the parking lot. So I pulled around the corner and parked in front of the building. I admired the two baskets of fuchsia petunias and white lobelia hanging on either side of the arches. A twinge of regret and a burst of pride flashed through my body simultaneously when I saw his name in black and white DYMO-tape—Bradshaw, C—beside suite 8C. My boy was all grown up. I pushed the white button and waited.

"That you, Mom?"

"Yes, it's me."

"Pull the door when you hear the buzzer. There is no elevator. You'll have to take the stairs, third floor, turn right. I'll meet you in the hallway."

"Okay."

An annoying buzzer sounded. I pulled on the door. It opened easily. Inside, I found the stairs, counting them as I went. Eleven stairs, a landing, eleven more stairs, a landing. The door at the end of the landing prominently displayed a sign that read Floor B. I turned and continued up eleven stairs, a landing, and eleven more stairs. Following Caleb's instructions, I pulled the door open on Floor C and turned right. There he was, standing in the hall, just outside an open door. Seeing him standing there, a wave of love washed over me. I was so glad to see him!

Inside, he showed me around. It was a small place, so it didn't take long to see it all. A galley kitchen, a small dining room, and a living room with a small balcony looking out over the back parking lot. The bathroom was still steamy from a recent shower. He pointed out the two bedrooms, one with a computer desk and a futon. The other bedroom door was closed. The place was immaculate, which surprised me. He was not untidy as a child, but this seemed obsessively neat. A feeling of pride filled me as I saw how responsible he had become.

"Want a soft drink or something?" he asked as he

led me through the narrow kitchen.

"Sure, what are you offering?"

He pulled open the fridge. "There's some cola or lemon-lime drink. I might even have a root beer in here, too."

"Root beer sounds nice."

He reached into the depths, produced a root beer, and then pulled a cola.

"Do you want a glass?" He was already opening a cabinet. He offered me a glass. We sat at the table together. I struggled to find something to talk about.

"How's the job?"

He was working at a bookstore for the summer, the same one he worked part-time at during the school year. It wasn't an exciting job, but it gave him some money to spend and an outlet for some of his energy.

"Job's good. I work tonight."

I nodded, taking a sip of my root beer. "That's good. You like it?"

He shrugged. "It's a job."

I sighed. Andrea appeared as I asked him about his college courses. Her hair was still damp from the shower. I stared, unsure of what to say.

"Yes, Mom, Andrea lives here with me."

He reached out and pulled her close, his expression defiant. Caleb was trying to show me a unified front, knowing I would take issue with this situation. Andrea, to her credit, showed a bit of remorse. At a loss for words, I frowned, unsure what to do. Should I pretend otherwise? My faith and upbringing said that waiting for marriage was the right way to go. However, I also lived in the world of today, and many couples lived together before marriage. It was normal to do things that way. In my day, it was normal to wait, but not everyone did back then, either.

"I see." I tried to smile. It wasn't wholehearted, but it was the best I could do.

Caleb's expression hardened. He became annoyed at my response. To salvage what had begun as a pleasant visit, I forced myself to smile again, this time with some feeling. "It's just a surprise, Caleb. I'm surprised, that's all."

The tension that arrived in the room with Andrea's appearance dissipated. Caleb smiled and let go of Andrea's waist. She moved into the little kitchen. Caleb watched her like a lost puppy that had found someone who loved him. She poured cereal into a bowl and grabbed a banana, the milk from the fridge, and a spoon. She then set it all on the table across from me. We all sat quietly, watching. Andrea looked up from her cereal, looked at Caleb, and made a face. He laughed, and the tension was now totally gone.

I cleared my throat. "So, Andrea, how's work going?"

She nodded, showing that she had heard me. She chewed her cereal slowly. "It's going well. I love the people I work with—we have a lot of fun." I smiled, and then I noticed Caleb's expression change. His body stiffened almost imperceptibly.

I thought the change in his attitude came because I was being nosey. Having heard Paul's story, though, I could see that even back then, months before the incident that took both of their lives, Caleb was having issues with Andrea's job. But why? What was it about her working or her co-workers that made him angry? Maybe he wasn't happy that they spent so little time together, but that happens sometimes when people are working toward their goals. It only means you must make the most of what little time you get together.

Maybe something was going on between her and a co-worker. I didn't have any answers. I probably never would. The people who could answer were no longer there. I could talk to their friends, but what good would that do? Had Caleb confided in them? Did Andrea talk to anyone? Was Caleb aware of what was going on inside his head?

CHAPTER THIRTY-FOUR

Sighing, I wondered if the manager would let me into the apartment. Opening my door, I walked across the parking lot. I was almost at the building when I remembered that Constable Harrison told me they would let me know when I could get into the apartment. I turned back.

Circling the parking lot on my way out, I stopped to allow a young couple to cross toward the building. I wondered if they knew Caleb. Were they—his neighbors? Had they been friendly? What difference would that make? If I proved Caleb was likable, friendly, and missed, would that make his death any more tragic? What if he kept to himself, was quiet, and nobody missed him? What was it I wanted to learn by coming here?

I wanted to find a way back—to wake up from this nightmare. Who was my son? What had he become? Who was he when I wasn't around? I wanted to understand—to find peace. My head was throbbing. I needed to go home and get some sleep. I had an apartment to sort out, and on Monday, I would begin my new job.

On the way back to my apartment, I stopped at a drugstore to get some pain medication. Passing down one aisle, I saw the writing paper and wondered if I should write a letter to Joe. At the cash register, I saw they also sold stamps.

Parked outside my building, I popped the lid off the pain medication and took three tablets without water. The weariness of the day crept into my bones. As I exited into the hallway, I experienced the sensation of my feet being mired in clay, as if every step was more than I could make. I opened the door, set the platters on the counter, and then threw myself onto the unmade bed. I lay there, too tired to cry, running the day's events through my mind, wandering down offshoots of my life here and there. My body relaxed and fell into a natural rhythm. I let go and allowed my breathing to lull me to sleep. I slept for a couple of hours.

When I woke up, my body was stiff and achy. After a hot shower and a bowl of soup, I sat on my lumpy couch with a hot cup of chamomile tea. With pen and paper in hand, I wrote my letter to Joe.

Dear Joe,

I am writing this letter because I was unsure if I could hold my temper long enough to say what needed to be said. I am at once too angry to speak and too brokenhearted to know what to say.

By now, you know that I have moved out of the house. The events of this past week have devastated me, both literally and figuratively. You made me feel like an enemy in my home. I don't know why you can't understand that regardless of what Caleb did or who he was—he was my son. He was our son. You may have been able to wash your hands of that, but I can't, and I won't apologize for loving him.

I still can't believe that you destroyed Caleb's things. That dresser and bed frame had been in my family for generations, but you burned them. Why? I don't understand. Because he touched them? You should have tied me to a stake and burned me in the middle of that flame, too, because that boy touched me, and I will not now, nor will I ever, be able to forget that it was my fault—our fault—he turned out the way he did. I know you don't agree with that, and I agree that ultimately, only Caleb is responsible for his actions, but the bottom line, Joe—we didn't equip him with the tools he needed, or this would not have happened. Things went sideways for us when Leah died, and I don't think we saw how deeply Caleb was affected. He needed us. My grief consumed me too much to see that he needed me.

I am not blaming you, Joe. I am just trying to help you understand that there are bigger issues here than we know. Maybe we'll never truly know why, but I won't rest until I can understand what caused Caleb to go off the rails and our family to implode.

Throwing me out of our room was beyond cruel. That revealed to me the level of contempt you held for me, and that's why I couldn't stay. How can I live in a house where I'm hated, hated only because I couldn't let our son go without saying goodbye? Funerals are for the living, not for those who have passed. I needed to say goodbye, and I think you do, too, but you missed the opportunity by not coming today.

I have moved into an apartment in Crawford. My cell phone is my only phone, as I haven't arranged for a landline yet. I don't want a divorce, Joe. I just need time to see this through and give you some time, too. Please try to understand that I wanted us to be a family—that's all I ever wanted for all of us.

And, like it or not, Caleb was part of that family. He was born of us. Your blood ran in his veins. I know you couldn't see the similarities between the two of you, but they were there. He is no longer with us, and I can't bear the thought of not being able to mourn for him.

When you shut down, Joe, you shut me out. I am all alone, and I think, in some ways, we've been apart since Leah died. My leaving is only making it visible. Jonathon has Debbie, but who do we have if we don't have each other?

I took some money from our account to give me a foundation and to pay for Caleb's funeral. Please don't be too angry about that. I had no choice. I will pay you back soon because the good news is that I will start work on Monday as a baker at Jack's Diner, that little place on Fifth. You must know the one I mean. I don't know how quickly I will make restitution, but I will.

You can call me anytime if you want to talk things over. Please contact me if you need me.

Love,

Joan

I read the letter over, wondering if I was right to sign "love, Joan." Did I love him? I wasn't sure. But if I didn't, I would have stopped loving him long ago. There was so much baggage to sort through with all that had transpired these past few years. I wondered if I would ever really know when things changed.

I decided that leaving it was the best alternative. It might assuage his pride. After addressing and stamping the envelope, leaving off the return address, I set it with my keys. A mailbox was on the corner—I would pop it in there in the morning. I looked at the clock. It was eight-thirty.

I pulled out my cell phone and dialed Jonathon's number. It rang several times and eventually went to voicemail. I left a message lamenting that he and his father had not attended the funeral. Then I advised him I wouldn't be home—I found an apartment in the Sam Goddard Towers downtown in Crawford. Then I told him I loved him but needed to do this for myself. The machine cut me off mid-sentence, so I just left it. My meaning was clear, and he could contact me if he wanted to talk to me.

I made my bed, wishing I could have washed the sheets before using them. I struggled to settle, tossing and turning for what seemed like hours. The light streamed through the half-opened curtains when I finally opened my eyes the next morning.

It took me a minute to remember where I was …

CHAPTER THIRTY-FIVE

After breakfast, I popped down to the corner to drop Joe's letter in the mail. My hand hovered over the slot for a few seconds before I pulled back and tucked the letter into my pocket. I wasn't sure if I needed to explain myself to Joe. He had made his choice.

Back inside, I worked diligently to organize my apartment, stopping only for a quick sandwich at lunchtime. I tackled the most complicated room first. The initial task was to clean and line the cabinets with shelf paper. It was time-consuming, to say the least. Once I completed that, I moved on.

Everything I purchased at the secondhand shop and at Wal-Mart needed to be washed. The thought of using unclean equipment turned my stomach. Even the new utensils could have a coating of dust or fingerprints. I filled and refilled my dish drainer, using every tea towel I had. I washed and dried every dish, pot, and piece of cutlery in the kitchen.

I contemplated the layout, planning the best use of space before I put things away. The groceries sitting on the dining room floor found homes. The dishes stacked neatly in upper cabinets and the pots, pans, and baking dishes in a lower one—everything found a place. When I was done, I opened all the doors of the cabinets and admired my hard work. I closed the doors, feeling satisfied.

I shifted the living room furniture around a few times before the placement suited the layout. There were no little nails to hang my picture, so I stopped at Ted's apartment after dropping off the cardboard in the recycle bin. Gracious to a fault, he followed me back to the apartment, carrying his laser level, his stud finder, his hammer, and a few picture hooks. He showed no surprise at my tacky furniture. Together, we sorted out where to hang the picture.

With the picture mounted, he squinted, put his hands on his hips, then glanced at me. "Looks good. And she's level."

I smiled. "Yes, it is. Thank you so much."

"You need anything else?"

"No, I'm good for now, but thanks. If I get more pictures, I will get you to help."

"That's what I'm here for." He walked to the door. "Goodnight, Mrs. Bradshaw," he called over his shoulder as he left. The door closed quietly behind him, and I was alone again.

I sat in the chair, looking at the picture hanging behind the couch. It was a pleasant image, and I was glad I had bought it.

A little later, I made supper and did the dishes. My phone stayed silent. I called Jonathon more than once that day. I received no callback. Joe did not call, either. I assumed Jonathon shared my news with him. Finally, feeling lethargic from all my hard work and anxious about starting my new job in the morning, I crawled into bed early, setting my alarm.

Again, I wrestled with sleep but finally drifted off.

The alarm shattered my dreams, which were dark and disturbing.

CHAPTER THIRTY-SIX

I was up and ready in plenty of time to walk to work, impatient to get started. Even the overnight snow didn't seem to settle my nerves. Looking at the clock did not allow me to relax enough to enjoy breakfast. I was eager for the day to go well, hoping I would enjoy the job.

I stood up and paced a little. After making my bed, I took my Bible and sat back at the table. I tried to read a passage but wasn't successful. My mind jumped. I read without comprehending. Pushing it aside, I looked at the clock and thought I might go for a walk.

I slipped into my winter boots and put on my coat, scarf, and mittens. Then, I took the mittens off so I could use the keys to lock the door behind me. Tossing my keys into my purse, I walked down the hallway. As I passed, I could hear dishes rattling behind one door, but it was mostly quiet. The elevator took a moment to arrive. It was getting warm inside my winter jacket. I laughed at myself.

I was used to opening a door and being outside, so I hadn't thought of the hallway, an elevator ride, and a lobby to cross before I hit the cold air. I didn't need to bundle myself before I arrived downstairs.

"Learning curves," I whispered to myself as I stepped into the elevator.

When it stopped, I stepped off, moving around the nicely dressed man standing there. As he walked into the elevator, I stopped because I realized I wasn't in the lobby. This looked like the hallway to my apartment, only the wall color was different. I must have looked confused because the man addressed me.

"This isn't the lobby, ma'am." He reached out and held the doors open. I walked back into the elevator, laughing with embarrassment.

"Learning curves," I said to him as I turned to face the doors.

He smiled and pushed the button to close the doors. I looked up at the panel above the doors and noticed a large number five displayed there. It was only the fifth floor—I had so much to learn, starting with paying attention. The man kept his focus on the panel above the door.

I didn't gawk at him, but I took notice of some things about him. He was wearing a long black wool coat, which was unbuttoned. In one hand, he carried a pair of gloves, a scarf, and a hat. On the other was a leather briefcase. He was obviously a professional of some sort. There was a newspaper tucked under his arm, the banner hidden, so I didn't know if it was the local paper or not. Glancing at his profile, I estimated him to be in his forties, his hair containing just a sprinkling of gray. I looked up at the panel again as the elevator came to a stop and saw a large red L.

The doors opened. My companion gestured for me to proceed, and I stepped out confidently this time, feeling a little lighter for having survived making a fool of myself. I pulled on my gloves as I crossed the lobby, pushed the latch, and stepped into the foyer. A blast of hot air hit me, so I hurried to the outer door. Pushing it open, the cold air snapped at me. I jerked back slightly before forcing myself outside into the brisk November morning. There was still an hour before I needed to be at the café.

The man from the elevator was standing inside the warm porch, buttoning his long coat. He wrapped the plaid scarf around his neck, tucking the ends under his lapel. He pulled the black cap over his locks, and as I watched, he slid his hands into his gloves. He picked up his briefcase and exited into the winter morning.

I watched silently as he came out the door and followed the sidewalk to the street. He turned left toward downtown and disappeared behind the hedges that framed the parking lot. I counted to twenty before following. When I got to the street, he was already crossing the avenue a block and a half away. I stood there wondering which way to go.

Following him would take me to the restaurant, so I turned in the opposite direction. I walked with no destination in mind, although eventually, I would head to work. Downtown Crawford was still sleeping. Stores were closed, and the streets were empty of parked cars. Only a couple of vehicles passed me, people off to work like me.

I thought about that—I'm off to work. This was new to me. I went from my childhood home to my husband's. Meals, housework, laundry, raising kids—that had been my life. I wondered what Joe was up to this morning. Was he angry that I wasn't home? It was cowardly not to call him to explain. He was so angry with me—he probably wouldn't answer the phone.

As I walked through the peaceful morning, wandering back toward the restaurant, I allowed the guilt of not being a good wife to overcome me. I pulled my cell phone out of my purse and dialed home. The phone rang once, twice, three times. I was about to hang up when Joe answered. A wonder of our modern age—Call Display—allowed him to know it was me.

His temper raged across the expanse. "Where have you been? I've been going out of my mind—you could have been dead in a ditch! You should have bloody called me!"

His angry words slapped me across the face. They echoed as they found their way to my heart. I realized my cowardice caused him to relive the night Leah hadn't come home. And maybe even the fear of the police would once again show up at the door with bad news. Feeling terrible for being such an awful person, I grimaced. I came back to the conversation when I stopped berating myself. I didn't know what I missed, hoping it was nothing important.

"… you've taken your things, eh? Moved out, have you? What are you going to live on? Wishes and dreams. Cause you are not getting one penny from me, darling. Not one red cent. And I want my vehicle back, do you hear me?"

I was stunned. There I was, scraping myself off the ground, feeling lower than a snake's belly about my lack of courage for not calling, when I comprehended the rest of his ranting. He hadn't been sitting up all night worrying about me. He'd noticed I had taken my things and knew I was gone. I was feeling guilty about torturing him, and he was probably sleeping, all tucked up nice and cozy. And he wanted my vehicle back. The one he gave to me for my birthday.

I had never expressed my feelings to Joe before, never vented at his rigidity. Sure, I pleaded or begged and tried to make him see sense, but I always did it with softness and humility. The rage that had become a large part of my life wanted to spew out the venom that filled my chest, but I choked it down.

My voice shook as I tried to appease the situation. "I'm sorry, Joe, I never thought …"

"That's right, Joan. You never think, do you? You never gave me one thought last night, or yesterday, for that matter. Now, I don't give a damn about you, but I want what's mine."

"Joe, listen, please."

"No, Joan, I've listened to you enough. You've gone against my wishes. You haven't considered my feelings at all. I'm done playing games with you. Just get that vehicle back, pronto."

CHAPTER THIRTY-SEVEN

The phone went dead. Standing for a few seconds with the phone still to my ear, I was unsure what happened. A whirlwind dragged me in, spun me around, and spit me out. I glimpsed myself in the glass in front of the store next to me and didn't recognize the image. There was no spark of life, no vitality. I dropped my phone into my purse, turned, and trudged down the street.

Within a few minutes, I arrived at the café. The original sparkle of the morning was gone, and my day lay before me with impending doom. The grief I buried rose and flooded my core. It was going to be a long day. The café didn't open until 7:30 a.m., so I found the door locked. I knocked on the glass and waited.

I saw movement and knocked again. This time,

Beckie noticed me and rushed over to open the door. "Sorry about that. I was busy getting the coffee on. Have you been waiting long?"

"No, just a minute."

"Well, come on in." She stepped back and allowed me to enter. The door closed behind me, and we moved toward the back. "You can put your coat back here," she called over her shoulder, leading the way. I followed obediently. She took me into a storage room. There were boxes of supplies on three of the walls and large white buckets stacked in the center. On the wall beside the door were several hooks. I took my coat off and hung it up.

Beckie handed me an apron that looked new and crisp. The design wasn't fancy, but it was clearly industrial in all aspects, save for the color. Bright yellow dye saturated the sturdy sailcloth.

"Now, Marta always wore a dark green apron. I decided I would retire those with her. While shopping for new ones for you, I saw this color, and it's perfect for you. You, I think, are a soul filled with sunshine."

A soul filled with sunshine! Tears sprang to my eyes. I wanted desperately to be that person, that soul filled with sunshine, but there was just too much despair inside.

"Oh, Joan, I didn't mean to make you cry!" She reached out and rubbed my arm and shoulder.

"Oh, no, it's not you. This is just a little overwhelming. It's very kind of you." I took the apron from her and slipped it on. She reached back and pulled four more aprons off the shelf behind her.

"Here are the others, a clean one for every day. You take them home—they belong to you, whatever happens."

I nodded.

"Okay, let's get cracking, shall we?"

I nodded again.

"First, a quick tour. This is the storage room. Everything you need in dry goods is here. If you need anything else, let me know. If we are running low, please mark it on this chalkboard." She pointed to a small blackboard attached to the back of the door.

"Our supplies get delivered every second day. I place the orders on Saturday, Tuesday, and Thursday for delivery on Monday, Wednesday, and Friday. Of course, I can go to the wholesalers myself, too, but if I can avoid that, all the better."

Beckie opened the door and moved down the hallway. We came to a large steel door. She pulled it open, letting a blast of cold air out. I followed her in. She let the door close loosely behind us. A stirring inside me, akin to excitement, filled me as I stood gaping at the shelves filled with products. For the first time in a very long time, I felt like maybe, just maybe, I was in the right place.

CHAPTER THIRTY-EIGHT

"This is the cooler. Here, you will find milk, butter, eggs, and other perishables. As with the dry goods, we also order these items three times a week. This time, though, you write what you need on the blackboard outside the door."

I nodded, so far understanding everything.

"Good." She turned to the door. "Now, don't worry about ever being locked in. If the door closes tightly behind you, you just push this, and the door opens." She pointed to a large, round button.

We left the cooler and crossed the hallway to the kitchen. It was larger than I imagined and was already busy. Jack stood behind a huge griddle, scraping it with a large black brick. The place sparkled with cleanliness, and the stainless-steel appliances gleamed in the light from the overhead fixtures. The squiggle in my tummy became more fervent.

"Jack, this is Joan. She's going to be our new baker." Jack turned from his duties, grinning.

"I'd shake your hand, but I'm a little dirty at the moment. Welcome aboard."

"Thank you." He went back to scraping the surface.

A couple of large, oversized pots sat simmering on burners. "Our soups for today," Beckie said, noticing my stare. I nodded.

I turned around, seeing for the first time an older lady working away behind me. She was rolling out pie crust. Several empty pie plates sat close by, waiting to be used. On a counter nearby, next to a bank of industrial ovens, inside of which were many loaves of bread, sat four large pans of cinnamon buns, already rising. Within the hour, these would come out of the oven, fresh for the morning patrons. My mouth watered in anticipation.

"Marta, this is Joan." Marta turned from placing a pie crust carefully across a pie plate. My eyes swept from her round, pleasant face—to the strong, floured hands she wiped on her apron. She reached out to greet me, and I took her warm, firm hand in mine.

"Good morning. I am glad to meet you." She spoke rhythmically, her German accent audible. "I am looking to spend more time with my grandchildren, no? You are a godsend." She beamed. "Now we go to work."

CHAPTER THIRTY-NINE

Beckie patted my shoulder, and the workday was underway. Marta walked me through the job—where to find the tools and how to operate the dishwasher. The pace was brisk. I hardly had time to notice that we opened, and the intensity on the other side of the kitchen increased proportionally. I would have expected the clatter of stoneware to create a tension-building cacophony, but to my pleasant surprise, it added a rhythm to the atmosphere.

"Now, we take a break, no?" Marta smiled. "Come."

She walked out into the front of the restaurant. She went behind the counter, grabbed a white mug, and poured herself a cup of coffee. Then she selected a bran muffin from the display case, which she set onto a side plate along with a pat of butter. I followed suit, only I used the hot water button and took a tea bag from the box. Chamomile tea. Marta watched.

"You want something to eat?" My tummy rumbled.

"How much is a cinnamon bun?" I cranked my head back to look at the board.

"It is nothing. You get your choice. You want one, no?"

She opened the case and liberated a large bun from the pan. She put it on a plate and handed it to me. I smiled appreciatively. Beckie scooted past us. We squeezed out of her way, took our supplication, and moved to the staff room just past the walk-in cooler. The room was windowless and a little stuffy—the door was no longer there, leaving the space constantly exposed and open. I could see that the room was also being used for storage, specifically for cleaning supplies. The broom closet. I was drinking tea in a broom closet.

The room wasn't much to look at, but above the small table was a beautiful photograph of Crawford at the turn of the century. I stared at the picture. Marta smiled.

"That is this street, no?"

"It is?"

"Yah, look, this building right here." She pointed to a building on the right side of the enlarged photo. "Look, this is the same one, no?"

I looked closely. Sure enough, there was the building in its early days. The large banner sign above the door read King's Mercantile. It spanned the space of Jack's Café and the computer store next door.

"King's Mercantile was owned by Harold and Herbert O'Dell," Marta explained. "It was called King's Mercantile because this was King's Street." She smiled with pride.

"I did not know. That's very interesting."

"Yah, this building has an interesting history, no?"

"How do you know that?"

"My husband was always interested in the history. He belonged to the Crawford Historical Society, and when the children were gone, I went along with him. When he died, I couldn't leave it. I came to enjoy learning about the history of my city. It's good to know such things, no?"

I nodded. Yes, I thought it was good to know such things. I spent my life sheltered in my little world, unaware of what was happening around me or what had gone before. I concerned myself with the details of my family, husband, and children. For the first time, I realized how I stepped out from under the cloak of safety for the first time since I left Joe. A vast land lay before me—I could go in a myriad of directions. None of them would be bad, and all of them would take me to places I had never imagined. I could go anywhere unless I allowed my fears to consume me. Then, I would crawl back under the safe umbrella and take up residence in my old comfortable world again.

"I like history. I think all old buildings are

fascinating."

"Yah, you come with me one time to a meeting, no?"

"One day," I replied noncommittally. I was excited to think I could get involved, but there was still so much to sort out in my head. She smiled and patted my hand.

The conversation turned to her plans for retirement. She was going south with some friends for a couple of months after Christmas. For the first little while, she would visit with her children. She had a large family—she told me all their names, and, except for Gertie and Fritz, the other names went in and out without hitching to anything inside my brain. Fritz and Gertie were the two who still lived in southern Alberta. The other eight scattered to the wind. She was going across Canada on her journey to spend time with her family. She was clearly excited about it.

"Beckie and I have been talking about my retirement for a long time. I could not go without having someone capable of the job, though—it would not be fair. You are a godsend, no?"

"Well, I haven't really done much yet."

"No, I know. You have it. You will do good, I know." She beamed at me.

I blushed under the weight of her unsolicited praise. A tear sprang to my eye, kindness overwhelming my overtaxed emotional system.

"No, don't cry, Liebchen, it will all be okay. The work is hard, but it is never too much. There is a rhythm to it. Each day is a different plan. I will teach you, and you will be fine. Now we go back and put that bread in the oven. The pies should be done."

We rose then, taking our dirty dishes with us. I followed Marta, and a surge of affection for her rushed through me. She was such a dear old soul, and I was going to miss her. Silly girl, I thought to myself. You don't even know her. A quiet voice deep inside agreed and then added, *But she's already like a mother to you.*

When I lost Leah so abruptly, I had thrown up a barrier between myself and God, and I used some pretty good cement a week ago to seal it completely. At that moment, a crack formed. It wasn't a large one, but the human kindness made me feel like I had some value. I couldn't remember the last time I felt worthy.

The rest of my day passed quickly. By two o'clock, the day was over. I was free to go, but I wasn't sure I wanted to leave the warmth of this family. Marta shrugged into her bulky coat.

"You come tomorrow early, no? Today, we were easy on you—tomorrow, you will learn it all. It is good, no?"

"Yes, thank you, Marta. Thank you for today."

She smiled, threw her arms around me, and hugged me to her sturdy form. I relaxed into her hug. She released me quickly, then turned and left. I pulled my coat off the peg. I pulled the scarf from the sleeve and wound it around my neck. Digging deeper into the sleeve, I found my cap. I was zipping up my jacket when

Beckie came in.

"So, how was your first day?"

"Oh, it was great, thanks Beckie. Marta is wonderful."

"I know. She's a gem—one in a million. She told you to come early tomorrow?"

"Yes, she told me to be here by five."

"Perfect. We go through a ton of bread here. Those loaves you left us today will hardly make breakfast. That's one draw here—fresh bread for sandwiches and toast."

I nodded wisely.

"Well, you go home, put your feet up. It's been a long day. See you tomorrow."

Dismissed, I went out the back door into the alley behind the restaurant. I walked down to the street, enjoying the warm sun on my face. Well, as warm as the sun attained in November. The sky was clear and blue. It helped put a bounce in my step. I made it through my first day at work. I wanted to celebrate, but there was no one to rejoice with …

CHAPTER FORTY

I arrived at my building, and within minutes, I was inside my apartment. The quietness settled around me. I hung my jacket in the closet and removed my boots before wandering into the living room. Sitting in the chair, I exhaled. I felt tired, but it was a good tired. I was content for the first time in a long time. What I had done today made me feel like I was part of a bigger picture. It had been a long time since anyone made me feel appreciated.

I arose and grabbed my purse—still sitting at the front door. Checking my phone, I saw no missed calls or messages. I dialed Jonathon's number. Nothing. I pulled the phone back, thinking I hadn't pressed send. No, the END button was visible, meaning I had completed the call. I put the phone back to my ear and waited. Nothing.

I pulled it away, pushed the end button, and tried again. Nothing. My phone wasn't working. Damn! Thinking perhaps there was a glitch in the phone's software, I turned it off. I counted to ten, and then, just to be sure, I counted another ten before initiating it again. Once completed, I dialed Jonathon's number again. Still nothing.

Without a phone, there was no way for me to find out what was going on. I was going to have to go to the mobility store. I dropped my malfunctioning phone into the depths of my purse, dug into it for my car keys, grabbed my coat, slipped into my boots, and headed back down. The mall was open until six. I hoped it wasn't a big fix. The phone functioned that morning, and I hadn't dropped it or anything. It was a puzzle.

Following the example of my downstairs neighbor, I didn't button my coat or put on my hat and scarf until I arrived at the porch. I was making progress—learning how to live in the city. Walking through the parking lot toward my vehicle, I marveled at how resilient I was. There were going to be hard days—it was common to feel moments of normalcy after losing my kids. When grieving for Leah, I did lots of reading about it, and, this time, I no longer judged myself unjustly when a little shred of hope poked over the horizon.

I stepped around a large white, windowless van, the older boxy model parked next to me, expecting to see my vehicle sitting beside it. The stall was empty. I could see that a vehicle had been there that morning because the ground had no snow cover. The snow around the bare pavement showed only a few footsteps had trampled it. I looked at them—they looked familiar. They looked like Joe's footprints.

Now, what do I do?

I reached into my purse and pulled out my phone. I dialed 911, then remembered my phone wasn't working.

"Shit!" I said aloud. "Shit, shit, shit, shit … shit!"

Then I laughed at myself. I was getting a serious case of potty mouth. I had never sworn before—Joe always said swearing was for people with lower intelligence. Now, there I was, swearing at the least provocation.

I returned to the café, stepped into the warmth, and approached the counter. The place was quiet, winding down before the supper rush. Beckie came out of the kitchen carrying a few pies for the pie case.

"Oh, hello!" she called. "Can't get enough of us, eh?" She smiled as she put the pies down, opened the glass case, and then slid them inside. Finally, giving me her full attention, she asked, "So what can I get you?"

"Can I use your phone?"

A puzzled look crossed her face. "Sure. You know where it is."

I didn't need to explain anything to her, but I did anyway. "My phone isn't working. I tried to make a call, but nothing happened. It won't seem to dial out. So, I was going to go to the mobility store and have them look at it, but when I walked into the parking lot, my Jeep was missing."

"Missing?"

"Yes, missing. As in, Joe took it."

"You're sure?"

"Pretty sure. I recognized the footsteps in the snow."

"That's terrible. How can he do that?"

I shrugged, unable to believe how calm I was feeling.

"So, what are you going to do?"

"I don't know. Maybe I should call Joe first before I report it stolen?"

She nodded but didn't give an opinion.

"What do you think?" I needed to know I was doing the right thing. I trusted her. She may not have been through anything like this, but to me, she seemed wise beyond her years. Working in this environment gave her access to people's lives and troubles, vicariously experiencing life's joys and woes.

"I think you need to do what you need to do."

CHAPTER FORTY-ONE

That was an unsatisfactory answer. Disappointed that she wasn't ready to swoop in and rescue me, I stiffened but nodded in agreement. I headed to the back, where I grabbed the phone book and looked up the number for Freyden Police Station, then dialed the number.

"Constable Harrison, please." I was told he was unavailable. "Thank you, no message." I hung up.

I sat for a minute. Beckie hadn't helped, and Constable Harrison wasn't in. No one seemed to be available to give me directions. My insides were twitching like I had swallowed a Mexican jumping bean, jittery and unsure of myself. I never had a lot of confidence, as I would often defer to Joe for big decisions. I just wanted someone, anyone, to tell me what to do.

When I called Joe, I was half expecting the phone to go unanswered, so I was slightly surprised when he answered.

"Hello?"

"Hi, Joe."

"Well, hello, *Joan*." The way he pronounced my name made it clear that this would be another ugly conversation. "How are you doing?" The question seemed benign enough. The tone, however, spoke volumes, and at that moment, there was little doubt that he had taken the vehicle.

I didn't answer his question. "Why, Joe?"

"I told you that you weren't getting anything, and I was serious. I paid for that vehicle—you can't have it."

"But it was a gift!"

"Sure, it was. And if you stayed, you'd still have it. You made the decision. It had nothing to do with me."

"Joe, please don't do this. I don't want to fight."

"There's no fight, Joan. I've taken back what's mine, and you won't find it, nor will you get it back. I will in no way support you in what you're doing. That includes letting you use my things. Now, if that's all you called for, I've got work to do." He hung up.

My things. Those words echoed as I put the receiver back into the cradle. *My things*. He turned off my phone, too. That was something he was paying for. Every ounce of energy and vitality leaked out of my body. I grew smaller and less significant. My breathing grew more shallow and rapid. My heart pounded—a dull roar grew in my ears. I was going to faint. I slipped off the chair onto the floor, bracing myself with my arms before lying on the cold tile. Closing my eyes, I tried to calm myself. I don't know how long I was there.

"Joan! Joan! Are you okay?" Beckie rushed through the door. She touched my shoulder. I stirred, trying to sit up. My head spun a little. I groaned and steadied myself with the chair. Beckie kneeled on the floor in front of me.

"Are you okay?" she asked, looking into my face.

I nodded. "Yes, I thought I was going to faint, so I dropped to the floor."

She sighed with relief. "Do you want to get up onto a chair?"

I nodded and leaned toward the chair. Beckie assisted me. Once on the chair, she sat across the table from me, concern written all over her face. She patiently waited for me to find my voice and tell her what had happened.

"Joe …" I said. "Joe took the vehicle. He's punishing me for leaving him. He told me this morning that he would not give me anything. I just didn't think he meant he'd take things away."

"He can't do that, can he? Is the vehicle in his name?"

"No, it was mine. He gave it to me for my birthday."

"Then you call the cops and get it back."

I shook my head sadly. "Yes, I could call, but I

won't get it back. He's stashed it somewhere. He's not stupid. It won't be sitting in the driveway at the farm."

"Oh."

"And he turned off my phone, too."

"What a jerk."

I nodded in agreement. "Yep."

She looked up at the clock on the wall behind me. "Well, let me drive you to the store. You need a phone."

"Thank you."

Beckie went out front and spoke with Ruby Sue, the afternoon waitress. I didn't overhear their conversation, but I presumed she was verifying that it was okay for her to leave. We went out the back door together. I followed Beckie to her vehicle, an older sedan. She climbed in and started the car. I grabbed the snow brush from the floor on the passenger side and brushed off the snow.

"Thanks," she said as I climbed in.

"No, thank you. I would feel so lost without you."

She dropped me at the door to the mall and then went to park the car. The parking lot was emptying. I hurried down the mall, not because I didn't have time, but because I was using Beckie's. The store was empty. A tall, thin girl sat at the display, looking at a computer monitor. She glanced up and smiled at me.

I told the girl about the phone, and she confirmed Joe had ended my phone service under his plan. The only option to get my phone working was to get my plan. She asked me if I wanted to keep my number. I thought about it for a minute and then decided I wanted a new one to reflect on my new life.

We discussed plans and options, and half an hour later, I walked out of the store with one more slice of independence.

Beckie was sitting on the bench outside the phone store. She rose as I approached.

"Everything fixed?"

"Yes. She verified Joe canceled my phone."

"Well, he's certainly not going to win husband of the year, is he?"

"No." I smiled at this, and then I laughed. We walked down the mall toward the doors, and I giggled, laughed, and chuckled intermittently. All the way back to my apartment, we were silent except for my laughter. Thanking Beckie for everything, I slid out of her car and walked toward the building.

I saw Beckie pull away before I noticed Mr. Fifth Floor—the name I dubbed the man from the morning ride in the elevator—walking down the sidewalk from the street. We reached the door at the same time. He held the outer door open for me. I entered the foyer and used my key to open the inside door. Reaching around me, he took hold of this door as well, allowing me to proceed ahead of him to the elevator.

We didn't talk to one another as we stood there waiting for the elevator to arrive from the tenth floor. When the doors popped open, an older woman and a younger man, possibly her son, stepped out. Mr. Fifth Floor reached out his hand to hold the doors, allowing me to enter the elevator ahead of him. Inside, I pushed the button for the twelfth floor. He stepped in, pressing the button for the fifth floor. The doors closed. We rode up in silence.

When the doors opened on the fifth floor, he nodded and wished me "Good evening." He left the elevator, and a few seconds later, the doors slid closed, and I was alone. I don't know why this hit me so forcefully—maybe because this was the time of day when our family would come together, and the house would be filled with loud, boisterous conversations and laughter. The silence was overwhelming. Trying to recapture the lightness of that moment in the mall, I failed to scoop up that moment. Tears filled my eyes.

I was alone and needed a friend—no, I needed my mother. But she hadn't called. I closed the door behind me and sat on the floor in front of the lumpy sofa, allowing my sorrow to leach the joy of the day. I focused only on what I had lost and soaked in a cold bath of self-pity and self-loathing.

CHAPTER FORTY-TWO

I don't know how much time passed. The apartment was dark, and the streetlights through the curtain-less patio doors cast dim shadows. Stirrings of hunger poked at my ribs. I pulled myself up off the carpet and walked into the kitchen. As I made myself a sandwich, I turned on the radio. I ate as I listened to the sultry tones of my favorite radio interviewer as she probed details of a harrowing experience from some man with an Australian accent. At first, it was simply background noise. Then, I listened more earnestly.

Despite his devastation, the man recounted his story with a detached demeanor. There was no emotion. Then I realized he was doing what I do—stealing himself to tell his story. He described how he lost his family in a random mudslide and how helpless he felt as he watched his wife being swept away, clutching their tiny son to her chest. He thought he was being punished and couldn't understand what he had done to deserve it.

I understood his pain. I could understand his words as they mirrored my situation. Although I still had family left, what good was that if they didn't want me? The interviewer asked him to describe his wife. As he shared the story of their courtship, I stopped listening to the words. Standing up, I turned off the radio and threw my unfinished sandwich in the garbage. Then, I made myself a cup of chamomile tea. Back in the living room, I curled up in the chair and sat there with my thoughts.

The past year and a bit were just as harrowing. There was no way around it. I don't know how I survived some days. I lost my faith because even though God hadn't stolen my future or my children from me—He allowed it to happen. Believing him to be benevolent was more than I could do.

I brought my thoughts back to more pressing details. How would I get Joe to understand why I was doing what I needed to do? Perhaps I should send the letter I wrote. Maybe that would appease him. If he reads it, that is. He may just burn it. I had no control. Then, I asked myself the hardest question. Did I still love him? Had I ever loved him? Yes, I loved him when we married, and there were days when my love burned bright, but Joe was pretty good at knocking me back, and there were days when I loathed him.

I thought back through our life. Joe was a very

particular man even before we were married. He was strict in his thoughts and ideas, showing little mercy for inadequacy and weakness. I remember thinking more than once that he could be cruel, and I also remember I dealt with it by shoving the incidents out of my thoughts. Because his dark, brooding good looks and natural athleticism enamored me, I dismissed all the raised red flags. I was certain he was my ticket to happiness, so I consciously decided those instances weren't important. Overall, he was caring. He loved God and wanted to make a life with me. That was enough.

CHAPTER FORTY-THREE

Our marriage in the early days hadn't been perfectly blissful, but in many ways, those days were idyllic for me. I went from my parents' silent home to the one where I was in charge. In retrospect, I thought I was the boss of the house, but I passed every thought, every decision, and every idea—through Joe. Agreeing with his color choice for the kitchen curtains, the furniture, and even the choice of bedding, I hadn't ever decided anything on my own.

I liked florals, and Joe liked symmetrical patterns. We never used soft pastels to decorate our bedroom. Instead, it was strong with navy hunter-green and mustard blocks. Bold, masculine patterns that never made me feel quite at home.

Even the meals I cooked, I verbally presented new

recipes to Joe in the early years. Once I learned his likes and dislikes, I could determine whether something new would be acceptable or if he would throw it across the table.

Jonathon was just a baby when sushi swept across the country like the latest craze. There were sushi bars everywhere. I had been shopping for Christmas presents and was late getting home. I usually picked up fried chicken on these odd occasions, but that night, I thought I would try sushi. Joe liked fish, and he liked rice. What could go wrong? I still shudder at the violence of that moment. It only happened once, but it was enough to show me I had to be more careful with my choices.

I always took new dresses or new blouses on approval. The clothing store in Freyden understood I purchased nothing outright. I took everything home for the green light. If Joe approved the outfit, I would call the store, and they would send me the bill. If it wasn't—I took the outfit back the next week. Eventually, I made better choices—muted colors, unflattering cuts, sleeves were a must, and nothing above the knee. Even my jeans, T-shirts, or around-the-house outfits couldn't advertise a product or present a slogan. I wore clothes that Joe approved of and not items I found attractive.

I think that's the thing I adored about Leah. Joe tried to maintain a level of control over her wardrobe and succeeded until she was twelve. Then, she dressed more like the kids she was with at school. This drove Joe nuts in the beginning, and if it had been anyone else, it would have destroyed the family. But it was Leah, the apple of his eye. She skirted around his control and made him feel that he'd given her permission. I loved her for that. She was always her own person—someone I could aspire to be. I snorted. Funny that my child would be the one I wanted to emulate and not the other way around.

I wonder what she would think of what's going on now. I think her father's lack of compassion would appall her. She would have been more understanding of Caleb—in fact, she might have been the only person to whom Caleb would have reached out. Sure, he bossed her around, but his affection for her was clear. It was her death that probably sent him spinning out of control.

My thoughts meandered through Caleb's life again. I saw areas where I failed him, where I bypassed or overlooked his sensitivities to keep peace in the family. If I had been a stronger person, I would have stood up to Joe. But would that have provided the answer for the family? Well, I argued with myself, I don't know, but could the outcome be any worse than the one I'm living now? Two of my children were gone forever, and the third one followed his father's wishes perfectly, regardless of his own will. How much worse could things have turned out?

Tired of running the gauntlet, I took my empty cup to the sink and went to bed. I set the alarm, pulled the covers up, and snuggled under my warm duvet. Deliberately focusing on my breathing, I lulled myself into a peaceful dream world.

I slept fitfully and awoke a few minutes before the alarm.

CHAPTER FORTY-FOUR

Again, disorientation welcomed me upon waking, but it didn't take long to remember.

I showered, dressed, and had a quick breakfast of toast and tea before heading to work. There was more snow overnight. At the early hour, though, the caretaker hadn't had time to clear the sidewalks. I walked the short distance to work, ringing the buzzer at the back door. Marta opened the door almost immediately. I stepped out of the cold. Another workday lay before me. There was bread to bake, muffins, cinnamon buns, pies, scones, carrot cake, and Marta's specialty—Black Forest Cake.

She taught me her secret, which surprised me because it was so simple that I expected it to be public knowledge. I promised her the secret would remain between us. She laughed and told me that when I was ready to retire, I would be free to share it with my replacement. Until then, it must remain between us.

The kitchen hummed with activity. It took no time to feel part of the fabric of this place. I couldn't believe it was only my second day. It was as if I'd always been part of things here. Marta patted my hand during our last break of the day.

"I think you are catching on beautifully, no? You are a natural. I may be able to leave earlier than I thought."

"No, you can't leave me, not yet. I can't do this without you."

"Yes, yes, you can. You are a strong person, no? You will run circles around me by the end of the week."

Tears welled up. I was losing another person. "Don't go," I said, surprising myself.

Marta smiled. "You will be fine, Liebchen. You are not alone." I know she understood me better than I did at that moment. This woman had been through this before—maybe not to the same degree—but she had lost the love of her life when her husband died. Her children all moved away to build their own lives, leaving her alone in the city. She understood what it meant to lose precious things. She was also wrong. I was alone.

For her sake, I pulled myself together and sat up straighter. "Please, don't go early, I need you."

"I will stay for a while," she assured me. "I will stay. Now, let's get back to work. We need to get that cake iced, no?"

I nodded, swallowing the last of my tea. I took our cups to the dishwasher before joining her in our corner of the kitchen. We gathered the ingredients for the icing when Beckie came into the kitchen, followed by a tall, official-looking man. She walked over to me.

"Joan, this man is here to see you."

Confused, I wiped my hands on my apron, preparing to greet him. As I extended my hand toward him, he whipped out a large brown envelope and shoved it into my hand.

"Joan Elizabeth Bradshaw?"

I nodded.

"I am Sheriff Ray Warren. Consider yourself served." He let go of the envelope as I took hold. I looked at it as if it were totally foreign to me.

"What is this?"

"Everything you need to know is inside. I wish you a good day, though I doubt it will be one, considering …" He turned on his heels and left the kitchen. We all stood together—Marta, Beckie, and I, watching his back as he disappeared from sight. Then, as a unit, we looked down at the large, brown envelope in my hands.

"You'd better open that," Beckie said, nodding toward the package.

My hands shook as I pulled at the corner, tearing it back. Having created a small opening, I slipped my index finger inside and tugged it toward the other corner, tearing a jagged opening in the top of the envelope.

I then pulled out an official document. Joe had filed for divorce.

CHAPTER FORTY-FIVE

Later that night, thinking back on that moment, I was surprised to find no tears, no rending of garments, and no wailing and gnashing of teeth. It was a surreal moment as if it were happening to someone else. I had no feelings about it. It was what it was. I slid the papers back into the envelope.

"Joe wants a divorce. My marriage is officially over." My heart fluttered.

Beckie and Marta reached for me simultaneously. Neither said a word. They just lay their hands on opposite shoulders. We stood there in solidarity.

"Well," I said, breaking the spell. "There's a cake to frost."

With that, we all went back to work. I stuffed the envelope behind some canisters in the kitchen and focused on the tasks still left to do. I barely remembered to pick up that envelope on my way out. It was insignificant to what I'd already been through. I had no intention of contesting. If Joe wanted a divorce, then I would give him one.

I tried calling Jonathon that night, but the phone went to his voicemail again. I hesitated before leaving a brief message.

"Hi Jonathon, it's Mom. Just wanted to let you know that I'm doing okay. I have a new cell number if you want to contact me." I listed it for him. Then, as an afterthought, I added. "Look after your dad for me. He filed for divorce today … well … I received the papers today. I'm okay. I never meant for any of this to happen. Keep well. I love you."

I hung up the phone. Sadness swirled in. Why was he avoiding me? Was he taking his dad's side, or did he also despise Caleb for what he'd done?

I made something to eat, then curled up with the radio and my book. This time, I tuned the radio to a music station that played songs from multiple decades. I don't think I read many pages. My thoughts kept circling back through the memories of my life. When I heard the song, I put my book aside and flashed back to Jonathon's wedding eighteen months earlier.

I relived that day, but this time through tears, not smiles. It was the day that changed our family and set us on the road that led here. I was still crying when the song ended.

I turned off the radio and, without wiping my tears, walked down the hallway and crawled into bed.

CHAPTER FORTY-SIX

Beckie cornered me shortly after she arrived at work the next morning. She was eager to know how I felt about the papers I received the previous day.

"I was thinking about you all night," she confessed. "How are you?"

"I'm good, getting on, you know."

She nodded. "Have you hired a lawyer to help you through this?"

"A lawyer, no? Do I need one? Can't I just sign papers or something?"

"I think you should see one, and that's what I've been thinking about. I know you don't have a lot of money, and the law firm Joe is using is a bunch of blood-thirsty cutthroats. You will need someone who knows the law to stand with you, or you'll get nothing."

"Well, that's okay. I don't want anything."

"You say that now, but I think you'll regret that in the end. You're entitled to something for all those years. If you walk away without a fight, he's won."

"Well, everything I have will go to Jonathon one day. Everything Joe has will also go to him. So, whether I have ownership for the years in between seems moot."

"Okay, I get you, but at least you might get your vehicle back."

That hit a nerve—she was making sense. "You're right. I hadn't really thought about that."

She nodded, clearly on a roll. "That's right. I don't know your financial situation, but honestly, you might get enough money to buy a tiny house. It would get you out of that apartment."

"It's not so bad, really."

She shrugged. "Just thinking. It's not bad now, but you don't have a garden, and you could have a tidy little one with a house."

My head was spinning a little. Overload! "Okay, I'll give it some thought."

She handed me a piece of paper. "Here's the name and address of a lawyer who will help. He is a champion of the underdog. He bases his rates on ability to pay, not the flat rates many other attorneys charge. You'll like him—he's a nice man."

I took the paper and stuffed it into my apron pocket, then went to work. Busy following Marta and making mental notes of everything I would need to know to do my job properly after she was gone, I never gave the note a second thought.

~ ~ ~

Saturday morning, I was preparing to do my laundry. As was my habit, I went through my pockets before tossing the clothes into the machine. I found that stray piece of paper. I set the washer in motion and took the paper to the kitchen. Using a magnet, I stuck the note to the fridge.

It took a couple of hours to finish the laundry. When it was done, I headed out to get my haircut. I was nervous. Other than having my hair styled professionally for Jonathon's wedding, I'd never been to a salon. Having taken Leah enough times, the routine was familiar. But the person who would cut and style my hair was a stranger, not a familiar face. I hoped she knew what she was doing. I had heard horror stories.

Beckie thought I made a good choice in salons. It was a block from the café. I walked there easily. Winter had truly set in. Although we had no snow for a few days, it was sticking around.

Inside the pleasant little shop, a young girl with a pierced eyebrow and a stud in her nose greeted me. Have I come to the right place?

"I have an appointment with Kathy."

"Joan?" she asked, raising her eyebrows.

"Yes."

"She'll be right with you. Please, take a seat."

She directed me to the seating area, where four chairs sat in a square. I obediently sat in the far chair. Looking around, I saw some style magazines. I picked up the top one and flipped through it. There were many styles, some you'd never see outside a fashion magazine, some more what I considered "normal" hairstyles. I wrinkled my nose at the fuchsia-spiky one. I was so engrossed in the pages that I jumped when a tiny woman called my name. She was perhaps thirty-five, her hair dark honey blond with lighter streaks. She looked normal.

"I'm Kathy. Please, come with me."

I followed her back to the sink. She gestured for me to sit, which I did. Kathy draped a towel across my shoulders and leaned the chair back. She washed and conditioned my hair, and it was lovely to have someone massage my scalp. A few minutes later, she wrapped a towel around my head and placed the chair upright.

"Okay, Joan, let's go to my chair."

She led the way to a chair in front of a long mirror. There were four stations here and four behind me on the opposite wall. Most of the chairs were busy with clients getting trims, colors, and perms. The chatter was endless. I looked around at these very ordinary people, some with extraordinary-looking stylists. The range of ages was wide, but all seemed somehow cohesive and connected.

She raised the chair to an adequate height, spinning

it slightly to ensure I was facing the mirror dead on. After rubbing down my hair, Kathy removed the towel. Then, she grabbed a comb from a jar of blue liquid and raked it through my long tresses.

"So, what are we doing today?" She kept combing my hair, assessing its length and condition with each stroke.

"I don't know. Seeing myself in the mirror the other day, I looked old and tired. I think I just need a change. My hair has no style. I need something."

"Okay, do you want to keep the length?"

"I don't know. I have always had long hair, but maybe it's time to change. But I don't own a curling iron or blow dryer—I never needed one. I guess I'm not too old to learn if I need to." I sat for a minute and then continued. "Maybe I should stick to something wash and dry."

She nodded, wrinkled her brow slightly, and looked at my hair in the mirror. Combing my hair again, she pulled it back off my face and then dropped it back again. She looked like she was thinking, and I was getting a little nervous again.

"Maybe I should just get a trim? Not too short, so I can still pull it back into a ponytail for work?"

"I can certainly do that, but I think we should try something different, too. What I have in mind isn't too drastic. You won't need a lot of tools to style it in the morning. Perhaps, just a little product, and you're set."

"Nothing too drastic?"

"Nothing too drastic." She assured me.

I watched her pull, pin, and manipulate my hair as the scissors clipped the tresses with finality. The first cut liberated me, but by the third one, I was feeling more panicked over my decision. I held my breath and waited for her to finish. A blow dryer, a curling iron, and some sticky product, and she was done. She fussed a bit with a few loose strands and then put her tools aside.

Spinning me away from the full-length mirror, she gave me a smaller hand-sized one so I could examine the back. When I handed it back, she spun me around to face the large mirror once more. Her hand gently resting on each shoulder, she smiled at my reflection. I stared. I looked ten years younger. My face was the same, but my new hairstyle stunned me.

Would I be capable of styling it? Probably, but I doubted it would look as professional as this. I bought some products she recommended to me and paid. When I stepped out into the street, the cold winter breeze nipped at my now-exposed neck. I reached into the back of my jacket and pulled my wool scarf higher.

As I passed storefronts, glassed display windows mirrored back an image of a young woman wearing my coat. I looked like a stranger.

For the rest of the night, every time I passed a mirror, my reflection surprised me. At one point, I spent fifteen minutes turning this way and that, back and forth, front and sides, trying to see myself from every angle—liking what I saw, even though it still seemed strange to have short hair.

I realized that my head felt lighter.

It was weirdly liberating.

CHAPTER FORTY-SEVEN

The next morning, I stood in the shower—the water running over my head and down my body. I poured some shampoo in my hand and washed my hair. My hair! I felt bald. There was no mass to it. I wasn't sure if I would ever get used to it. I cried for the first time since seeing Kathy's work. Why had I done this? What was I thinking?

Drying off, I pulled back my emotions and forced myself under control again. As instructed by Kathy, I rumpled my hair with my hand, fluffing it occasionally to add volume. I dressed for church. I wasn't sure I was going to go. In the time since Leah died, Joe and I had stopped going, and the coolness toward God had not warmed. With Caleb's death, I had to admit that letting my faith go produced guilty thoughts. What if I'd been more fervent—more open to God? Could that have saved my son? Had my anger at God caused Him to be deaf to my prayers?

Before I left the apartment, I put a wee bit of the paste on my hands, rubbed them together vigorously, and then ran my hands through my hair, rumpling it into some form. I wiped my hands on the towel, pulled a stray hair this way or that, and looked at my reflection. Not as professional as Kathy, but not bad. I looked smart and sexy.

On my walks around the neighborhood, I spotted a couple of churches but hadn't taken in the denomination of either. I meant to ask Marta and Beckie if they knew anything about them, but the subject just never came up. I stood outside the first church, the one with a ten a.m. service. A few elderly folks were climbing the cold, bare concrete steps and pulling open the heavy honey oak doors that led inside. I admired the building. It was gorgeous. I looked at the sign. It read St. Mary's Catholic Parish. A Catholic Church. Not that I had anything against them. I had never been to a service in one, but I doubted that this was the church for me. I walked one more block to the next church.

It was as lovely as the first one, very similar in size. The stairs were forbidding, but the doors were darker and arched, not square. It appealed to me a little more. The sign out front read Jubilee Christian Fellowship—Pastor Maxwell Harvie. Early Morning Worship Service: Eight-thirty a.m.—Prayer: Nine a.m., Morning

Worship Service: Eleven a.m., Evening Fellowship: Six-thirty p.m. I left the apartment at nine-thirty. The service at the first church was just getting underway. This one was already in between services. I walked past the church, turning at the corner to walk along the side.

From there, I could hear singing. It sounded lovely. Turning around, I headed back, then stopped again. Should I? I turned away as the singing ended. This time, I walked past and kept moving. Arriving at the next street, I turned east and moved back toward the center of town again. I kept moving, enjoying the walk, thinking about life, Caleb, Joe, Jonathon, Leah … My thoughts turned to Beckie and Marta, too. People who came into my life and helped make me feel normal again. I even thought about Constable Harrison and wondered what he was doing today. Was he working? Did he go to church?

I laughed at myself. What did it matter? I'd probably never see him again, anyway.

Then, I thought about Joe's petition for divorce. I kept walking, thinking about Joe's hastiness in filing. It had been just over a week since I left. His willingness to throw away our marriage hurt me. As I assessed my feelings about the petition, I realized he hurt me far more deeply by what he'd done to Caleb's belongings and moving me out of my bedroom. That bothered me far more than being sued for divorce.

CHAPTER FORTY-EIGHT

Given the situation, I wondered if Beckie was right in thinking that I should protect myself. Everything I owned would go to Jonathon when I passed, and everything Joe had would do the same. Did it matter who had possession of it in the meantime? I didn't think so, but I also didn't want to have to live hand to mouth, so to speak, working all the hours God made just to keep a roof over my head.

Of course, working the hours I received would give me enough to pay the rent and what I estimated the utilities to be. But that was based on the caretaker's guess. I had not received the bill yet. What if I was sick and missed work? What would happen to me then? If I ever fell behind, I'd never be able to catch up. That made me quiver.

I decided Beckie was right. I'd better take care of myself. No one else was going to.

In addition, I really wanted my vehicle back. I had no freedom without it. Public transport was foreign to me. I always drove. If I wanted to visit Leah's grave, I'd have to find a way to Freyden. Even taking the local bus, it didn't go out there. What about when the time came to scatter Caleb's ashes? Again, I'd have to rely on someone else to take me out of town. It was insane. Besides, that vehicle was mine. It wasn't right that Joe took it.

By the time I came to myself, it was well past eleven. I walked a fair distance, up and down streets, heeding neither the display in the windows nor the signs above doors as I went. My mission when I left the apartment was to worship God—instead, I cleared my head. I was walking by a low, nondescript building when I noticed the sign Crawford Public Library. I walked up the steps and pulled the door open.

What a lovely space. Books as far as the eye could see. Tables and chairs sat randomly around the room, some in groups. I noticed computer stations on one side. Removing my coat as I walked up and down the aisles, I looked at the books, finding hidden nooks where readers could lose themselves inside pages and stories. I hadn't used a library since leaving high school. Any books I read came from the used bookstore—trading them in for new ones to keep costs down. Joe didn't like clutter, so I couldn't keep them. Caleb was the only book hoarder in our family, and he had an extensive selection of sci-fi and fantasy books, many in a series. Those he had left behind were gone now, a heap of ashes that would soak into the earth when the snow melted.

I meandered through the building, noticed a set of stairs, and took them. More books. What an amazing building! As I wandered the aisles, I saw I was in the nonfiction section on Lifestyle and Family. A large, bright yellow and black book practically leaped off the shelf: *Divorce for Dummies* by John Ventura and Mary Reed. Really? I pulled the book from the shelf and skimmed through the table of contents. What would they think of next?

Debating whether to sign the book out, I wandered the rest of the area with the book tucked in my arms. Deciding it wouldn't hurt to know a bit about what I might face, I kept the book as I left the section. Even if I hired a lawyer, I would not be unfamiliar with the procedures.

I wound through a hallway until I came to a brightly colored area. Even if the tables hadn't been low to the ground, I would have recognized it as the children's section because of the use of vibrant colors. I did a cursory walk-through, then took a set of stairs back to the main floor.

I looked around for an indication of where to sign out books and finally found a desk where a young girl sat in front of a cash register. She was tending to a lady with a stack of books, eight or ten—I didn't count. Their transaction was complete, and the woman stuffed the books into a green canvas bag she had brought with her for just this occasion. When she moved away, the young girl smiled at me.

"May I help you?"

I stepped forward and set the book on the counter. "I'd like to check out this book, please."

CHAPTER FORTY-NINE

Since I didn't have a membership, I had to purchase one first. Once that was in place, it was easy to check out the book. The librarian gave me a paper receipt that provided my name, the date, the return date, and the book's name and author.

As I walked toward the doors, I noticed a little coffee area. I ordered hot tea and took it and my borrowed book to a nearby table. For the next hour, I sat reading. My tea grew cold, but I drank it anyway. My fury flared as I skipped past the parts about children. Fury at the fact that two of my children were no longer here. Fury at Joe for forcing me into this situation. I was so angry I wanted to smash something or someone—angry that I had to do this on top of everything else I had to deal with. Angry that life was a shitty excuse for breathing right then. Alone and weak and unsure I was ready for what lay ahead, I closed the book and took a sip of my lukewarm tea.

Agitated, I stood up and pulled on my jacket. As I left the library, I noticed the return slot for books. Hesitating for a moment, I dropped the book in. I didn't want to know anything else. A lawyer could deal with this. I had too much on my plate to fight with Joe over a divorce I wasn't sure I wanted.

Going back to my apartment didn't appeal to me. There was nothing there, so I wandered the streets for a little while longer. Finally, hunger forced me to head back home. Inside, I relished the warmth. It wasn't freezing out, yet winter would grow more bitter before it was over. However, it was significantly colder than my apartment.

I hung my jacket in the closet and tucked my boots on the floor underneath before stepping into the kitchen. After putting together a quick lunch, I withdrew to the living room and turned on the radio.

I walked for hours. Ten minutes after I sat down, the pull of sleep tugged at my sleeve. I didn't argue. In my bedroom, I slipped out of my clothes, crawled under the covers, and slept for nearly three hours. When I arose, disgust welcomed me. My grandfather had always told Susan and me, as girls, that people die in bed. It was his way of reminding us not to waste our lives. Yet, there I was, sleeping a Sunday afternoon away. I could have been doing something productive. I should have been doing something worthwhile … like making supper for my family.

The tears sprang from nowhere. I missed my family. I missed my home. It was only a few days, but I was so homesick. At that moment, if my vehicle were in the parking lot, I would have driven out there—begging Joe to forgive me. But, of course, I couldn't do that. He took my vehicle.

With that thought, the pendulum swung across the range of emotions, and I flared with anger. The need to strike out rose again. I ran back to my bedroom, jumped onto the bed, and smashed the pillows. I didn't realize I was screaming until I heard someone in the next apartment bang loudly on the wall. This brought me up short. Stopping mid-punch, I lay down and cried until I had nothing left inside.

I lay there, looking at the bare walls, wishing I had someone to talk to, someone who would help me and be my friend. The face that rose before me was Marta—lovely, kind Marta.

I didn't know her phone number. I looked in the phone book, but M. Kunkel was not listed. Her phone number might be under her husband's name, but I was no further ahead since I had never asked her what it was. I could have tried the six or seven people listed but decided not to.

Instead, I made some soup for supper. By the time I cleaned the dishes, it was dark outside. I pulled out my Bible and then tossed it aside. Relieved—there was no more pretending that God and I were talking. I tried to read my novel and couldn't concentrate on the romantic hero and his chiseled good looks. I chastised myself for not keeping the book from the library.

Finally, I took out Beckie's note, which included the lawyer's name she thought would help me. A pleasant male voice answered.

"Douglas and Grimshaw. Brad Douglas speaking."

I paused. I had expected voicemail, not a real person. "Hello, Mr. Douglas. I'm sorry. I didn't expect to talk to a real person at this time of night on a Sunday."

He chuckled softly. "Well, normally, I don't answer the phone this late on a Sunday, either. So, what can I do for you, Ms. …?"

"Oh, sorry. Bradshaw. Joan Bradshaw." I sighed. "I, I mean …" I sighed again. "My husband is suing me for divorce, and my boss suggested I call you."

"Your boss?"

"Yes, Beckie … I mean, Rebecca Driscoll."

"Oh, over at Jack's Diner. Beckie is a wonderful lady. I go there often, but I don't recall a Joan. You must be new. Do you wait tables?"

"No, I'm the new baker. I'll be taking over for Marta."

"I see. So when can you come in?"

"I guess, just about any time, after about two o'clock."

I could hear him flipping through papers. "How does Tuesday sound at three o'clock?"

"Perfect."

"Okay, bring the petition with you, please, and I'll see you then."

"Thanks, good night."

"Good night." He hung up.

I stood with the phone in my hand for a minute. He sounded normal. I didn't know what I expected. I had little experience with lawyers. The only one I knew was the one Joe and I used for our wills, and he was an old stuffed shirt. He was so clinical and distant that he was more mechanical than human. I remember telling Joe that Mr. Perkins was the man with the missing personality. We laughed together, and Joe remarked he was good at his job, and that was what mattered.

I hoped that since Mr. Douglas seemed to have a personality—he wasn't terrible at his job.

CHAPTER FIFTY

Monday mornings at the café were a flurry of activity. Both Marta and Beckie commented on my new hairstyle. The compliments embarrassed me, but soon, the duties called for all my attention. It was a snowy day, made for coffee and fresh cinnamon buns.

After the lunch rush wound down, Beckie came back into the kitchen. "So, Joan, did you make an appointment with that lawyer?"

"Yes, as a matter of fact, I did." I explained my phone call to her and gave her my first impression of the man on the other end of the line.

"Oh, yes—Brad Douglas is a wonderful man. You'll like him." She agreed.

I smiled at her, suddenly seeing what I hadn't seen before. Beckie liked Mr. Douglas. I think her feelings were more than professional courtesy—she really *liked* him. I remembered he had complimented Beckie to me, and I wondered if I should tell her. No, not yet. I was going to feel him out first.

Marta noticed my mood. "So, what makes you smile, Liebchen?"

I told her my suspicions. She nodded. "Beckie is a good woman, but she works too much. She could use a good man, no? I don't know this—Mr. Douglas. I hope he is worthy."

"Well, I don't know him, either, but I can tell you that Beckie perks up when she talks about him. She knows many men, and I presume she knows many lawyers since several of them come through here regularly for coffee and lunches. She gave me his name, and I think it was because she admires him, but for all I know, he's married. I will check it out."

Marta patted my arm. "You are a good girl, no."

We returned to work, and an hour later, we were done. As I slipped my jacket on, I remembered I had wanted to call Marta the night before. So, I asked her for her phone number. She gave it to me and took mine, as well.

I walked home in the haze of fat snowflakes drifting slowly from the sky. I loved lazy snow. It was perfect for making snowmen. After this type of snowfall, the kids and I would always make a couple of snowmen in the front yard. We used sticks for arms, carrots for noses, pebbles for mouths, and some rocks for their eyes.

Cleaning up that first spring, I collected the snowman parts except the carrot noses and kept them under the porch in a plastic tote. I added to the stash as the number of snowmen grew. One year, Jonathon brought home some shiny black spray paint and painted the rocks we used for our eyes. Then, they looked like lumps of coal. It was brilliant.

We added old scarves and hats to the tote as snowman costumes. It was something that brought the family together and an activity that always invoked lots of laughter. It had been years since we'd made a snowman, though. Why had we stopped?

Arriving at the apartment, I noticed a stack of booklets sitting on a wire rack. "Don't Hibernate This Winter," the front page advertised. Take a class. I grabbed one and took it upstairs.

Sitting at the dining room table, I flipped through the pages quickly. There were language courses, French and Spanish. I read about yoga, fitness, pottery, and photography classes, too. There were culinary art options and other artistic ventures, so much from which to choose. I circled the sessions that interested me.

Spanish might be fun. I took French courses at school and found them hard, and Spanish might be hard, too. Did I need to learn another language? I flipped the page. Photography would be fun, but I'd need a camera. I didn't have a good one. It was just a simple digital thing I had for several years. I looked at the required supplies. I might be out of my depth on that one.

Cooking classes—making Chinese food from scratch. Introduction to baking. I could probably teach that course. What else? Italian cuisine. That sounded fun. I looked at the cost. It was not too costly, but it was only one night after all.

Learn calligraphy or learn to paint. Okay, what were the costs of those? A supply list of materials with an approximate cost of $200 plus the course fee of $100. That was steep. I needed to be frugal with my pennies, and now there were lawyer fees to consider. I tossed the pamphlet onto the coffee table. Why did I let myself believe I could afford to have fun? What was I thinking? Joe's decision to throw a divorce into the mix would keep me from doing anything fun for a very long time. Maybe that was his plan. What a jerk.

CHAPTER FIFTY-ONE

As anger rose, I stood up. I needed to move, to walk, to work it out.

I'd just come in, but I grabbed my coat again. Slipping it on, I grabbed my boots. I was about to put them on when my anger dissipated—and despair set in. I dropped my coat onto the floor and headed back into the living room.

No! I won't let him win. Turning back, I picked up my jacket again. I could cry until the sun stopped shining, and it would never be enough. Losing two of my children in the most brutal fashion possible was unimaginable to most people. Forced to leave the only home I knew because of Joe—only added to my burden. I was trying to make my way in a world I didn't yet understand, and I would not let Joe's pettiness reduce me to tears every day.

Enough!

As I strode down the hallway, I confessed to myself that even though I cried every night before I fell asleep, thoughts of my children throughout the day brought tears to my eyes, often flowing down my cheeks, yet I wasn't sobbing with despair anymore. If I gave in to despair now, I may as well crawl into bed, pull the covers up over my head, and cry until death came to claim me.

I needed to honor my children by living my life. Living it to the best of my ability, not living it under the thumb of a man. My thoughts turned to Caleb and how I forgot him so often while I labored to keep my husband happy. Flashes of my boy, his sad face, his big wide eyes staring with such longing. My breath caught in my throat, and as I stepped into the elevator, a sob burst through. I sucked in the stale air, sucked it deep into my lungs to push back the sorrow that rose at the vision of my son.

The trip down seemed to take forever—I was eager to move, walk, and escape the swirling thoughts. A burst of rage flared as I thought of the one place I'd love to go right then and the one person I needed to talk to—Leah. But her grave was in Freyden, and I had no way of getting there since Joe had stolen my vehicle. Clenching my hands into fists, I wanted to punch something or someone. Why was this elevator taking so long?

The doors finally opened on the main floor, and I

stumbled out, nearly knocking over the man from the fifth floor. He stood holding his briefcase, his coat unbuttoned, his scarf still jauntily wrapped around his neck.

"Oh, excuse me," I muttered as I slipped past him, tears beginning to flow.

Catching the edge of his concern as I rushed past, I didn't stick around for further conversation. I might burst into flames if I didn't put some distance between those thoughts and myself.

After buttoning my coat in the elevator, I was ready to go when I reached the foyer. I stepped out into the city's night lights. The sky was a dark blanket above my head, yet there was no darkness. The streetlights burned brightly, dissipating the darkness with forceful intensity.

I turned left instead of right, moving away from downtown and walking until I came to a residential section. As I passed big old houses with warm, glowing windows, I wondered about the people who lived inside. Were they happy? Were they living a good life or just going through the motions? I walked past house after house, a few dark, but most of them beacons to a lonely heart. My thoughts swirled, unsettled and volatile. I kept moving.

I finally thought of the farm and wondered what I'd be doing if I were there. The supper dishes were washed and put away, and Joe was in his recliner, having a nap with the paper lying across his chest. A subtle but familiar snore would weave its way across the house, and I would feel the peace of knowing all was well.

Ha! All was well. What was I thinking?

I had just been going through the motions for years. Since the first miscarriage, the first look of disappointment in Joe's eyes. Since I judged myself with the harshness of a stranger, without love and acceptance. Since Caleb emerged as a gentle soul, not the dynamo like his brother. Each passing year sucked a little more of Joan out of me.

Who was I?

CHAPTER FIFTY-TWO

Walking on, I was thankful for the clear sidewalks to stretch my legs. I crossed roads, turning if I saw an interesting street, interesting architecture, or trees on the boulevard. Each step helped me work through my feelings, draining the septic thoughts from my psyche. It was cathartic. I felt looser and more alive.

Eventually, I was so turned about—I didn't know where I was. The city was more of an unknown than the familiar streets of Freyden. Walking on, I passed a house with a For Sale sign on the lawn. I stopped and looked at the house. It was average-looking, white with green trim. A large shrub on the left side of the lawn set the stage for a winding sidewalk that curved gently around it. A few steps farther, the sidewalk split into a Y, the right branch going around toward the back of the house, disappearing under a gate that barred access to the backyard. The other branch led to the front step.

The house appealed to me. I stood there looking at it with longing, trying to imagine what it might look like inside. What colors had they used? Was it in good repair? Catching myself, I snorted. I couldn't afford a painting class. How was I going to afford a house? I was simply kidding myself.

I walked on. The house, or stopping at the house, stripped the urge to walk farther. I turned back when I reached the corner, walking by the house again, and taking another look. I sighed and continued up the street.

At the corner, I looked at the street signs to see where I was, not paying attention to them as I walked. I would need to know them to find my way back. I turned left and walked straight, no longer searching for interesting streets. I was simply walking home.

Snow fell again, light, fluffy flakes. It wasn't falling hard at first, but as I neared the apartment, it came down more fervently. I was glad when I recognized my surroundings. It wasn't much farther.

I looked up at the brick building, really looked at it—as I walked toward it. It was huge. I wondered how many people lived there. That little house flashed into my mind again. I shoved it out.

Inside the apartment, I made a cup of tea. I sat with my steaming brew, warming my hands on the mug before picking up the calendar again. I slowly flipped through the pages. Nothing was interesting to me or that

I could afford right now. I tossed the booklet into the recycle bin. I'd have to find something else to occupy my evenings.

With that settled, I walked down the hall. I brushed my teeth, changed into my nightgown, and climbed into bed. In the darkness, I allowed my thoughts, as they always did, to flutter back to happier days when the kids were small.

Perhaps the snow outside brought back the memory of Caleb's fourth birthday. It fell on a Monday. Leah had been born the previous July, and since her birth, I had been tired most of the time. Caleb was a quiet child—he never cried or asked for much. He simply accepted what was. This birthday was the first time he ever showed a passion for something.

He helped me make invitations, applying little stickers haphazardly. We invited all the children from his Sunday school class—eight kids in total, all three to five years of age. The weather had been unseasonably warm as the calving season began in earnest. The night before the party, however, a storm blew in. Joe headed out to stay with the herd. I watched the wind whip the snow into drifts and prayed everything would turn out okay.

When I went to bed that night, I realized I would have to cancel the party. Even if the snow stopped, it would be late in the day before the county cleared the roads, but it was more likely the storm would continue into the next day.

It was still snowing the morning of the party. I called all the mothers, and they all felt bad, but no one would risk a trip out onto a drifted country road. When Caleb came down for breakfast, I told him we would have to postpone his party. He didn't understand what that meant. He didn't cry. He just sat there staring at me. I don't know why, but guilt sidled up to me like I'd gone out and poured snow onto the roads to prevent people from coming. After a few minutes, he left the table, leaving his cereal mostly untouched.

Joe came in later that morning and went to bed. In the afternoon, Jonathon and I tried to throw Caleb a party. We played pin the tail on the donkey and tried to get Caleb to walk the right way. Leah was giggling away on her blanket nearby. I guess we got a little loud because Joe came down, shouting that he was trying to sleep.

Caleb pulled his mask off his eyes. Jonathon sat down on the couch. I stared at Joe, knowing we weren't making that much noise. He was just being himself. A flare of rage burst in my chest, but being the dutiful wife, I stuffed it down and apologized to him. As he went back up the stairs, the kids and I retreated to the kitchen, our game forgotten. I served cake and ice cream to the boys and sat with Leah on my lap. We remained at the table quietly.

Joe stomped in, commented about not feeding my children properly, and then asked Jonathon if he wanted to go with him to check on the cows. Jonathon jumped at the chance to spend time with his dad, and the pair disappeared. Caleb finished his cake and then asked to be excused. Permission granted, he slid off his chair, thanked me for the party, and left the room. We never had an actual party for him that year.

The next year and for a few more after that, when I asked if he wanted a party, his answer was always no. I eventually stopped asking. Jonathon and Leah had parties at the pool or the bowling alley and even a couple of summer tenting sleepovers for their birthdays. But Caleb, being our winter baby, never had another party.

Why hadn't I insisted? Why hadn't I ever arranged a surprise party? What kind of mother was I?

As I lay in my bed, my heart heavy with grief, I rewrote this memory. The snowstorm never came. Happy, laughing children filled the house. Joe came down the stairs, ready to play games with his children. He even carried Caleb on his shoulders when he won the "Pin the Tail on the Donkey" game. We took lots of pictures and had a lovely day celebrating our boy.

I fell asleep with the deep understanding that if I had been a proper mother to Caleb, the outcome of his life would have been very different. Maybe I would still be home with Joe because in these mini before-sleep movies I created from real circumstances and my imagination, Joe was not the same, either. He was compassionate and caring. He allowed people to be themselves rather than expecting them to be what he wanted them to be, including me.

I allowed my world to be Utopian and fictional.

CHAPTER FIFTY-THREE

The new week saw me taking over the baking. Marta became my helper.

"I will help you this week, and by Friday, I hope you know the routine so well—I can sit on my tuchus and watch without helping, no. Then I will know that you are ready to fly solo."

"It's too soon, Marta, you can't go." I smoothed down my bright yellow apron.

"I promise I will not go until I know you can fly, no? But you are a strong woman. You just don't see it."

With that, she walked into the kitchen. I watched her go, feeling at once strong because she believed in me and weak because I wasn't sure she was right.

"Okay," I said, coming into the kitchen behind her. "The first order of business is to get some dough rising.

Marta, could you please heat some milk?"

"Sure, boss lady, I will do that." She grinned at me. I smiled back, a small tear in the corner of my eye.

We worked hard and by Tuesday I noticed Marta did less and less, always waiting for my instruction rather than jumping in as she would have in the previous week. She gave me the opportunity to do the work, as much as I could, without her. It was a brilliant plan because it gave me confidence as the day went by. The last loaves of bread came out of the oven at 1:55 p.m., right on schedule. I turned them onto the cooling racks with a great deal of satisfaction. Marta smiled, patting me on the shoulder as we left the kitchen together.

"You did good today."

I nodded. My body was weary from the labor. It was good, though, and I proved to myself that I could do it. Having that extra pair of hands was nice, but when push came to shove, I'd manage all on my own.

"Thank you, Marta! It was a good day."

Marta turned to retrieve her coat. I went into the small staff room.

I untied my apron. Normally, I would have left it on and walked home, but I had my meeting with Mr. Douglas at three o'clock. I didn't want to see him with my apron on.

Beckie walked in as I folded my apron and stuffed it into my purse. "You off to see the lawyer?"

"Not until three. I think I'll have a cup of tea first. Maybe put some thoughts down."

"I'll grab you a tea then."

"No, I can get it myself."

"I'm sure you can. I'll still get you one, though." With that, she spun around and hurried off. I sat down at the table with a notepad from my purse.

Marta poked her head in the door, her coat buttoned to the top. "Good luck with the lawyer, Liebchen. See you tomorrow."

I nodded. She nodded back, a friendly smile on her lovely face.

Beckie returned with a pot of tea and a mug. She set it down beside my blank notepad.

"It looks like you've decided a lot."

Smiling sadly, I set the pen down. "I tried to put things on paper, but I didn't even know what I wanted. All of this is too much." My voice cracked, so I stopped speaking. I cleared my throat, shoving my emotions down. "I didn't need this on top of everything else."

Beckie brushed her hand across my shoulders, soothing me with her gentle touch. "Everything will be fine. Brad Douglas is a smart guy. He'll help you figure it all out."

I nodded, staring down at my blank paper.

"The one thing I know I want is my vehicle. I wanted to go to Leah's grave …" I choked again. Beckie sat down across the table. She took my hand and squeezed. I looked at her with tears in my eyes. Neither of us spoke.

"Well, I'll let you drink your tea in peace," Beckie

said as she stood a few moments later. "My only advice to you is to trust Brad. He won't steer you wrong. He's not your typical lawyer."

"Thanks, Beckie … for everything."

She slipped out the door without another word. I looked down at the paper. I reached for my pen and wrote one word.

Vehicle.

I put the pen down and poured the tea into the mug. Taking a sip of the hot tea, I sighed deeply before taking another. Sitting with my hands circling the hot mug, I thought about my upcoming meeting. Quivers of butterflies fluttered in my belly. I took a deep breath, then another, settling them down. It was just nerves, fear of the unknown, uncertainty of the process. I didn't know anyone who'd divorced their spouse. Not that there weren't people splitting up, sure there were. But details of a divorce were private, circumstances that didn't concern me.

Bob Farley's wife left him for a feed sales agent. That was probably the closest I came to exposure. Bob and Helen lived on the next farm. She never gave me the impression of being a farmer's wife. She always wore city clothes, which were not suited to hard work. Where I wore jeans and a denim shirt, she would wear a linen skirt and a silk blouse. She always wore makeup and styled her hair in a trendy way. She disappeared one day, and no one saw her again.

I don't remember Joe mentioning the word divorce

in connection with Bob. Huh, that was funny. Maybe she didn't run away. Maybe she's buried in the wheat field. I snorted. Sure, Joan! Bob Farley murdered his wife! Well, it's a good thing I left before Joe could make the same decision.

I snickered. I gulped, trying to calm down the rising hysteria. This was ridiculous. I purposefully sat up straight in my chair, closed my eyes, and cleared my mind. I did this often during my marriage to keep myself from going off at Joe. It worked well.

Once in control, I opened my eyes. It was already twenty-five minutes to three. There was little time left. I sipped the tea—it was tepid but still satisfying. I drained the cup. Then, I used the facilities, taking a moment to pat some color on my cheeks. On my way to the storeroom, I poked my head into the café, caught Beckie's eye, and waved. She gave me the thumbs up sign.

I smiled and headed out.

CHAPTER FIFTY-FOUR

Inside the foyer to the lawyer's office was a set of stairs leading up and two frosted glass doors on either side. One of the glass doors led to a travel firm, Journeys Begin Here. Cool name. The other glass door was Douglas and Grimshaw, Barristers and Solicitors. I took another deep breath before I entered.

An older, beautiful woman sat behind the desk. As I entered, she looked up from her computer monitor, and her smile welcomed me silently.

I told her my name and why I was there. She told me Mr. Douglas would be with me shortly and asked me to take a seat. I turned back to the stylish seating area filled with fake plants, comfortable chairs, and tables stacked with magazines. I perused the stack of magazines for something that might interest me.

Canadian Homemakers. I picked it up, sat in the big, overstuffed chair, and flipped through to the recipes. Bruschetta Burgers. Interesting. I read the ingredients and the instructions, looking back at the picture of the burger in a bun on the opposite page.

I flipped to a recipe for potato corn chowder. Skimming the ingredients, I noticed it was very similar to the one I made. I looked up before flipping to the next page. A man approached from the inner offices through the opening behind the reception desk. He looked like the man in the elevator from my apartment building—no, he didn't look like the man. He was the man. I nearly gasped.

He noticed me, too, and his eyes widened in recognition.

"Well, hello there." His voice was soft, his tone welcoming and warm. He extended his hand toward me as I stood up. "We meet again. I'm Brad Douglas."

"Hello, I'm Joan."

"Right. Well, follow me, please."

We walked back through an archway, passing through a hallway with a few closed doors before arriving at his office. Mr. Douglas gestured for me to enter. This room was spacious and elegant. The desk was bare of anything save a pad of yellow paper on a clipboard. He pulled out a chair in a casual seating area to the right. He offered me a beverage, but I was too nervous. With the preliminaries over, he picked up that clipboard and sat in the chair across from me. He set it on the coffee table and sat back in his chair. His relaxed manner helped me to unwind a little.

"So, shall we begin? Let's start by seeing what we're up against. May I see the petition?"

I pulled the envelope out of my canvas bag and passed it across to him. He pulled the papers out and perused them. He said nothing. I stared at the floor, only looking at him with cursory glances. He was a pleasant-looking man. I noticed that as I rushed out of the elevator on the fifth floor that day, I'd first seen him. He had brown eyes. Silver threads sprinkled his hair, but it was still full and thick. He'd probably never go bald.

Setting the papers down, he picked up his clipboard. He made a few notes before speaking. "Well, the petition is standard stuff." Brad sat back in his chair, setting his notes on his lap. "Okay, why don't we start with your story? You needn't go back to the day you met or married, even. Just to where things fell apart."

I nodded and opened with the day of the wedding. Brad listened intently, making notes from time to time. A box of tissues appeared as if out of nowhere when my tears overwhelmed me. I told my story right up to the day I received the petition, including Beckie's encouragement to call his office.

When it was over, my eyes were puffy, and my nose was red. Going through this story in bits was hard. Going through it in one chunk was exhausting. I sat back, wiping my eyes. Turning in my chair, away from Brad, I blew my nose as delicately as I could. Thinking again that this was such an unpleasant result of crying, I reminded myself that I was going to ask God why a person's nose had to run when they cried. I never could understand it, and God owed me an explanation.

Brad stayed silent throughout the story. He waited patiently for me to compose myself.

"The only thing I really want from this is my vehicle back. I wanted to visit my daughter's grave the other day, but it's in Freyden, and I had no way of getting there and back. That is wrong. I shouldn't have to hitchhike."

Brad wrote on the pad. "So, you'd be willing to settle the assets with the receipt of your vehicle. You know, you have the right to more? What about spousal support?"

"I have a job—I don't want to fight with Joe about support. The way I see it—if it belongs to Joe or belongs to me, it's going to end up going to Jonathon anyway. He's the only one left. I don't need to prove anything to Joe. I don't want to cause anyone grief or anguish …"

"You are too kind." He smiled at me—his brown eyes warm. "What are the marital assets as you know them?"

I told him what I knew, how much land, how much money we had in the bank, and that we had no debt of which to speak. Credit cards, utilities. No loans, no line of credit.

"What about living arrangements? You want to live in an apartment building? You don't want to have a house?"

That thought gave me pause. A tiny house with a garden would be welcome. I spent my summers in the garden every year since I was married. How would I feel cooped up in a tiny apartment, never getting soil under my fingernails? Then, remembering the neighbor pounding on the wall, I blushed. And a place where I could cry without bothering the neighbors would suit me, too. The lack of privacy wasn't something I was used to. The desire for a space of my own sprouted up inside. I agreed that having my own place was necessary, though I doubted Joe would agree.

"If his lawyers have any influence, they may get him to settle without going to court." Then Brad summed up the assets as I had explained them to him.

"Yes, that's about right. The money came from the sale of gravel. It sure allowed us to breathe easy. Joe and I hardly touched that money except to upgrade some of the machinery. We lived rather simply. Of course, we were subsidizing Caleb's education. We bought him the vehicle and paid his rent and utilities. He was going to come out of university debt-free. It was the least we could do. Not that it matters now, I guess." I took a deep breath and focused.

"Jonathon, of course, has a trade. The children weren't aware of our financial status. We never lived like we had any money. Joe thought it was important to their well-being. He also didn't want neighbors talking or thinking they could borrow from us. That, and Joe was rather private."

"How did he manage that? Wouldn't people know you sold the gravel?"

I nodded. "Sure, people knew, but Joe downplayed the value, and many neighbors believed the company had swindled him. He didn't care what people thought of him. Well, until Caleb. Caleb brought him shame. That he couldn't handle."

Brad nodded. "Okay, if I were to ask for a cash settlement and your vehicle, how much money do you want?"

Since I hadn't thought about buying a house, I hadn't come up with anything for that. My vehicle was the most important issue. "I don't know how much real estate is or how much it would cost to buy that house. I really don't know."

"Do you want all the money in the bank? That's about a third of the marital assets, not including the livestock."

"Oh, no, I couldn't take it all. Maybe … half?" I said this with uncertainty.

"Does that sound like enough? Let's put in a statement of claim for the vehicle and the cash in the bank. It's the least of what you deserve."

That was a lot of money. I nodded. "I don't want Joe to lose the farm. That's important that it stays for Jonathon to take over."

He advised me of the legal steps he would take on my behalf. When he received a response from Joe's lawyers, he would make another appointment. Then, we would know our next step.

I gathered my belongings and stood up. Brad stood, too. He set the clipboard on his desk, walked across the office—and opened the door. He stood back, allowing me to precede him back down the hall. Once in the foyer, I stopped and turned back to him.

"Thank you, Mr. Douglas. This was easier than I imagined."

"You're welcome, Joan, and please call me Brad. Now, if you need anything, just call Marjorie here. She'll set you up." He gestured to the woman at the front desk. He reached his hand out to me. I shook his hand and turned to go.

"See you in the elevator," he called after me as I pulled open the door.

I laughed. "Yes, I'm sure I will."

The sun set while I was inside. The streetlights lit the avenue, but the dark sky above made me feel lost. I hurried down the sidewalk toward the apartment, eager to get home and close the door on the day. Brad made the process seem simple, but I doubted very much that it would be so easy.

Joe was no fool. He already proved to be one step ahead of me, not that I was prepared for what he had in mind. But I also didn't think tactically. I followed my heart, unaware of how to win a war. I sure hoped Brad was a fighter. Without him, I would be at Joe's mercy.

CHAPTER FIFTY-FIVE

Considering my state of mind when I went to bed, it surprised me that I slept. I don't remember dreaming—I just fell into the welcoming net of oblivion and woke several hours later feeling like I hadn't closed my eyes. I don't know if there is an actual term for it, but I call this sleeping hard. I don't pretend to understand the physiological aspects of sleep. It was nights that maybe I didn't breathe deep, maybe I didn't dream, and I awoke feeling like I was heavy on the inside, not refreshed.

I prepared for work by grabbing a bagel and peanut butter for breakfast and washing it down with a tall glass of milk. It snowed again during the night, so I rushed to work on snow-covered sidewalks, thankful that at least it wasn't icy. Knocking on the back door, I realized that in a few short days, I would have the keys and be on my own. Was I ready for this?

Marta opened the door, still wearing her overcoat. "I just got here, Liebchen. Good morning!"

"Good morning, Marta. How are you?"

"I am well, you? You look tired, no?"

"I feel a bit tired actually."

"How did it go with the lawyer?"

"It was fine. He's really nice, and it's hilarious. I'd already met him. He lives in my building."

She raised her eyebrows but said nothing.

"Yes, he's the man on the elevator. Remember that morning, I walked off on the wrong floor." I laughed at the memory.

"Oh, yes. That's the lawyer?"

I nodded. Then I leaned in and whispered conspiratorially. "I think he and Beckie would be good together. I just don't know how to make that happen."

Marta chuckled. "Well, you throw circumstances in the way, toss the situation to God, and see what happens. If it is to be—it will be. Now, let's get to work."

Just like that, we were up to our elbows in flour and sugar. I was about to try the dreaded jelly roll. Feeling intimidated, I hoped to do it well and feared that I probably wouldn't match Marta's skill. I worried about nothing, though. It worked beautifully. Marta's tips and encouragement helped me to get it done.

When I finished the job, I stood back, and Marta clapped her hands. Then she wrapped one arm around me and hugged me close to her side as we stared at the finished product. I took a deep breath and smiled. I had passed the test.

After work, I stopped at the grocery store, picking up a few items for supper. I had made a call to the bank on the corner for an appointment. I remember the days when you could go to the bank and do business. Now, everything was by appointment. I made an appointment to see an officer to get my account moved. I could not get the information Brad needed from another branch of my bank, so I needed to move to my home branch. Without a vehicle, I wouldn't be able to make the journey to Freyden, so I needed to first move my account and then give them the paper to complete for Brad.

My appointment was for Friday, so a few days away. Taking a new route home, I passed a knitting shop. Impulsively, I stopped in. I used to knit once. I knit booties and blankets for all my babies, then attempted a sweater once. That was so much work. By the time I finished it, Jonathon had outgrown it. I made slippers for everyone in my family—a new pair every Christmas until Leah died. Then, I put my needles away.

Mittens and scarves were easy to wear but stopped being cool when kids hit their teens. Wearing the least amount of outerwear to school was more important than dressing for the cold. I won't ever claim to understand the teenage mind. When I was young, we wore our hats, scarves, coats, and mittens because our parents mandated it.

Shifting my groceries as I walked through the wool

aisles, part of me wanted to feel the skeins, but I knew I shouldn't touch them. A pleasant-looking older lady approached me.

"Can I help you?" Her name badge read Linda.

"Perhaps. I'm feeling a little at loose ends during the evenings. I used to knit, and when I passed your store, I just thought, on the spur of the moment, that maybe I should take up knitting again."

"Wonderful, we always love to see more knitters. Do you want to start with something easy, or do you want to tackle a more complex project?"

"Oh, easy, I guess. It's been a few years."

"Okay, maybe a scarf and tam set? We have some wonderful wools over here."

I wandered behind her, listening and dreaming. We settled on a nice royal blue to brighten up my winter look. A toque, a scarf and mittens. I figured if I knitted the scarf first and then the hat, I could tackle the mittens.

"We have classes, too," Linda said as she rang up my purchases. "There's a beginner's class on Monday nights at seven, an advanced class on Wednesdays, and an intermediate class on Thursday. On Tuesday night, we host an open house where knitters of all abilities gather to chat and knit. It's very informal. We talk and help each other if needed, but mostly, it's just getting together and knitting. The other classes are already in session, but the new ones will start again in January." She slipped a piece of paper into the bag with the wool and needles. "I've given you the class information and registration form." She passed the bag across the counter to me. "I hope to see you again. Please drop in on Tuesday, even if you don't need help."

"Thank you, Linda, I will."

I left the shop with a smile on my face. Now I know why there was nothing for me in that brochure for winter classes. This is where I should be. It was within walking distance, not across the city, and I already knew one friendly face. The stirrings of anticipation squiggled in my tummy. I might enjoy this, and I plan on attending the following Tuesday.

CHAPTER FIFTY-SIX

It was my last day with Marta. I couldn't believe it. I'd been working at Jack's Diner for three weeks. Tears filled my eyes every time I thought about her not being there. I had to refocus my attention on the task at hand.

Two dozen loaves of bread were cooling on the rack, and more were in the oven. Cinnamon buns were rising in pans. We had a few special orders to prepare. Someone ordered a carrot cake to be picked up at five o'clock, and there were a few pie orders and one Black Forest cake. Most of these were available at local grocery store bakeries, but honestly, the quality of the ones we baked far surpassed those, in my humble opinion.

The busy afternoon ahead was more on my mind as Marta and I slipped off to the staff room for a quick break. I needed something to eat and something to wet my whistle. A hot kitchen does much to ward off the winter chill—however, it takes a lot of water to quench the thirst. I opted for just that: some water, a large cool glass, and my cup of tea. That and a turkey and lettuce sandwich with mayo and salt and pepper should hold me over until supper. Marta was having a pita stuffed with tuna and vegetables.

I sighed and sank back into my chair after taking my first bite. I enjoyed a sandwich with perfect proportions, crisp and wet lettuce, tangy and tart mayonnaise, and tasty real turkey. Jack slipped in a couple of strips of bacon. I smiled. He was always doing something generous. He was a nice man.

Beckie had warned me that there was going to be a surprise Bon Voyage party for Marta. She told her regular customers, and many of them were coming back for the celebration. I found an activity book for retirement at the mall. Despite not being a big present, I couldn't afford to buy her something more. The book contained over one hundred activities to stimulate or inspire the mind. I hoped she would get years of enjoyment out of it. Flipping through it, I found the puzzles and games intriguing.

During our break, the conversation remained on the work left to do, planning what needed to be done first and what could wait. There were also silences as we munched away.

After draining the last of my water and swilling the

last of my tea, I gathered our dishes and prepared to take them to the dishwasher. I immediately set them down again, spontaneously threw my arms around Marta, and hugged her tightly. She sputtered a bit and then hugged back. Neither of us said anything. Not looking at her for fear of bursting into tears, I gathered the dishes and rushed out of the room.

I stacked them into the dishwasher, but noticed it was full, so I pushed the rack into the machine, added soap, and pushed the button. The dishwasher roared to life. I walked back to our corner. Marta hadn’t appeared yet, so I went to work. Several more loaves of bread came out, the cinnamon buns went in, and I measured the ingredients for the carrot cake.

Marta finally appeared, her eyes puffy and red. I nearly burst into tears when I saw her.

How silly I was. All this time, I was so sure it was me losing her. I never considered that Marta had emotions about leaving. She was moving on—she was retiring. She was going to sleep in, see her kids, and relax. Perhaps she also felt scared. How had I not noticed that?

I didn’t know whether hugging her again would help or worsen things. Should I mention it or keep quiet? I wasn’t good at this. I decided that maybe now wasn’t the time. There would always be time to talk.

“I’m getting that carrot cake started.”

Marta nodded and smiled sadly. “I will do the Black Forest, no?”

I nodded. She didn't need my approval or authorization. She was just making sure I understood she had passed the baton. We worked in silence then, each to our own task. I was so blessed to have spent the past few weeks with this woman. It had been a wonderful training ground.

What Marta didn't know was that the special orders were not for pick up. They were for her party. The café was closed to the public at two p.m., the time Marta and I usually went home. She didn't know about it. I had mentioned we should get together for lunch to celebrate her freedom, but she had some packing to do before catching the bus late Saturday afternoon. It was unfortunate that I left it too late. We promised we would get together the moment she came home.

Beckie decorated the café surreptitiously by edging the tables with swags and streamers and setting little balloon bouquets as centerpieces. She hung a HAPPY RETIREMENT sign across the long wall. It was my job to ensure Marta didn't poke her head out. It wasn't hard. I think she was emotional and, therefore, paid strict attention to the tasks at hand and did not wander too far afield. She was quiet and introspective, not her usual bustling self.

I couldn't wait to see her face. She was going to feel incredibly surprised.

CHAPTER FIFTY-SEVEN

"We need to box the pies, no?" Marta said as the clock crept toward the hour.

"Yes, Marta, but they aren't quite cool enough. Give it another few minutes."

She walked over to the pies and held her hand over them. "They feel pretty cool." She went to lift one to prove it.

"Oh, okay." I was scrambling now. "Well, I can do that. I must get used to doing it myself, anyway. Why don't you put your feet up?"

"You don't need me, then maybe I should go home." Tears welled up in her eyes.

"Oh, Marta!" Rushing to her side, I threw my arms around her neck. "I need you—Lord knows I do."

I let go, stepped beside her, and, with one arm across

her shoulders, walked her to the staff room. She sat on the chair I pulled out. I sat next to her and took her hands in mine. Tears welled in my eyes as I scrutinized her watery blue ones.

"Marta, I do not want you to go. If I could keep you here and still have my job, I would never let you leave. I feel a little like I've stolen your life from you."

"It's okay." She squeaked out a response. "I am being a silly old woman. I didn't know that retirement was going to be so hard. A few weeks ago, it was all I could think about, and now that you're here …" She paused, her face crumpling even further. "I have loved working with you. You have been a breath of fresh air, no. You helped me to find the passion in what I do again, and now, I don't want to go. I want to work with you instead. I don't want to leave."

"Oh, Marta!"

I hugged her again, and the two of us sat like one, blubbering on one another's shoulders. I needed her, and she needed me. Neither of us was happy with the outcome, but life's not always fair. Once she overcame the shock of being free, she would wonder why she was afraid. With the routine in place, I would manage. The work was going to go well. It was the rest of my life that was a mess. The impending divorce, the financial settlement. All of that was tenuous. The job would be a piece of cake.

We finally pulled apart.

"Marta." I cupped her face in my hands like I'd done

to my children many times. "You are a treasure sent from heaven. You are going to have so much fun, beginning tomorrow. Focus on Sunday. You will be with your daughter and your grandchildren. You will hug them and love them, and you won't even once give a thought to me or this place. The best years of your life are about to begin, so don't be afraid. You'll have the freedom to play. This is your reward after all your hard work. And when you get back, we will have lunch and properly celebrate. Okay?"

She nodded, but I had a feeling that she still had doubts. The clock was at two. Beckie stepped into the doorway. She smiled brightly.

"Well, Marta, this is it, eh?" She noticed Marta's tear-stained face and looked at me. I smiled to reassure her.

"Marta's just a bit wobbly at the moment. Last-minute jitters."

Beckie rubbed her hand across Marta's shoulders and then squeezed the left one reassuringly. "Marta, you will always have a place here. You have been a vital force. So much of what we have accomplished over the years is because of you and your expertise. We have been so blessed to have you here. You are going to be missed, believe me."

I could see Marta brighten a little.

"How about if you come out front to have a coffee with us? Then, if you want, you can leave by the front door to symbolize your new beginning?"

"That would be nice, no. I'll just go wash my face." She rose and headed down the hall toward the washroom. When we heard the door close behind her, I filled Beckie in. She smiled at me.

"I'm so glad you understood what was going on."

"Well, it was an impulse, really. I put myself in her shoes and asked how I would feel. When I verbalized it to her, I was right. I could have been way off the mark."

"But you weren't, that's what counts." She smiled again. "Are we ready?"

"Oh yes, the pies are cool. That's what started this. I told Marta she didn't have to put the pies into boxes and that I would do it. That was the straw that broke the camel's back. She doesn't know they weren't going into boxes at all."

I slipped off my apron, fluffed my hair, and applied lipstick, using the mirror on the back of the door. Ready for the party, I stepped into the hallway just as Marta came around the corner. She looked calm and refreshed.

I reached out my hand toward her. She took it, squeezed it gently, and together, we walked into the café. It took her a moment to figure out what was happening, but once she realized it was a party in her honor, she burst into tears again. Many of the guests came up to hug her. It was a receiving line of hugs after that. Everyone stood in line, patiently waiting their turn. With Marta in excellent hands, I slipped away to help Beckie set out the rest of the food.

CHAPTER FIFTY-EIGHT

Eventually, Marta found a table, and people took turns sitting with her and talking to her. She grew animated when she spoke of her plans. She would be okay. Maybe she didn't know it yet, but she really was ready to go. A few people came over to introduce themselves to me, saying they were glad to meet me and hoped to see me again.

People came and went, and many came bearing gifts. A few did not. Marta opened her presents graciously, thanking the givers individually. She had quite a haul and would need a truck to get it all home.

At about 3:30, Beckie tapped a fork on a glass to get everyone's attention. In a wave, the crowd stopped speaking, turning their attention toward Beckie. She cleared her throat. Before she could speak, though, Brad

Douglas came through the door, a blast of cold air sweeping in behind him. He noticed immediately that all the attention was on him.

He raised his eyebrows, glanced around the room for an empty chair, and, spotting one next to me, made his way across the floor. "Sorry, everyone, please carry on."

Beckie waited for him to sit before she continued. She wasn't usually nervous, but I noticed a tremor in her voice. I didn't know what affected her—Brad's appearance or Marta's farewell. I hoped it was Brad.

"Thank you, everyone, for coming." She looked around the room. Almost everyone was staring at her.

"It has been a great honor to have Marta with us all these years. She has been the perfect employee for Dad and me, hardworking, lovable, and very much a part of our family. We are losing a valuable asset today, but I know that this is what she needs. It is time for her to hang up her oven mitts, let down her hair, and play for a change. Dad, the girls, and I all wish Marta the best as she travels to spend time with her family. We hope that when she returns home to Crawford, she will come back and join us for breakfast or lunch.

"Marta, this is from Dad and me. We hope you enjoy your golden years, and may this go a long way to making that possible."

She crossed the floor to Marta, handed her the envelope, and then reached down to hug her. Marta pushed her chair back and stood for a proper hug. The two women, the tall, thin blond and the short, round senior, rocked together with fierce affection.

I glanced at Brad and noticed that he had a fixed gaze on Beckie, with a smile of admiration and, dare I say, affection on his face. Someone clapped, and soon, the whole place was clapping. Brad and I joined in. Beckie and Marta parted. Beckie's eyes were moist. I couldn't see Marta's face from where I sat, but I figured she probably shed some tears as well.

The applause finally died down, and the crowd resumed their conversations.

"Do you want a coffee or something, Brad?" I asked.

"Sure, but I can get it. Do you want anything?" He stood and took a step away from the table.

"No, thanks."

Brad nodded courteously and made his way across the room to the coffee urn. I watched Beckie, who was watching him. She must have sensed I was watching her, for she turned to me, blushed slightly, and smiled. I gestured her over.

She arrived at the table just as Brad did, carrying his coffee and a large cinnamon bun. He hesitated slightly, then set his food on the table and pulled out a chair for Beckie. She sat down, and he sat directly across from her. I looked at them, feeling a bit like a third wheel. Neither spoke as they tried to pretend the other wasn't there, both looking off in different directions. What a pair! They certainly needed some help.

CHAPTER FIFTY-NINE

"Marta sure is going to be missed."

"Huh?" They both looked at me.

"Marta," I gestured to the woman of the hour sitting a few tables over, surrounded by friends, enjoying her moment, "is going to be missed." This time, they looked at Marta and nodded.

Rolling my eyes, I tried again. "I'm certainly going to miss her."

"Well," Brad said as he lifted his cinnamon bun in the air. "I'm going to miss her baking."

Sitting up straighter, I said, "Actually, those are my cinnamon buns, start to finish."

He looked at me, his eyebrows raised. "Really? They taste the same."

"They should. The recipe is the same. It's just that

the effort of putting that recipe together was mine."

"Well, then, I say, let Marta have a happy retirement."

"Aren't men all alike, Beckie?" I said conspiratorially. "Just look after their tummies, and they have no complaints."

Brad laughed, and after a few seconds, so did Beckie. Good grief, she had it bad. I didn't know if I should stay and keep the conversation going—or leave and let them work it out for themselves. If I left, would Beckie even stay? This was harder than giving birth.

With that one little innocuous thought, I flashed through the birth of my children. I saw, for a moment, each of their precious little faces. Tears filled my eyes. I took a deep breath, then another, trying desperately to keep the party mood going. Beckie looked over. I ducked my head, but I wasn't fast enough.

Taking my last sentence as the one that had set me off, she scooped up my hand. "Men, most men, are good, Joan. There are always rotten apples, but Brad is one of the good guys. He's in your corner. It's just hard, I know."

I didn't know Beckie well enough to know if she spoke from experience. She had shown me a great deal of care and affection, but I didn't really know much about her. I guessed she was about thirty-five years old, perhaps five or ten years younger than Brad. I didn't know if she'd been married. Her last name was the same as Jack's, but you can pay to change your name. Maybe she only lived with someone. That was quite common these days. Many couples lived together for years before marrying or parting. Come to that, I didn't know Brad's situation, either. Maybe I was hoping for something that neither of these two wanted. Who am I to play matchmaker?

"No, it's okay. That was not the reason for my tears." Shoving my emotions aside, I continued. "I'm not sure how I feel about what Joe is doing. I feel he's not the same person, yet the more I ponder our lives together, the more I realize that he's true to form. The one who's changed is me."

She let go of my hand, wrapping her fingers around her coffee mug. She glanced up at Brad, who was staring at her with such intensity I would burn my hand if I waved it in front of his eyes. This negated all my silly, worrying thoughts.

I waved Marta over. She sat in the chair opposite me. I don't think our table companions even noticed. She raised her eyebrows, and I nodded. We had discussed the Beckie and Brad situation, and now was the time to implement our plan—well, her plan.

When Brad finally noticed her, he gushed about how he would miss her. She patted his hand and thanked him. Then she leaned toward him and asked, "You like movies, no?"

"Some, I guess. Not all," he answered hesitantly.

"You hear of this new movie, no?"

Brad nodded. He knew the movie Marta was

speaking of. Sitting across from me, I saw Beckie's expression go from serene to shock and embarrassment. She shook her head. She guessed what Marta was up to because Marta had asked her these same questions a few days earlier.

"I've heard of it," Brad responded, unaware he was being led into a trap. "I've even heard that it's pretty good."

As bold as anything, delightful little Marta set the trap. "What are you doing Saturday night?"

Brad tensed, unsure if Marta was asking him out on a date. He sputtered a bit before finally answering that he didn't have any firm plans.

"Well, neither does Beckie. I know because I asked her to take me to the bus station. So, there you go. You two have a date on Saturday to see a movie, no?"

They looked like lovesick teenagers, smiling shyly at each other.

"There you go. That was not so hard, no?" She stood up. "Now, I can enjoy my party, and I can go off and visit my family and not worry about you, no?" Marta patted Beckie on the shoulder.

I stood and followed Marta. When we were out of earshot, I leaned into her and whispered, "You were brilliant back there. I am going to miss you terribly."

She hugged me tightly. "You will be great—you are a strong woman. I go, with no worries, Liebchen."

Tears sprang to my eyes at her praise and her affection. Had it only been three weeks? It felt as if I'd known her all my life. I was going to miss her desperately. I drew back.

"Thanks, Marta. We'll talk soon."

With that, I made my escape. I slipped into the back room, grabbed my coat, and headed out the back door. I have the keys now.

Monday morning, I would come into the kitchen alone.

Hurrying down the street to the bank, I tried not to think about being on my own.

But the thoughts wouldn't leave me.

CHAPTER SIXTY

Maybe it was Marta's leaving, but when I arrived at the apartment, I reran my losses. I went to bed, using my pillow to muffle my screams of rage and howls of anguish. I continued to kick, flail, and pound my fists until I reached a point of physical exhaustion. Then, I curled up and slept, hoping to wake up with lighter thoughts.

I finally did. At about four o'clock on Sunday afternoon, I woke up feeling hungry for the first time since Friday. My head cleared, and the storm passed—as I ate some cereal and sipped a cup of tea.

After I ate, I took a quick shower. As I lathered my hair, I thought of my mother and realized she didn't have my new number. She had no way of reaching me, as she was unaware that I wasn't home and that my old cell number was no longer in use. I berated myself for not realizing this sooner. Dressed in sweats, I dialed her number and braced for the backlash. There was no answer, so I left my new phone number on her voicemail.

I turned on the radio, picked up my knitting needles, and worked on the scarf. Wasting an entire weekend feeling sorry for myself was something I vowed to never let happen again.

Thinking about my first day without Marta, I mentally went through the list for Monday morning. I wanted to reward Beckie for her confidence in me. Maybe I lost a weekend wallowing in self-pity and regret, but come five in the morning, I wanted to be ready to take on the world. I was so lost in thought that I dropped a stitch when the phone rang.

Without looking at the caller ID, I knew who was calling. Picking up the phone, I saw my mother's name. I sighed. Did I have the strength to talk to her? I debated through another ring, knowing I would have to talk to her sometime. I answered.

"Hello?"

"Joan, is that you?"

"Yes, Mom. How are you?"

"I'm fine. Why didn't you call me after the funeral? I have been worried sick! I called you so many times at the farm, but no one answered until last week when Joe finally picked up. He wasn't very pleasant to me."

"I'm sorry, Mom. I should have called."

"Harrumph."

"I've already apologized. What more do you want? I realize I've disappointed you again, so maybe my not calling was so I could avoid a lecture, maybe I just wanted to … I don't know, maybe, I just wanted to …"

"What did you want, Joan?"

"The honest to God's truth is, I want my kids back!"

"Oh."

There was a long silence as I wrestled with new emotions. This time, my anger didn't strip me of my dignity. Instead, my rage felt powerful and righteous.

"Well, that isn't going to happen," she whispered.

"I know that, Mom." I spoke with such vehemence that I shouted at her.

"Don't you yell at me, Missy. It isn't my fault!"

I hated it when she called me "Missy." She only did that when she was angry and thought I was misbehaving. It made me feel ten years old.

"Don't call me that!"

"Call you what?"

"Don't call me *Missy*."

"Okay. But I really wish you wouldn't take your frustrations out on me."

"Okay."

More silence as we collectively pulled back our tempers.

"Now, Joe tells me you're getting a divorce. That's rather sudden, isn't it? Are you sure that's the right thing to do?"

"I didn't want a divorce. Joe's the one who started it. There was some stuff … um … well …" I wanted to tell her what he did to me, how he destroyed what I had left of Caleb, but I couldn't seem to find the words.

"So, Joe started it. He threw you out?"

"No, I left."

"You left, but he started it."

I could feel the anger build again.

"I left because he gave me no choice."

"No choice? What do you mean?"

"Well, he refused to allow me to have a funeral for Caleb. He didn't want to pay for one. He said the government should put him into a pauper's grave or not even bother burying him at all, just toss him in the landfill with the rest of the garbage." I choked and sputtered on the words.

"You're kidding. Is that why he wasn't at the funeral?"

"Yes, he knew when it was. He's turned Jonathon against me, too. I have called Jonathon every day since this whole mess began, and he never answers or calls back." I was speaking freely now.

"I see."

"So, I left him and found an apartment and a job."

"You are working? Doing what? You're not qualified for anything?"

This is where she would express all her disappointments. She wanted me to go into nursing or teaching, to have a profession I could call my own. I disappointed her by marrying Joe right out of school. The lecture she pulled out occasionally reminded me that I had settled for a life of no value when I could have had a career that was about to begin.

"You know that little café on Fifth? Well, I'm their new baker."

"Baking? Well, I guess you certainly are qualified for that."

Pulling my phone away, I looked at the screen. The voice was my mother's, but those words were not.

"Thank you." I put the phone back to my ear.

"Well, you've always been an excellent cook."

Another compliment! "Thank you."

"And I'm sorry about Joe. If it's any consolation, I never liked him."

I laughed. This was not news to me. My mom and Joe mixed like oil and water. They didn't like one another. "I gathered that when he threw you out of the house. Sorry for all the times that I didn't take your side. It was easier to keep the peace if I stayed on his."

Following a long pause, Mom said, "Joan, it was a nice funeral for Caleb. I'm sorry I never came home for Leah's. I was furious at Jonathon for having his wedding in May when he knew I was away until the middle of June. What would a couple of weeks change? What difference would it have made to him?"

I wondered what difference it would have made to her, too. It would have put her home three or maybe four weeks before schedule. But I didn't say that.

"It wasn't like he did it deliberately. From what I could gather from Debbie, they were trying to remain chaste until the wedding and waiting another month … well, you know about young hormones."

"I suppose. I can be a stubborn old woman sometimes." She chuckled at her admission. "I'll be leaving for Arizona in a few weeks, but I was wondering if I should postpone that until after Christmas. Maybe we could have Christmas together if you'd like, presuming you'll be alone."

With everything else going on, I hadn't thought about Christmas. I did not know what I would do, but having Mom there would be something. Her generous offer warmed my heart. She hated being here in the winter.

"Unless Jonathon and Debbie come to their senses, I'll be by myself. But I don't want to impede your plans."

"Well, Wally and I won the title of king and queen for the New Year's Eve ball, so I must be present for that. But I could stay for Christmas."

She reminisced about Christmas in Arizona and her wonderful community of friends there. I had to admit I was a tad envious of my mother and felt quite sad that I was unaware of this part of her life. How many years had I wasted thinking she was selfish and didn't care? Somehow, I forgot to see her as a human being with feelings. I chastised myself for judging her and keeping her at arm's length.

When she mentioned Wally for the second time, I questioned her. She told me he was her boyfriend, and I smiled. Sounding like a teenage girl, she told me a little about him. Curious to meet the man who had captured my mother's heart, I suggested she invite him to share our Christmas.

"I'll think about it," she said. "I have to go. It's time for *Jeopardy!*, and Wally and I watch it together."

"How does that work? You're in different time zones?"

"Yes, we are. Wally has the time surfing channels, so he watches the same station as I do. We sit on the phone and try to beat each other to the answers. He's very smart."

She sounded like a woman in love.

"Okay, Mom, thanks for calling back and thanks for ... you know."

"Yes, I know. Good night." She hung up.

I set the phone down, a wave of melancholy washing over me. Suddenly, I didn't feel so alone in the world. My mother loved me. I hoped she did, but she'd never given me any proof until now. She really surprised me.

I went to bed that night feeling lighter than I had in a long time. It was one thing to know your strength. It's quite another to know that no matter how strong you are, someone is willing to hold up your arms when you get tired. For the first time since I left home, I knew my mother was in my corner, and that seemed amazing.

CHAPTER SIXTY-ONE

I opened the café on my own for the first time. Walking into a dark storeroom was a little spooky. As I moved forward through the building, I turned on the lights. I removed my coat before heading into the kitchen to begin the morning preparations. That morning, I would need to make bread, buns, pies, and cake. There were cookies in the freezer, so they could wait until tomorrow.

I went to work. When Beckie and Jack arrived, the kitchen smelled like a proper bakery.

"How are you getting along?" Beckie ran her hand across my shoulders.

I smiled. "They are going very well. I am simply following Marta's game plan, and even though it was much simpler with her, it really is manageable without her."

"Good to hear! I knew I'd picked a winner." She patted my shoulder.

I blushed at the unsolicited praise.

"Okay, is there anything you need help with before I get cracking on the menu board?"

"No, thanks. It's all under control."

"Good." She stepped away and then turned back. "Oh … by the way, Brad and I have another date this Friday. Thanks to you and Marta." She winked, grinned, and then left the kitchen with a spring in her step.

All right! I thought to myself. Progress! Beckie's news put a bounce in my step. I was so glad we pushed them together and hoped they would live happily ever after. Well, as happy as anybody lives, or happier.

The day passed quickly. I didn't find much time for breaks. I took a few minutes to make tea, then returned several minutes later to drink it warm, not hot. For lunch, I ate my sandwich and returned to work in fifteen minutes. It would get easier once I was totally in a routine.

At two o'clock, I pulled the last loaves of bread out of the oven and set them on the rack to cool. There were only a few dishes left to wash, and as I headed to the sink, Beckie stopped me.

"We can finish those—you get off now. You've hardly had a break. Go home and put your feet up."

"Thanks!"

I squeezed her hand briefly, then headed out. The

wind had picked up, and the walk to the grocery store and back to the apartment was brisk. It was certainly getting wintry out there.

I put the few groceries away, sat on the couch, and put my feet on the coffee table. I sat staring out at the whiteness on the balcony, thinking about winter in the country. Here in the city, there was an eagerness to clear out the snow and move forward. In the country, it shrank the world into a small, manageable space. If drifting snow blocked the road, sometimes it was days before Joe took the time to clear it. Of course, they plowed the main highway, but they considered secondary roads less important and gravel roads even less.

On wintry days, when the kids didn't always get to school, we sat closed inside the warmth of the house, in the kitchen, drinking hot chocolate and making cookies. It was family time. When the storm passed, we would don our warm outerwear and head out to the hill for some tobogganing.

Ice skating on the pond was another fun winter sport. Joe would take the heavy metal snow shovel down and clear away the snow, smoothing out the bumps that would have formed if the wind had blown while the temperature dropped. That was usually late in the season when the ice was thick enough to hold the weight. The kids were all excellent skaters, but they didn't play hockey unless there were more kids around because Caleb refused to play as he always lost. He did like to skate, though, taking corners at breakneck speed.

Leah would spin and twirl in the middle of the ice, and Jonathon would shoot pucks into an empty net. Sometimes, Caleb had to dodge a wayward puck, which never caused a fuss between the boys. They played just fine on the ice.

After an hour, they would troop into the house, where I would have hot chocolate waiting. Their cheeks would be rosy, and their eyes bright. As the snow melted, abandoned snowsuits and skates cluttered the porch, creating puddles under their boots.

I thought and smiled. Those were the days and memories that would live forever. I looked around the table at those smiling faces: Jonathon and Leah chattering away, Caleb silently listening but not retreating. My heart swelled with such love that I wanted to scoop each of them up and hold them tight. Memories. Memories.

I snapped back to the present. Tears were streaming down my cheeks. Once, I had it all—didn't I? Now, I had nothing but the wispy smoke of those memories. Intangible and elusive. I closed my eyes against the pain those thoughts inflicted. When was this going to get easier?

I worked on my scarf that night, knitting after supper for a good hour. When I tied it off, I held it up, feeling satisfied that I had done a passable job on my first attempt. Now, to tackle the toque. Tomorrow, I was going to go to the knitting circle. They would help me if I had trouble.

CHAPTER SIXTY-TWO

Following another busy day at the café, my excitement about going out again surprised me. It had been a long time since I'd joined anything. I hoped I would like it and that they would like me. The fear and anticipation of something newly created tingling in my belly. Butterflies. That's what we called them when I was a girl. How long had it been since I had butterflies?

Gathering my gear, I headed out for the short walk to the store. The wind had died down, but the cold air nipped at my face. I pulled my scarf up over my nose, hurrying down the sidewalk.

I thought about the call from Brad I had received earlier. He'd heard from Joe's lawyers, and the impression he gave was the news wasn't good. It didn't surprise me. Joe was a planner, and I'm sure he organized his affairs long before he filed the papers to petition me for divorce. I had an appointment to go over the details on Thursday.

Outside the Knitting Shop, I stopped and took a deep breath. Here I go! I pulled the door open, stepping into the warm room. Linda met me before I could remove my scarf, grinning.

"Good to see you again. Welcome. Come on in."

I followed her through a small doorway into a large room. Many mismatched chairs, some already occupied, were sitting in a semicircle.

"Sit anywhere." Linda motioned with her hand. A bell rang, and she scooted back the way she came. I heard her greeting others as I moved toward a chair on the opposite side of the room from the others. I debated taking the rocking chair, but I took a soft-looking chair next to it.

"Oh, don't sit there. That's where Thelma sits," one knitter called as I sat.

With that one comment, I became uncomfortable and unsure about my decision to be there. Territorial women always scared me.

"I didn't know."

Gathering my stuff, I moved backward toward the chairs closer to the door. I glanced at Linda, who ushered a few more ladies into the room. She was scowling. I couldn't determine if Linda's annoyance focused on me or the two women across the room.

"Thelma can sit somewhere else," Linda said with

finality. "Sit where you want, Joan."

"Oh, that's okay. I don't want to be in anyone's way."

"You're not."

I didn't go back to the original chair. Instead, I chose one closer to the door, where it would be easier to make my escape.

The two ladies who just entered greeted the others warmly and took chairs at the far end of the room. The doorbell chimed again, and Linda moved off. Soon, three more women entered. They separated, taking chairs in different places in the room. A tall, thin woman came in, holding herself with the regal air of royalty. Her outfit was impeccable, and her hair was perfectly coifed. She oozed elitism, crossing the room to take the chair I abandoned. This was Thelma. I instinctively didn't like her.

With haughty gestures, she fluffed and preened until she settled into the chair like a bird upon the nest. Roosted on her perch, she glanced around the room, nodding hellos to a few of the other women. All those present greeted her as if she were someone to be reckoned with. She looked down at everyone over a hawkish nose. She glanced over at me, looked away, and then back again. Her beady eyes settled on me, and I squirmed in my chair.

"You're new." Her voice dripped with disdain. "What's your name?"

"Joan," I replied obediently.

"Joan? Joan, what?"

Another woman swooped in, filling the room with fresh air. The atmosphere changed—it became brighter.

"Hello, ladies!" she trilled. "Isn't it a brute out there tonight? My goodness, you'd think that someone forgot to pay the heating bill."

Polite chuckles echoed around the room.

"Hello, Maxine!" a few called back.

She looked around the room and settled on the chair next to mine. "Hello, I'm Maxine."

"Hi, Maxine," I replied quietly, smiling at her. Her warm brown eyes penetrated mine. "I'm Joan."

"Nice to meet you, Joan. Have you been knitting long?"

"Well, I used to knit, once upon a time, but I haven't for so long, I thought I'd come and reacquaint myself with it. This knitting circle, where you can get help from other knitters, seemed like a good idea to me."

"It's fun, too, getting to meet new people." Then she leaned over and whispered conspiratorially into my ear, "Despite a few bad eggs."

Instantly, I understood to whom she was referring. I looked guiltily down the row to find Thelma hadn't forgotten about me. She was eyeing me like a cobra staring at its prey—she was just waiting to strike.

A shiver ran up my spine.

CHAPTER SIXTY-THREE

Linda breezed into the room, clapping her hands together. "Okay, ladies, it looks like this is us for tonight. I'd like to welcome Joan Bradshaw, our newest member of the knitting circle." She gestured toward me. Everyone politely clapped, and my face flushed at being the center of attention.

"Now, before I sit down, does anyone need help with their patterns or stitches?"

A lady across the room raised her hand. Linda went over to stand in front of her. The rest of the women returned to their knitting, some rocking in their chairs, others settled comfortably in softer ones. Conversations became whispered. The clacking of needles settled into a rhythm that soothed the room, lulling us all into a place of serene calmness.

I took a deep breath and exhaled slowly, feeling content and at peace. I paid attention to my knitting, working the band of the hat to complement my scarf.

Linda finished her instructions and made a pass around the room, checking on each participant before she settled down to her own knitting. She didn't settle, though, like the rest of us, as she kept her eyes on the group. Occasionally, someone's hand would go up, and Linda would put her knitting aside, cross to that person, and attend to their question.

When Linda disappeared into the store with one lady, Thelma came to life. "Bradshaw. You're Joan Bradshaw," she called from her chair down the circle.

Startled, I looked up and nodded. Everyone in the room turned to look at me. My face flushed. I hated being the center of attention.

"I've been sitting here wondering where I heard that name."

With those words, all the blood drained from my face. My breathing quickened as fear rose in my heart.

"You're the mother of the coward who shot those two girls, aren't you?" She didn't wait for a response. "What was his name, Calvin? No, Carl? No, it was something like that." She snapped her fingers, trying to jar her memory. "No, it was more biblical, wasn't it? Cain? That would have been fitting, but that's not it, is it?"

Involuntarily, I shook my head. She smiled, not a kind one, but the predatory, sly sneer of someone who could smell blood and was moving in for the kill.

"No, it wasn't Cain. It was Caleb! Caleb Bradshaw, son of Joe and Joan Bradshaw, fatally wounded Brenda Taylor and Andrea Pritchard before cowardly taking his own life. He was a coward, wasn't he?" She paused, waiting for me to answer. "Was he always a coward, Joan?" The weight of her message pulled down a dark veil of unwelcome hostility.

I shook my head again, wanting to spare my son the judgment she was making. The room was deathly quiet. Every eye was on me, watching with frightened fascination, willing me to respond.

Shame overwhelmed me. My breath grew more shallow—tiny beads of perspiration formed across my forehead and upper lip. The room spun, and I wanted to get up and run out of there, but I didn't trust my legs to work. Tears sprang to my eyes, spilling down my face. My mouth opened and closed as if I was going to speak, but no sound came out.

"Come on, Joan, enlighten us!" Thelma sneered.

When I finally decided to leave, Maxine slid a protective arm across my shoulders, grounding me to my seat. I was prepared to run out into the frigid night without my jacket or purse to escape this persecution—this unwarranted judgment of failure.

"That's quite enough, Thelma! You stop right there." Linda spoke with quiet authority as she re-entered the room. Everyone turned their attention to Thelma. Linda looked outraged as she re-entered the room.

"I'm just asking," she snapped.

"Well, you've said more than enough. This is neither the time nor the place for this conversation. Joan is here as a fellow knitter. Her life outside this circle is none of our business unless she makes it our business. As far as I'm concerned, since Joan didn't pull the trigger, whatever happened has nothing to do with her. Now, either you accept that, or you can pack up your needles and leave. I will not tolerate this in my store."

Thelma's face darkened with embarrassment. She huffed indignantly before she stuffed her knitting into her leather satchel. She stood with a flourish and slipped into her stylish winter jacket, buttoning it up angrily. Squaring her shoulders, she snapped, "Well, I will not stay where I am not wanted!" She turned on her heel and flounced out of the room.

Linda followed her. The bell rang as Thelma left. Linda returned a few seconds later, having locked the door behind her. As Linda entered the room, all the women clapped. Calls of congratulations rang out.

Maxine leaned over to me, pulling me closer with the arm still slung across my shoulders. "You are like Dorothy from the Wizard of Oz. You have just ousted the Wicked Witch of the West."

"But I didn't do anything," I stammered.

"You didn't need to. You were the catalyst, and in this group of women, you are a hero."

CHAPTER SIXTY-FOUR

I looked cautiously around the room. Every woman met my gaze, and each had a warm smile on her face.

"Thelma is a bully. She comes from a wealthy family, and even as a girl, she had an unpleasant personality. I've heard that she was so mean-spirited her father paid Bobby Graham to marry her. Bobby has the Porter's wealth at his disposal as long as they stay married. We like to think that no one would have married her if not for the money." Maxine paused. "We tolerate her presence because of her husband. Bobby might be a powerful man, but he is very likable. She might bluster that he'll ruin someone, but he rarely involves himself in Thelma's peccadillos. She is no longer here, at least for tonight, and we can relax knowing that she isn't pouring out her special blend of poison over us."

Maxine's words helped, though I must confess that the shock of being attacked in such a purposeful way scared me. How many people in this world wanted to take a swipe at me because of what my son had done? Surely Andrea's parents might want that, and Brenda's parents, too. Besides them, was there anyone else who had a stake in what happened? No, but when has protocol ever stopped people from entering places they didn't belong?

The group went back to knitting, the atmosphere in the room warmer and friendlier with the vanquishing of that nasty woman. I focused on my project, my needles clacking away as if I knew what I was doing. I kept knitting, going round and round, pouring out row after row. When I finally stopped to look, I could see an error. I sighed, pulled out my needles, and wound the wool back into a ball.

Maxine looked over. "What are you doing?"

I looked down at my project. "I was so intent on just knitting that I failed to follow the pattern. This hat would fit the jolly green giant and his wife." I laughed. It felt good after the tension Thelma had unleashed in me. A few women looked up from their work, smiling.

Getting serious, I really looked at Maxine for the first time. I took in her warm brown eyes and kind face, which wasn't classically beautiful but pleasant and appealing in a way that made you instantly want to like her.

"Thank you for standing with me tonight. I don't have many friends, and even fewer since that night."

Maxine nodded. "You're okay, Joan, and you're welcome."

Minutes later, Linda stood, clapping again to get our attention. "Well, time is up, ladies. We've had another glorious night. Please, come back again next week."

Knitting needles stilled, skeins of wool collected, and everything was tucked neatly into bags and satchels around the room. There was a distinct chatter among the group, and heads turned toward one another.

"Some of us go for coffee at the Java Drop-In, and you can join us if you'd like," Maxine said as I collected my paraphernalia.

"No, thanks. I work early in the morning, so I should go home, but thanks."

"Anytime. Are you walking? Do you need a ride home?"

"No, thanks. I don't live far, and the walk will help me calm down, so by the time I get home, I'll be ready for bed."

"If you're sure."

"I'm sure, thanks."

With coats on, hats pulled onto heads, and scarves wrapped jauntily around necks, the group dispersed. Some women left alone, and others were in packs of two or three. Linda gently touched my shoulder as I prepared to leave.

"Please come again, Joan. I hope Thelma didn't

scare you off."

"Oh no, I'll be back, thank you." I nodded.

"Good!" She squeezed my upper arm gently. "Good."

I left, following two older women out the door.

"Goodnight, Joan!" They called as we parted outside.

I was heading across the street alone, the other women turning left or heading off to the right.

"Goodnight," I called back. I smiled.

Despite Thelma's attack, it was welcoming there. I would do my best to return.

CHAPTER SIXTY-FIVE

Walking along the street with the wind at my back, I kept my head down, my thoughts focused on getting home and going to bed. I noticed a car sitting along the street ahead because it was running. The door popped open as I neared, and a tall, thin figure climbed out. The door closed, and the person walked around the front of the car to meet me.

I stopped, fear pricking my skin. Taking a deep breath, I looked around for a way to escape.

"Not too sure of yourself when you're all alone." It was Thelma. "It is fortuitous that we meet again like this, isn't it?"

I didn't respond. Like a deer in the headlights, I stood there trapped.

"Well, my dear, I just wanted to let you know I think

you are abominable. You don't deserve to breathe the same air as the rest of us. You raised a monster, yet you show no shame. God will surely make your life miserable, and I'm here to make sure you know you are a horrible person."

From somewhere deep within, courage rose. "What's it to you, Thelma? Why does my living well or not matter? What have I ever done to you?"

She sputtered, perhaps unaccustomed to the challenge.

"And just for your information, the Bible says, 'Let he without sin be the first to throw stones.' Are you without sin, Thelma? Have you lived such an exemplary life that you can throw stones?"

Her face darkened again—her eyes flashed angrily. A car came around the corner, slowing as it neared us. The window came down, and Maxine called out.

"Joan, do you need a ride?"

Thelma turned without a word, climbed back into her car, and sped off. I walked to the middle of the road to speak with Maxine.

"Are you okay?"

"Yes, thank you, Maxine. I don't know what came over me, but I stood up to her, and she had nothing to say. Mind you, you came along before she could."

"Well, good. I had a feeling she left the store a little too easily, so when you wouldn't take a ride, I thought I'd make sure you made it home okay."

"But how did she know which way I would go?

That's the eerie part."

"If you look down the street, back toward the knitting shop, you can see for yourself that the door is visible. She was waiting there to see which way you were going. Thelma would have chased after you, but lucky for her, you were walking this way. She's no fool, that's for sure."

"Do you think I've seen the last of her?"

"You never know with Thelma. She only picks fights she knows she can win. Since you stood up to her, she may leave you alone. Just know that you are not by yourself, okay?"

Tears welled up again. "Thanks, Maxine. I appreciate that more than you will ever know."

"Here." She handed me a piece of paper. "Here's my number. Call me anytime."

I took the paper and stepped away from the car. She pulled away, waving her arm out the window and calling goodnight. I stood in the middle of the road, watching her taillights grow more distant. Her signal came on, and she turned right toward the Java Drop-In. I drifted back to the sidewalk and made my way home.

I had lost so much, and there was no way I would ever get it back. Sure, I could live in the sewer of despair, and no one would blame me. How do you live with so much grief? I didn't want to end up bitter and angry like Thelma. She was the one person I never wanted to be, an ugly hag, so angry at the world I would try to tear people down to my level.

I climbed into bed that night, strangely warmed by the possibility of friendship.

I slept well, not dreaming for the first time in many weeks about Caleb and Leah and life without them.

CHAPTER SIXTY-SIX

The next few days passed quickly. I wasn't looking forward to meeting with Brad only because I was unsure what he had found out.

Thursday afternoon, I was busy icing a Black Forest cake. My carrot cake was in the oven, and two apple pies and one cherry were ready to go. Beckie came into the kitchen, grinning ear to ear.

"Joan!" she trilled, her voice rising and falling in a cadence. "You have a visitor."

"What? I have a visitor?" My heart pounded. Joe? Jonathon? The way Beckie spoke, it had to be someone I wanted to see, so probably not Joe.

"Okay, I'll just check on my carrot cake."

"I can watch that for you. What time does it need to come out?"

I looked at the timer. "In about eight minutes. Then the pies need to go in."

"Okay, go. Take your break. If you want to invite your guest back into the staff room for more privacy, that is allowed."

I smiled awkwardly and moved out of the kitchen. I glanced out the large window but didn't see any familiar faces. When I came onto the restaurant floor, Constable Harrison was at the end of the counter. Dressed in street clothes, he looked handsome and powerful. I hadn't seen him since Caleb's funeral, which was over a month ago.

He looked up at me and smiled, rising to his feet. Bending down, he picked up a brown storage box from the floor. When I was beside him, he lifted the lid.

"I brought you Caleb's journals." He reached inside and pulled out the top book. I recognized it. It was one I'd given him for Christmas. The leather-bound book had a magnetic catch. The hand-tooling displayed the shield of Zelda. Tears filled my eyes. "I wasn't sure I should take them to the farmhouse after that bonfire. I thought if you wanted them …" He didn't finish.

"Let's go into the back. We can have a little more privacy there."

He nodded. I picked up his coffee mug while he grabbed the box, and I led the way into the back room. Once there, I set his cup down, pulled out two chairs, gesturing for him to sit. He set the box on the table and then waited for me to sit before taking his chair. An awkward silence filled the room.

"How are things, Joan?" he asked, finally breaking the silence.

"Oh, good, I suppose. I love my job. It is hard work, but it feels good to get out and be busy."

"I can imagine."

Nodding, I didn't know where to go next.

"You gave Caleb a good sendoff. There was a nice turnout, too. Nobody there who shouldn't have been."

Nodding again, like a bobblehead doll, I chastised myself. Stop being so shy—after all, he was only here out of duty.

Glancing up, I caught a look on his face that caused me to blush. Well, maybe not. My tummy flipped over.

Constable Harrison cleared his throat. "I should tell you that our investigation is complete. We can now return all the stuff that was taken from his apartment to you. I brought the journals, of course, and his laptop and cell phone are in the box, too. You are now free to enter the apartment and clear it out. If you don't, the apartment complex manager will do it, but he'll send you the bill."

"Thank you." Thinking about Caleb's furniture, I compared it to the stuff I had. "I'll have to figure out how to get it out of there. I have no vehicle."

"What happened to your Jeep?"

"My husband took it. I was naïve enough to let Jonathon know where I was living, trying to keep the lines of dialogue open. Joe came one day while I was at work and took it back. He had the spare keys. I didn't think to take them the morning I left."

Anger flashed across his face.

I continued hastily. "He's suing for divorce. I received the papers a couple of days after the funeral. He's not wasting any time getting rid of me."

"Oh, I don't think he's trying to get rid of you. I think he's trying to force your hand."

"That's what my lawyer thinks, too. Unfortunately, it will not work. He's going to get his divorce. The only thing I want is my vehicle so I can go out to my daughter's grave. He can keep his money and the farm."

"You deserve more than that, you know. You were married for what? Twenty-five years?"

"I might deserve more, but I don't want more. I'd only manage it long enough to give it to Jonathon when I die. Joe's not stupid. It all goes to Jonathon in the end. Who cares if I manage it or Joe does? I'm just frustrated that I don't have a way to get out to see Leah."

"Well, I hope your case gets settled quickly then. In the meantime, I can take you to the cemetery."

Surprised at his generous offer, my eyes widened. "Are you sure? I wouldn't want to inconvenience you."

"I wouldn't offer if it was inconvenient. Of course, I can't do it if I'm on duty, but I surely can if I'm not."

"That's very kind of you." I blushed again, looking down at my hands.

He reached into his jacket pocket and pulled out a card. He then took out a pen and wrote his cell number on the back: "Call me, and we can set something up."

I nodded. "Thank you, Constable Harrison. I really

appreciate that."

"I think you can call me Ben." He smiled.

"Okay, Ben. Thank you."

"Well, I'd better let you get back to work. If I can do anything—anything at all, please let me know."

I walked him out into the restaurant, where I stood awkwardly, unsure how to say goodbye. Should I shake hands? Or just say goodbye. Should I hug him? No, that was too familiar. I stuck out my hand.

"Thank you for coming and for bringing me those journals. I really appreciate it."

He took my hand gently but firmly smiled, his blue eyes twinkling. "You're welcome. Talk to you again." He squeezed my hand gently before letting go. I stood there watching him walk out the door. When it closed behind him, I exhaled and went back to work.

The journals infiltrated my thoughts for the rest of the day. I was eager to take them home, but I had my meeting with Brad. With some sorrow, these would have to wait until tomorrow. Then, I would have the entire weekend to delve into Caleb's world. I couldn't wait.

CHAPTER SIXTY-SEVEN

A few hours later, Brad ushered me into his office. He gestured for me to sit at the table before moving around his desk to pick up a file. Then, he took the chair next to mine. He opened the file. The first page was an affidavit duly signed and witnessed. It related all Joe's assets, which I noticed were nowhere near what I thought they should be.

"Your expression tells me you are a little shocked?"

I nodded.

"It's only a guess, but I think your husband moved assets, probably into Jonathon's name. Joe probably did this immediately after you left, mere days before he filed for divorce. He wanted to make sure there was nothing left for you. He's taken an enormous risk in moving everything, including the farm, into Jonathon's name.

Should he and his son fall out, he stands to lose it all. But that doesn't help you."

I sat there, feeling defeated. I wasn't cunning enough for this cutthroat business. Tears welled up and rolled silently down my cheeks. Brad reached over, squeezing my shoulder as a sign of solidarity.

"We can get a forensic accountant and petition the court. It'll be expensive, and even if we can prove that he moved the funds, it'll cost a lot to get them back."

I shook my head, feeling beaten before I even began. Fighting dirty took more energy than I had to spend. I was ready to throw in the towel and let him have it all. Except I wanted my vehicle back. Despite Ben's offer, I wasn't ready to share my visits to Leah with anyone, let alone someone who never knew her.

"I'm done, Brad. All I want is my vehicle back. I don't care about anything else. Let him keep it all. It's not mine, it's never been mine. It would feel like blood money anyway."

Brad nodded, frowning slightly. "I think we should request half the farm. That's worth even more than the money in the bank."

"At what cost, though? I cannot afford your fee as it is, and Joe will fight this until I have nothing left. He doesn't care if he loses half the farm to lawyer fees as long as I don't get one red cent. It isn't worth the fight. In the end, it goes to Jonathon. I don't want to steal from him just to get one over on Joe."

"You are a better parent than he is."

"That may be, but Jonathon's allegiance is with him, so let's just leave it, shall we?"

"If that's what you want, I must abide by your wishes." We sat there in silence for a moment, letting the situation settle. "I'll draw up some papers, and you can come in and sign them. It should take a day at the most. How about you stop by after work on Monday? Then we can get this done with little more cost incurred."

"Sounds good, Brad. Thank you."

"Are you okay?"

"Right now, I'm weary, bone tired. I know that I will eventually get angry about what's happened, but I'm not there yet. In the end, I will be okay. I have no choice. Well, I do, but it's not an appealing choice."

Brad looked puzzled at my statement.

"Suicide. Believe me, there have been days in the last few years—when I have wondered what life was all about. There have been days when I thought it was too much to bear. Those feelings have been stronger and more urgent since Caleb's death, but I know I cannot give in to that kind of thinking. I know I must be stronger than them."

"You are a survivor, aren't you? You've had much to bear." Compassion filled his eyes. "Have you seen a counselor?"

I shook my head, remembering the phone call I made but never completed.

"Well, I suggest you call the Mental Health Clinic.

They can help you through this better than I. I feel a little helpless with the emotional battle you're facing."

"You've done lots, Brad, really you have. It's nice knowing that I'm not alone in the world."

He nodded. I smiled at him, tears glistening in my eyes. He smiled back.

I cleared my throat, hoping to relieve the tension. "Speaking of not being alone and changing the subject, how are things with you and Beckie?"

He threw back his head and laughed. "You are too much, Joan Bradshaw!" he howled. "Things with Beckie and I are good, ticking along at a comfortable pace. I owe you and Marta a load of thanks for your help in getting us together."

"You're welcome." I smiled.

I gathered my belongings and put on my winter jacket. Brad quickly assisted me, and soon, I was heading out into the evening.

"Well, Joe, I guess you've won. I hope you can live with yourself," I muttered as I scurried down the street. At the grocery store, I selected a few things for supper, some apples, and some tea bags. Spontaneously, I also picked up a tin of hot chocolate. I didn't drink it too often, but it would make a pleasant change from tea occasionally.

At home, I kicked off my boots, hung up my jacket, and set the groceries on the counter. I walked into the living room and sat on the couch, letting the exhaustion take over. I curled myself around a cushion and wept.

Why does life have to be so hard? I railed at God for His lack of compassion, for His lack of care, for His downright neglect. I was so angry with Him that I might have punched Him in the nose if He had miraculously appeared.

Those thoughts made me feel worse. I grew up believing God is good, great, powerful, all-knowing, and loving. Yet, my life had been a series of misfortunes in which God allowed evil to be perpetrated without restraint. My anger at Him burned again as I thought of the injustice Joe meted out.

I was a good, dutiful wife, following the Bible's guide. I held my tongue and served my husband well, always doing my best. Cautioned that a third pregnancy could be fatal, I went ahead with it at my peril. I did it all because I believed it was my duty. And where did it get me? It was me living in a tiny apartment with limited means, with no family to call my own. The only thing of value I possessed was my wedding ring.

Looking down at it now, I pulled it off my finger and set it on the coffee table. A deep sadness settled into my soul.

It was done.

It might take a year to be declared "divorced," but in my heart, it was over.

Even though I had picked pork chops for supper, I had no appetite for them. Instead, I made myself a grilled cheese sandwich after I put the chops into the fridge.

CHAPTER SIXTY-EIGHT

Friday, after work, I hauled the box of Caleb's belongings home. The box was heavy. I also arranged for Beckie to go to Caleb's apartment on Saturday afternoon. She was so good to me. I could have gone on my own, but with her vehicle to haul small stuff, I could make headway. Movers from the charity shop could take the furniture away.

That night, after I cleaned up my kitchen, I brought the box of journals and set it on the table. Grabbing the top journal, the one that Constable Harrison had pulled out, I flipped it open at random and read.

> The dancers swirled in a circle, the bells on their ankles jingling a rhythm. They moved so quickly that their costumes blended into a

whirlwind of color. It was mesmerizing. The audience seemed to fall under a spell as they watched with rapt attention. No one moved.

The music rose to a crescendo as the dancers spun faster, and then, with a loud crash of the cymbals, they dropped to the ground. The audience held their breath for a split second before rising to their feet, applauding with appreciation. Shouts of bravo echoed across the amphitheater.

Marcus turned to his companion. "The time is right. We must make our move."

The two men slipped out unnoticed as the dancers rose from the ground to begin a new dance. This one promised to be less dramatic as the music swelled. They moved down a short alley and emerged onto the main street. It was quiet, devoid of life. Looking both ways, they scurried across the wide road and stepped into the cool and quiet apothecary.

This was some of Caleb's fiction. I had read none of his writing in years. There was a time when he would show me his work, but I couldn't remember the last time. I set the journal aside. As beautiful as it was, I didn't want to read his imagination. I wanted to read his heart. I pulled out another journal. From the date inside the front cover, he was fourteen.

It is a typical Monday here at Chez Bradshaw. I got special honors with my writing, a story that my teacher wants to submit for an anthology of student writing from across the province. It was exciting, and I couldn't wait to tell everyone. Imagine my story being read by kids from all over Alberta! Of course, I hoped that this news would make Dad happy, that he'd finally see me. But guess what? Today was also the day they announced that Jonathon's basketball team made it to provincials, as if anyone would care about my story when they could celebrate the sports hero.

Just as I predicted, his news trumped mine. All my dad could talk about all night was his precious Jonathon and his pride. When I finally had the chance to tell everyone, Mom clapped her hands, trying to push this accomplishment further. Leah thought it was great, too. I looked at Dad. His face was passive at first, then he broke into a big smile. I couldn't believe it—Dad was happy for me—maybe even proud? I was a fool. He clapped Jonathon on the back as he said, at least he had one son he could be proud of. Mom's face crumpled, but she let it go. She always lets it go.

As I read that passage, my heart shrank. These were my son's honest feelings. He felt invisible. How was I going to reconcile myself to that? I flipped over a few pages.

Dad is such a prick. I know the Bible says

> that I am supposed to love my parents, honor and obey them, but I can't do that. I am seriously going to Hell. Tonight, at supper, he humiliated me again. He makes me feel so small and insignificant—so worthless. I just hate him. Why does he do that? I don't understand why he doesn't love me. What's wrong with me? Sure, I'm not a jock like Jonathon, I don't like sports. Well, not competitive ones. If he thought computer games were amazing, he'd see I'm pretty good at them, way better than Jonathon or Leah. But he doesn't care about computers or games. He just hates me. I can never do anything to please him. I wish he would just die.

Caleb's tears on the paper made the rest of the page almost illegible. But I think it read …

> I'm sorry, God, I really didn't mean that. Maybe you could change his heart or something. Make him love me or take me away. I don't want to live like this anymore. It's too hard. I wish my dad were like Mr. Turner. He likes me. Maybe I should go and live with him. Maybe then I could have a real dad.

My son would rather live with another family. How abysmal was that?

CHAPTER SIXTY-NINE

I put the book aside. I read enough to know that, indeed, my son was in trouble years before it manifested into something horrid. If only he'd been confident enough to talk to me. Maybe I wasn't approachable enough. Can you imagine my kid was afraid to confess his fears to me? Afraid that I might tell him some hard truths that were unpalatable. How unfortunate for both of us. I pulled out another journal. He wrote this journal when he was sixteen.

> I like Mr. Fitzpatrick. He's a cool teacher. I watch him being patient with some kids who don't understand chemistry. He's even asked me to partner with Aaron because he is struggling to get it. I get a little frustrated with

how dense Aaron is. I mean, come on! No one can be that useless and still breathe—can they? Once or twice, I wanted to smack Aaron when he asked me the same question for the twentieth time. Only Mr. Fitzpatrick's watchful eye kept me from doing it.

Ha! I've decided that "Dumb Ass" is going to be my nickname for Aaron. I don't know how long Fitzy is going to keep us together. Five minutes was long enough for me. Good grief. Why can't people accept their limitations? Aaron totally should drop this class. He's never going to get it and there are other options—like cooking. He could totally burn the school down the first time he had to turn on the oven. That would be funny!

I read and reread this passage. Caleb was acting just like Joe. How had I never seen this before? His intolerance of someone different or someone he perceived as weaker is so clear in his words. Did he want to impress someone, or was it sheer mimicry? An angry boy became an angry man.

I grabbed another journal, this one from the year he graduated. I was feeling a little more apprehensive, wondering how much angrier he would be. Was I going to see an escalation in his aggression?

What a day! Jonathon was so much fun today. He's getting married in a few weeks, and today, we went for our final tux fittings. Dad didn't come, nor did his best man join us. It was just the two of us for once. I can't remember the last time we spent any time together.

After the fitting, he took me to the shooting range. That was a surprise for me. He had brought our rifles, so he had it all planned. We had a lot of fun trying to outdo one another in target practice. I did better than him on the moving targets, but he was way better than me on the stationary ones. He put six rounds through the same hole. I was too impatient—that's what he said. And he said I needed to breathe, not hold my breath when I was aiming. I got better after he told me that. I will practice more once I live in Crawford and go to school. Then we'll have a rematch.

Afterward, we went for burgers. We were eating, and this woman came in with her husband. He looked like he weighed all of ninety pounds, and she was gigantic—and I mean gigantic! Jonathon said she probably weighed four hundred pounds. It was like Jack Sprat and his wife—right out of the nursery rhymes. We both found that hilarious. That woman used two chairs when she sat down. That's how immense she was. I was a little disgusted. I mean—how could someone let themselves go like that? It was gross.

When we left, we passed a battered old Chevy truck with stock racks on the box parked in the handicap space beside the door. Jonathon suggested the lady was so large she probably had to ride in the back. I laughed and asked Jonathon if that made her a cannibal. He looked confused for a minute, then I said—I mean a cow-ni-bal. He finally caught on, and we both laughed all the way to the truck. When I asked if he thought she mooed, Jonathon slapped me on the back and said I was funny.

That felt pretty good. For the first time, I had a brother, and today was the best day ever.

I had never heard of either of my boys being deliberately cruel, and the comment about that poor woman disgusted me. Had I taught them nothing? They both showed a lack of compassion for people struggling and no understanding of human frailties.

This was two weeks before Leah died. The weekend before the wedding was Jonathon's stag party. He wasn't home that weekend. He and his best mates went to Calgary for the weekend. They had hoped to see a hockey game, but the team got eliminated from the playoffs a few weeks before. They were too busy with last-minute preparations, and I don't remember what they had planned.

I was glad they had fun together that day, but never had a marksmanship rematch. Between his work for the electrical firm and coming home to help Joe on the farm, Jonathon had little time for anyone but Debbie. Even though they lived in the same yard, I only saw him when

I invited them over for supper on Sundays.

I flipped forward a few more pages. It was late August, just after Caleb had moved to Crawford.

> I thought I would be glad to be on my own, away from Dad and the farm. But I feel homesick. Maybe it's just because Leah is gone—and I miss her. I still can't believe she's not here anymore and it's my fault. There is a secret that I'll take to my grave.

What is he talking about? How is he responsible? He wasn't even there. I read on.

> I really didn't know Ryan all that well. He was new to town. His dad bought the local hardware store. He was popular with the girls because he was new, and I guess he was handsome. When I saw them getting ready to sneak away, I wasn't happy. I told Leah as much, but Leah was always so sure of herself. I remember telling her that if she just wanted time alone, why not just sit in the car in the parking lot? She laughed and said she wanted to feel the wind in her hair.
>
> I thought then that she must be drunk, and realized that she was. If Dad saw her like that, he'd surely kill her. So, instead of stopping her, I let her leave. When she didn't come back, I was worried. I mentioned something to the group, and Simon told me I shouldn't have let her leave

> with Ryan. He said he was the worst driver he knew. The boy had already had a couple of accidents because he drove too fast on the gravel roads.
>
> The longer they stayed away, the sicker I felt. I tried not to let Mom know, hoping they would return and no one would be the wiser. I even hoped she was getting it on with Ryan because she wasn't answering my texts. The alternative—that something terrible had happened was unthinkable. But I finally had to come clean, and the rest is history. If I had intervened and allowed her to face the consequences of underage drinking, she would still be here. I thought I was doing her a favor. Her death is totally—one hundred percent—my fault.

My heart sank. I did not know that Caleb bore this burden alone all these years. It wasn't his fault. It was Ryan's fault and Leah's for trusting him enough to go with him. If she had been drinking—she wouldn't have made the best decisions, despite that they were hers to make. I should have known. If only I had ensured Caleb went to counseling or something. But I was so consumed by my grief that I didn't realize he was holding this in. He thought he failed Leah, but the truth was, I failed him.

I dropped the journal into the box and stashed it in the bedroom closet. I didn't want to read anymore. I was tired—tired to my very bones—tired of trying to figure out how I could have saved him. It was too late to do that, anyway. Opportunity may have knocked, but I wasn't listening.

I went to bed—my dreams mixed up and crazy.

CHAPTER SEVENTY

Saturday dawned. I hardly slept. After a light breakfast, I headed out to Caleb's apartment to assess what was salvageable. I called the city the day before to find out which bus to take. I walked to the central bus stop, the one place downtown where they all parked for their breaks. Finding the bus I needed, I paid the fare and stepped on.

I had never ridden a bus before, so I stepped into a foreign land of public transport. A few people were already seated. A young man was lost in some handheld device, and an older gentleman with a toque pulled down over his ears, his face lined with years of experience, neither smiled nor greeted me.

Sitting close to the front, I watched as other riders boarded—none smiled or looked at me. They found seats behind me. Finally, the driver stepped in, sat down, and closed the door. He looked in the mirror at his passengers, then signaled and pulled away from the curb. We wove through the streets, stopping when someone pulled the cord. I was grateful I was going so far because I did not know I was supposed to pull the cord. I simply expected him to stop when I needed him to. Did I have a lot to learn?

The young man stepped off—his eyes still glued to his handheld as he exited. A woman with her young daughter walked on at the next stop. They debarked with me at my stop but headed down the street toward the seniors' complex. Must be going to visit Grandma. I headed to the apartment. I rang the buzzer for the manager.

"Ya?" the gravelly voice jumped out from the mechanical box.

"It's Joan Bradshaw. We spoke on the phone yesterday about my son's apartment."

"Oh, ya. Come on in. I'll meet you up there."

A loud buzz rang into the tiny vestibule. I pulled open the door and headed up the stairs to my right. I climbed to the third floor and stood outside the door when an average-looking man arrived. His face was unshaven, his hair matted to his head. A stained gray sweatshirt with the sleeves cut off covered his ample abdomen while a pair of equally filthy sweatpants hung low on his hips. I shuddered.

Mumbling to himself, he unlocked the door and

pushed it open. I stepped into the room. The smell of rotting food hit me first. My stomach lurched. I stopped in my tracks. The greasy little man squeezed past me, his hairy arms brushing against me. My stomach lurched again. I took a slow, deep breath through my mouth, trying to ease the panic rapidly building inside me.

"Lots of damage here," he said, walking into the living room.

I followed, still breathing through my mouth. My jaw dropped. The damage was significant. There were holes in the wall. One side of the drapes lay on the floor, and the other, torn to shreds, hung from the attached end of the bent curtain rod. I shook my head.

"Right mess, this is," the manager proclaimed. "Going to cost a pretty penny to fix. Way more than the damage deposit will cover. So, who's going to pay for that, eh?"

"I'm sorry?" Focusing on the fury behind the damage and Caleb's state of mind, I didn't understand what he was asking.

He repeated his question, slower and more loudly. "Who's going to pay for this?"

"Oh. I guess you'll have to send the bill to his father." Feeling responsible, I wasn't trying to get away without paying, but I didn't have any money. Joe was equally culpable, so he would have to step up to the plate.

"Not you?"

"Well, my husband takes care of the bills." He

didn't need to know that I wasn't living with him anymore.

"I prefer a cheque today."

"Well, I'm sorry. You might have mentioned something on the phone yesterday. I didn't bring my checkbook with me. Can't you send a bill?"

"I thought you women carried everything in your purses. No? Well, I guess I have no choice." He whipped out a tiny notepad, pulling the pen hanging on his collar. He licked the end of the pen before setting the nib on the page. When I said nothing, he looked at me expectantly.

"Oh." I gave him Joe's address and phone number.

Slapping the notepad closed, he shoved it back into his pocket and clipped the pen to his collar again.

"Well, I'll get out of your way. Let me know when you're done. Everything needs to be out by the end of next week, or we will remove it at your expense. I'll order the restoration as soon as that is done." He moved toward the entrance, leaving me alone. Pulling open the door, he turned back. "I always liked Caleb. He was a decent kid. I don't know what went wrong, but it was recent. He'd been an ideal tenant before this ..." He gestured to the holes in the drywall.

"Thank you." I nodded, feeling a little of my distaste for him dissipating. He nodded, turned, and left, shutting the door behind him. I closed my eyes for a minute.

I walked to the patio door and pulled it open. Even though it was the last day of November, I needed the fresh air. Then I went to work. After removing two garbage bags from my satchel, I slipped on rubber gloves and opened the fridge. The rotting milk practically leaped out at me. Gagging, I grabbed dishes, scraping the filth left on them into the bag before stacking them into one sink. I upended the milk jug into the now vacant sink, rinsing the rotting mess down the drain.

The pungent half-head of cauliflower went into the bag, along with some fuzzy green oranges and two slimy peppers. I kept breathing through my mouth, willing my stomach to settle. Pizza scraps sat in an open box on the counter. I dumped the box and contents into the bag, feeling a tiny niggle of guilt for not recycling the cardboard.

I dumped the ketchup bottles, mustard, half-eaten jars of pickles, moldy cottage cheese, and sausages long past their best-by date.

The freezer contained hamburger, a steak, and pork chops, which I also put into the garbage bag. When I was done, I tied the bag closed and took it to the dumpster. I stuck the dustpan under the door to keep it open in my absence.

Back in the apartment, I found a bucket and some cleaning fluid under the sink. I filled the bucket with water and cleaned the fridge from top to bottom. I'd already turned it off, so the freezer part was easy to clean. It sparkled.

I did the dishes, mopped the floor, and wiped out the cabinets. After tossing all the spices and open packages of pasta into the garbage, I placed the canned food in a separate bag. This could go to the food bank—someone could use it.

With the kitchen done, I tackled the bathroom. Tubes of toothpaste, shaving paraphernalia, half-used bars of soap, emery boards, and bubble bath—everything went into the garbage. There were some cleaning products under the sink. I cleaned the toilet using the brush. The shower curtain was hanging on one ring. I took it down, folded it as tightly as possible, and shoved it into the bag. When the bathroom was complete, I carried the second trash bag down to the dumpster. It startled me to see it was already one o'clock. Time was flying.

CHAPTER SEVENTY-ONE

I moved into the bedroom. The closet door was lying on the floor. I lifted it, moved it into the closet, setting it against the back wall. I bagged up all of Caleb's clothes, noticing there were no items belonging to Andrea. Had her parents already been here? The dresser contained none of Andrea's things. Caleb's clothes were all that remained. Underwear, socks, and some T-shirts. I shrugged. They must have been here. Why wasn't I told that?

I was going to have to talk to Constable Harrison. It would have been awkward if they showed up while I was there or vice versa. I couldn't believe how much that annoyed me. Then I remembered Paul's story. She had left him. That's what set this whole thing in motion. Andrea's parents hadn't been there. There was nothing there that belonged to Andrea. She'd gone at the end. That thought saddened me. Tears welled up. I took a deep breath and shoved them aside. I didn't have time to dwell on Caleb's pain.

Stripping the bed, I folded the sheets nicely before tossing them into the garbage bag. They would take up less room, folded. The curtains in the room were also missing, but the rod remained intact. I did a quick once over with the vacuum cleaner I found in the front closet. They would shampoo the carpets before the next tenant, anyway. I hoisted the bed onto its side, moving it against the wall. I moved into the next room.

When I finally finished, I had taken down eight garbage bags. I had a bag of clothes and some canned goods for Goodwill. I had put most of the music CDs and DVDs in bags to go to the charity shop, along with most of the books in the apartment. But there were a few things that I wanted to keep—Caleb's Bible, his ratty copy of *To Kill a Mockingbird* by Harper Lee, all the homemade CDs because I didn't know what was on them, his iPod, his *Lord of the Rings* DVD box set and the six-volume book set by J.R.R. Tolkien. The last item I would keep was the framed landscape I'd given him when I saw he had no pictures on his walls.

I gently placed the box set of DVDs in the bottom of the canvas tote I had brought with me. I smiled, knowing how often he had watched them. He had seen the movies at least ten times in the theater and then refrained from buying each DVD separately because he wanted the set. I remember how annoyed he was when he heard they were making The Hobbit into a movie. His set would no longer be complete. He had ranted.

I put the books in next and then fondled *To Kill a Mockingbird*. He read this book often, and I remember that after finishing it one time, he told me he wished his father was like Atticus Finch.

"Me, too, son. Me, too!" I said it aloud. Then I laughed at myself—I was talking to Caleb as if he'd just spoken to me, not like I was remembering words from years ago. I must be losing my mind.

Before I put the book in the bag, I slid a few pictures I'd found inside the pages. Snapshots taken from our albums at home. Before the fire, Caleb taking these pictures without permission would have annoyed me, but after the fire, I was grateful to have a few mementos of Caleb despite Joe's attempt to eradicate him from our lives. A framed photo of Andrea and Caleb captured happier times, with the two of them smiling into the camera with no hints of what was to come that I found between the couch cushions.

Throwing away the cracked glass and broken frame, I removed the photo. Underneath, I discovered two others taken the same day. One of Caleb, lost in thought, unaware of the photographer, and one of Andrea, smiling boldly into the camera. She was so beautiful.

For the first time since the day of the funeral, I wondered about Andrea's parents. How were they doing? Should I contact them and apologize? Would it help if they knew Caleb wasn't a monster? Or would my presence pain them, knowing I had brought that boy into the world? I was at a loss about what to do and unsure if I should do anything at all.

The apartment was now stripped of Caleb's belongings. I called Beckie to tell her I didn't need her to pick me up. Then I called and talked to the charity shop. They would send their driver over next week—the manager would let them in to clean out the furniture, clothes, and dishes. I took one last look around, wondering again at the damage this place had seen in the last days of my son's life. He must have gone totally off the rails. I hated to think of him like that—in so much pain. I sighed. Had he been able to communicate with me, maybe this would not have happened. My heart was heavy, but what was done—was done.

I walked down the street to the bus stop. The bus came ten minutes later. I climbed aboard, dropping my coins into the machine. The driver watched me but said nothing. He was a different driver from the one this morning. I was a stranger. I rode the bus, looking out the window at the cars beside us—families, single drivers, couples. Many cars and trucks—everyone going somewhere.

Back downtown, the bus emptied. Some passengers moved to get onto other buses nearby, most heading to other destinations. I crossed the street, heading home, weary from my hard day's labor. I was looking forward to having a lazy morning the next day, but I still had to get through the night.

Feeling lonely and at loose ends, I took out Maxine's card. After a morning with the ghost of my son, I didn't want to spend the entire night on my own. I debated whether to call her and then decided to just do it. I dialed her number.

When she answered, I invited her for coffee. She rambled on about family plans and suggested we meet at Jack's Diner for coffee after supper for one of their famous and oh-so-delicious cinnamon buns. She expressed surprise when she found out that I worked there.

"Oh, I've never seen you there. I always eat there—but I haven't seen you waiting tables. You must be new."

"Actually," I chuckled. "I make those delicious cinnamon buns."

"Really? I thought a little German woman, Martha, or Margaret or something like that made them?"

"Marta. She is such a grand lady. She retired, and I took over. I've been on my own for two weeks now."

"Wow. You learn something new every day. Let's go somewhere else anyway. Despite having great food, if you work there, you're probably eating there all the time. There's another place, and it's farther out. They also do their own baking but on a much smaller scale. Have you ever been to Emerald's House of Tea? They are open until eight, too."

"No, I've never been there, but I know where it is. On the bus today, we passed right by it, and I wondered what it was like."

"They specialize in tea, there's a hint to that in the name, but they make their own soups and stews. The bread isn't homemade, but the desserts are good, other than the pies. I don't think they are homemade. Then again, with a little ice cream, who cares."

We settled for six forty-five, and I agreed to meet her there since it wasn't too far from home. Smiling, I hung up the phone. I hadn't had a date with a friend in many years, long before Leah died. I was really looking forward to it.

Jumping into the shower, I washed away the grime of the day. When I was ready, I pulled out my knitting. Before long, it was time to go.

CHAPTER SEVENTY-TWO

I walked into Emerald's House of Tea, so bundled up against the cold that it took me a minute to undress. It was a chilly night, made colder by a north wind.

The café was small and cozy. Tiny round tables with red gingham tablecloths graced the space. Small and delicate floral bouquets were in the center of each table—the chairs were a mishmash of assorted wooden ladder-back styles. It felt like home.

Maxine was already there, sitting patiently at a table close to the back. I made my way across the room, noting that she looked stylish in a lovely mauve cardigan over a crisp white blouse. A silver pendant and matching earrings graced the ensemble. She'd tastefully applied her makeup, enhancing her chocolate brown eyes, and there was not a hair out of place. In my old sweater and blue jeans, I looked frumpy in comparison.

She smiled as I set my bulky outerwear on an empty chair at the table and slipped into the one opposite her. A menu lay on the table in front of me.

"You look nice. That color suits you." I glanced at the sleeves of my old blue sweater. It was one of my favorites.

"Thank you." I smiled at her. When was the last time I heard an unsolicited compliment?

"Your cheeks are all rosy, too. Did you walk?"

I nodded. "Yes, I walked. My husband has my vehicle, so I have no other transportation." I laughed and said, "These boots were made for walking."

"Your husband has your vehicle? That sounds like a story."

"I suppose it is if you're not living it."

"So, tell me. Oh, wait. Let's order first, and then you can tell me."

My heart skittered, unsure about opening fully. I picked up the menu and stared at the array of delicious sandwiches and hearty soups. I selected a chicken salad sandwich and peasant soup—a tomato-based soup with lentils and vegetables and a berry herbal tea blend. Maxine, having already eaten, ordered a pot of Earl Grey tea.

The young server brought our tea in tiny white porcelain pots and two mismatched china cups and saucers.

"Tea is best when served in a china cup," Maxine

informed me as the server walked away.

I smiled.

"Okay, Joan Bradshaw, I'm all ears, but before you begin, please don't feel pressured to share anything you're not ready to share. I am not trying to get the low down or the gossip. I'm just interested in you and your story."

Nodding, I was grateful for the qualification. I already figured she wasn't a gossiper, but I knew nothing about her. She was powerful enough to feel she could take on Thelma and come out unscathed. What to do.

"Well, after all that's happened in my life, I decided I couldn't stay with my husband. I needed to grieve, but that would not be possible at home." Clearing my throat, I shifted uncomfortably in my chair. I looked across the table. Maxine was watching, a look of concern on her face. "So, I moved out, not forever, but just for a while."

"I see." She nodded. "So, where does the vehicle come into it?"

"Well, I rented an apartment, then told my son where I was. Joe, my husband, came with the spare keys and took the vehicle one day while I was at work."

"Wow. That must have made you angry?"

"You know, I don't really know how I feel about it all. It was Joe's money that paid for it, but not having a vehicle has prevented me from doing some things I've wanted to do." Tears welled up. "I can't get to Freyden to visit my daughter's grave for one thing. I used to go weekly, but now it's been over a month. It's wrong, and I guess I'm angry at Joe for taking that away. But the vehicle was just a tool. I don't need it for anything else. I love going out there to walk. And the bus system is pretty good for those longer trips."

"I've not ridden the bus in ages."

"Well, I must confess that I've only used it once, but I'm sure I'll get the hang of using it if I use it more. I found an apartment close to Jack's Diner so I could walk to work. There's the grocery store downtown, which is easy to get to, and I can go there every day on my way home. It's a few blocks out of the way, but certainly doable."

"You sound too reasonable, Joan. Your husband gave you a raw deal, yet you have somehow accepted it all."

Tears sprang to my eyes again. "What were my choices? Sure, I could have wailed and had a tantrum, but that would serve no purpose. I have so much grief bottled up—there is no room for bitterness. Maybe I am deceiving myself. I just don't have the energy for all this anger."

Maxine nodded like she understood, but I think she was just appeasing me. People who haven't been to the depths of hell don't understand what it takes to make it through a day.

"So, tell me about you."

"Me?" She blinked, surprised.

"Yes. I think you know a lot about me. I'm rather

infamous, what with my son's tragedy. But I know nothing about you."

"Well, my story is basic, really."

Feeling she was being evasive on purpose, I hit her with a tough question. "What do you do for a living?"

"Oh, that. Well, I am …" The waitress arrived with my sandwich and soup.

"Yum, this smells good."

Maxine smiled at the waitress.

"Is there anything else you need?" We both shook our heads. "Bon Appetit!" she replied, leaving us alone. Two ladies settled around the table next to us.

I lifted my spoon from the bowl and tasted the soup. It was good, not as good as Jack's, but delicious.

CHAPTER SEVENTY-THREE

I ate in silence, the conversation not forgotten but deferred as I tucked into my meal. The sandwich was also tasty, but I couldn't help comparing my meal to one I'd have at Jack's. The fresh bread made our sandwiches moist, but my meal was a darn good comparison. I was delighted to have found this place. Where they surpassed Jack's was tea. But that was their focus. They had many varieties of tea for sale and consumption, along with teapots, tea cozies, and tea sets.

There was something about tea made in a pot and not a mug. I'd been so used to mug tea that I'd forgotten how delicious a cup of properly steeped tea could be. I thoroughly enjoyed the meal, my tea, and the company. Maxine was funny, spontaneous, and witty. But a tiny niggling in the back of my mind told me she was hiding something.

When the dishes were gone, we settled back into our chairs, sipping our tea. Maxine smiled. I smiled back and then turned serious.

"Okay, before my food arrived, I asked where you worked. You didn't have time to answer."

A cloud fell across her face momentarily. "I work for the *Crawford Sentinel*," she sighed, and my eyes widened. A battery of thoughts raced through my mind, none of them good. Seeing my expression, she put up a hand to ward off my thoughts.

"I promise you, Joan, that our friendship has nothing to do with my job. My position is in fashion and the arts. I won't say that I am not interested in your story. As a reporter, it piques my curiosity—however, I will not abuse our new friendship to gain ratings for myself. There is no interest on my part in winning a Pulitzer or elevating myself in the paper's eye. I just want to be a friend."

The tornado inside my stomach ceased and fell apart, like particles falling to earth. Could I believe her? I wanted to believe her.

"I didn't tell you about my job because I didn't want to scare you off. That night at the knitting circle, you looked so alone. My heart went out to you. Then, when Thelma attacked you, and you sat there taking it … well, I had no choice. People like Thelma think they can run roughshod over others and get away with it. I don't think many people have stood up to her because she is the granddaughter of Herbie Crawford, and her husband, Bobby Graham, is president of Graham Ventures. Have you heard of them?"

I shook my head.

"Well, Maurice Graham was his grandfather. He was one of the founding fathers of Crawford, along with Herbert Crawford and George King. The family owns half the city—Graham Ventures constructed many of the buildings in this town. They have most, if not all, city contracts sewn up. The family has considerable clout and the money to back it up. Bobby is a perfectly pleasant fellow. I've spoken to him often over the years. He's mild and laid back, but don't let that fool you. Rumors are that despite who sits in the mayor's chair, Bobby Graham runs the city."

"I had no idea."

"Well, don't worry about them. Bobby doesn't take Thelma's ranting too seriously. She is a far more formidable force than he is, and she hasn't the force of a twenty-K wind. She blows and blusters, and people give in to her because it's easier than facing her sharp, bitter tongue."

"Yes, but not everyone has my history."

"I can't say with certainty, but I don't think that Bobby Graham cares that the mother of someone who did something that does not affect his family or income is working in the city. If he were going to have a vendetta against people who sully the name of our city, there would be far too many people ahead of you. You are small potatoes, and I mean that in the kindest way. Suppose you had done those things yourself, then maybe. But most people know children don't always turn out like we hope and dream they will. Sometimes, they do daft things, like taking drugs. How many kids have died driving drunk, who've killed others?"

I shook my head. "I never thought about it."

"Of course, you haven't. Most people don't think about things like that because kids grow up and most of them turn out well. Most, if not all, families have skeletons in their closets, including Thelma. So, don't give that old battleaxe or her husband another thought. Focus on Joan."

Relieved, I took a sip of my tea. It had gone cold. I set it back down.

Maxine gathered her things together. "It's been delightful, Joan. I do hope that I've reassured you and that we can do this again. But I will understand if you don't think you can trust me." She picked up the bill from the table. "This is on me, okay?"

"Oh … no …"

"I insist. You can get it next time." She smiled sadly, like she wasn't sure there would be a next time.

"Thank you, Maxine. We can do this again." I stood up, slipping into my coat. "I'll see you on Tuesday at the knitting circle?"

"Yes." Maxine nodded. "I will be there."

I waited for her to pay the bill, and then we walked out together. She moved toward her car. "Can I drop you home? It looks like it's going to snow."

"No thanks, it's still nice enough. I like to walk. It's not too far anyway."

With a wave of her hand, she drove off. I watched her go down the street, turning right at the corner two blocks down. When she had disappeared, I went back inside Emeralds and bought an inexpensive teapot—a Brown Betty. I was going to make tea properly.

Arriving home, I shed my warm coat and put the kettle on the stove to boil before washing my new acquisition. A few minutes later, the kettle shrieked. I poured a small amount of the water into the pot and swirled it around, warming it like I saw my mother often do when I was a child. Emptying the now tepid liquid, I dropped two tea bags into the depths—filling the pot with the contents of the steaming kettle. I even tossed a towel over the top to keep the pot hot while it steeped.

While I waited, I went into the closet and pulled out another journal. This one looked worn. The cover was teal—the pages had assorted colors in stripes. I didn't remember seeing it before, but then, I didn't know everything about Caleb. I took the journal into the kitchen, where I poured myself a cup of tea. Placing the towel over the pot again, I took my tea and the journal into the living room. I settled on the couch and took a sip of my tea. It was so much better than mug tea. I savored the warmth.

Outside, the snow that threatened to fall earlier swirled. Sitting inside, with my feet tucked under me, there was a modicum of peace. I had lost so much, but I couldn't dwell on that. I needed answers, and I hoped these journals would help me. I took another sip of my delicious brew before opening the journal to a page at random.

The first thing that struck me wrong was the penmanship. This wasn't Caleb's clipped, sharp lettering. The words on these pages were round and loopy. This wasn't Caleb's journal—it must have belonged to Andrea. I closed it sharply, then set it on the coffee table like it had burned me. I stared at the book, seeing why I hadn't recognized it as Caleb's. It was feminine.

I stood up to look out the window. Should I read Andrea's journal? Would this help me understand what happened to my son? To her. I stared out at the flakes of snow drifting from heaven. Tiny little flakes piled on top of each other on the railing. It wasn't deep yet, but it didn't show signs of stopping.

I looked at the clock. It was eight-thirty. Maybe I should just go to bed. I changed into my pajamas. I slipped my fluffy robe over the top and moved back into the living room. Weighing the issue, I decided that although part of me understood that reading her journal violated her privacy, another part considered what I might see inside those pages that could help me see what was happening inside my son's head. I needed to know, which seemed more important than whether I trampled on the rights of someone who was no longer there.

CHAPTER SEVENTY-FOUR

I read it, yet I still pulled it onto my lap with some reluctance. I took a deep breath and started with page one.

> November 28th—It's been a wonderful day. College is so great. There's this one guy in my classes, he's so cute!!! His name is Caleb Bradshaw. He's kind of shy, but he's very smart. When Professor Hicks calls on him, he always has a well-thought-out answer. He never shirks the questions, even the tough ones. I must have a crush on him because I see him wherever I go. I don't talk to him, but I am very aware of him. Maybe one day, he'll ask me out. I hope so.

That was sweet. I flipped the page and read on.

> December 1st—Today, I saw him at The Edge. I've never seen him there before. Brenda and I went in, and he was there with some of his friends. I know he saw me, but he pretended not to. That is a good sign. Pretending not to see me means he likes me and is playing hard to get. There are butterflies in my tummy even now. Brenda thinks he's cute, too. She says she reserves the right to date him if he's not interested in me. I laughed because I know he is. Oh, he is so fine!

Having met Andrea, hearing her voice in these innocent passages was easy. A budding romance. I kept reading.

> December 4th—I had Tyler introduce us today. I've seen Tyler talking to him occasionally, so we planned a random encounter in the cafeteria. It worked great. I had borrowed a book from Tyler and needed to return it anyway, so I met him in the café under the pretense of returning his book. He was so funny about it, teasing me mercilessly. So, I walk into the café, see him, and walk over. He and Caleb are sitting there talking. I sit beside Tyler and pull the book out of my pile. "Here's your book, Tyler. Thank you so much for lending it to me." He nodded and then asked if I knew Caleb. I say I think we have a couple of classes in

common, but I've never actually met him. Tyler does the honors. I shake his hand, and whammo!!! An electric shock goes right up my arm. Zap! Not an actual electric shock, but something passed between us, and I know he felt it, too!

December 8th—Caleb had been aloof and arrogant since our introduction. He avoided me, walking out of the room when I walked in, not coming to class until I was seated, and then sitting as far away as possible. What a jerk!! I hate him. I smiled at him, and he looked away. Who does he think he is?? I'm going to blow him off when he talks to me.

December 10th—EEEEEKKKKK!!! I'm going out with Caleb Bradshaw!!!! I am sooooo excited. He just walked right up to me in the cafeteria. Brenda and I were there with Sharon and Chelsea. He came up behind me, but I knew something was up by Brenda's face. I turned around just as he got to the table. I want to write this down so I don't forget. He said, "Andrea, would you do me the honor of accompanying me to the movies on Saturday night!" The honor!! Who talks like that? No one, it was sooooo romantic. I just looked into those blue eyes, and my heart simply melted. How could I refuse? So, we're going to see *Frozen* because I didn't want to see *Crossing Fire*. I hope it's good, but I won't care. I'm going to be with Caleb.

December 13th—Caleb came by and

picked me up. I was sooooo nervous—I hadn't been able to eat. I don't think I've ever been this nervous, not even with Lee when we did it the first time. Mind you, that was sort of unplanned. I guess I didn't have time to think about it. Caleb even came to the door. He didn't honk his horn like a lot of guys do. He's a proper gentleman. When we get to the movie, I pull out my money, but Caleb won't hear of it. "I asked you out. Put your money away." He bought a big bucket of popcorn, too, and a drink for each of us. I don't even think I watched the movie. I was so aware of him. Every time our hands accidentally touched the popcorn bucket—it was electric. When the bucket was empty, he set it aside, and then took my hand. We sat through the last half of the movie, holding hands. I don't think you can wipe the smile off my face. He likes me. He really, really likes me. After the movie, we went for coffee. I suggested The Edge, but he didn't want to go somewhere we might run into our friends. He stated it is not advisable to share dates. When he took me home, I got nervous again. I had such a good time.

We talked about so many things, including his childhood and mine. Our teachers, our faith. So, as we drew closer to my place, I panicked. Do I kiss him? Do I not? I didn't know what to do. I didn't want to give him the wrong impression, but I also wanted him to know I was interested. He walked me to my door, and then he kissed me quickly on the lips before skipping back down the stairs. "I'll call you later," he said over his shoulder as he left. I stood there watching him drive away. What a hunk! I think I'm in love.

December 17th—Caleb still hasn't called me. What sort of game is he playing??? I see him in class, and he smiles, but he disappears before I can talk to him. I don't like this, not one bit. Who is this person? He was so witty, funny, and engaging on Saturday, and now, in the last days of classes before the Christmas break, he's being evasive and mysterious. I don't like it. He's playing with my emotions here. Brenda said that I should not go out with him again. She says that a proper man doesn't do what he's doing. She thinks he's wrong in the head. But she hasn't talked with him, and she hasn't listened to him talk about things. When he talks, the world disappears, and all I see is the wisdom behind his blue eyes. Why, oh why, can't he just speak to me?

December 18th—I got a call from Caleb today. He called me, apologizing for ignoring me this week. He told me that besides the finals, we both needed to study for—he had a special assignment for Professor Henderson that needed his focus. He told me it had been so hard because he had thought about me all the time, and it was even harder when he saw me. He said he wanted to pull me into his arms but that if he did that, we'd get nothing else done. We'd both fail our classes, and that would not be good. I couldn't believe how relieved I was. What's wrong with me? Right up to the minute he called, I wanted to tell him to go to hell. Then I heard his voice, and suddenly, all I could think about was being in his arms and leaning against his chest. I must be crazy. Brenda wasn't happy, either. She told me he would walk all over me if I didn't set some ground rules. I don't think Brenda's ever been in love.

December 19th—I gave Caleb his Christmas present today. It wasn't much. I gave him a journal and a pen. He gave me mine, too. It was a Rose Quartz Crystal on a silver chain. He said it was a love stone. It's lovely. I will wear it every day. He's going home to the farm tomorrow, but we have plans for New Year's Eve. I can't wait. He is so gorgeous. I just get tingly thinking about him. When he left today, we kissed for a LONG!!!!! time. It was delicious. I could have stayed there all day, but he had to go. I can't wait … New Year's Eve can't come fast enough for me.

CHAPTER SEVENTY-FIVE

With my finger marking the pages, I reflected on that Christmas, Caleb's last one with us and the first one without Leah. It wasn't a happy Christmas for many reasons. Leah had always brought such enthusiasm for the day that without her, it seemed like we simply went through the motions. Jonathon and Deb brought her dad to the festivities, which provided a distraction.

After we opened the presents, Joe switched on the football game. The men sat in the living room, burying their feelings under the plays, the end zones, and the touchdowns. Looking back now, I noticed that when I poked my head in to see how things were going, Caleb was missing. He was up in his room. I was worried he was grieving. Now, I wondered if he was thinking of Andrea. I sure hope so. I opened the book and read on.

December 25th—Caleb called me today. We talked on the phone for twenty minutes. He told me he wished he could be with me. He didn't say, but he gave me the impression that home wasn't a good place to be. I wonder what's going on. Well, he'll tell me when he's ready. Christmas at Dad's house was great. I always love having Christmas here. Mom came over for a while. I hate her latest boyfriend, though. He's such a creep, especially in how he looks at me. YUCK!!! What does she see in him, anyway? My dad is the salt of the earth. He's generous, funny, and kind. Even the other guys my mom has been with, the four or five who never made it to the altar and the three who did, were all better than this guy. He's a creep with a capital C. Sleazy. I couldn't wait for them to leave. Then, some of Dad's friends came over, and the party got underway. He has great friends. It was a great day. I got lots of loot, too! New clothes I can't wait to wear, an iPad. Yes! My dad rocks!! But my favorite gift is still the simple necklace Caleb gave to me.

December 28th—It's been a boring holiday. The weather was cold and snowy. Ginny phoned today. She told me she isn't coming back to school in January, so I will have to find another roommate. That just sucks. How am I going to pay January's rent without her? I told her I needed the money, but she refused. Going into her room, I discover she's already taken her stuff—I just hadn't noticed. Furious, I called Caleb, but he didn't answer. When I dialed his number, my heart pounded like I was doing something wrong. I didn't leave a message. I'll see him in a few days, anyway. Brenda came over for a while. She's so lucky. She lives in her own place, which her parents bought and paid for, so she doesn't need the money. I thought about moving in with her, but she didn't have any room. She rents her rooms to other students, and of course, none of them will be throwing school in January. I could move back in with Dad, I suppose. I only moved out to get some freedom, and it's been lovely not having to tell people where I am going, who I am seeing, and when I'll be back. All questions Dad asks! Well, I'll have to go back now, won't I? Big sigh!!!!

December 31st—Today is the day!!!! He's coming to pick me up at seven! I don't know what he's planned, he just told me to wear a dress. I've been trying on dresses all day, and I think I have finally found the right one. The dress is red, with see-through bell sleeves and a gauzy skirt with an uneven hem. A slim silver belt finished the outfit, and I had silver shoes to match. I look taller in this outfit. I can't wait until he gets here. Brenda came over and helped me with my hair and makeup. I LOOK amazing!

January 3rd—It's been a few days since I wrote. So much has happened!! I think I'm in love. Well, if I'm not in love, I'm on the brink. Caleb is amazing. He's so funny and witty. He took me for supper first at the swankiest restaurant in Crawford—Top Hat. The waiters there all wear tuxedos to serve, well, maybe because it was New Year's Eve. They even wore white gloves. I did not know such sophistication existed outside of the movies. After supper, we slipped across the street to The Landing, where they were having a good bash. The music was superb, the dance floor writhing with warm bodies, all in high gear, getting their party on. It was so energizing. Of course, it was loud! When we sat, we sat close so we could talk. I was smiling, just happy to be there, and Caleb kissed me. That kiss went right down to my toes. I'm not really experienced, but at that moment, I wanted him. Looking into his eyes, I saw the same passion there. It was only ten-thirty, and I didn't know how I would wait to be alone with him.

Okay, this was getting into dangerous territory here. I didn't want to know the details of what went on in my son's bedroom. Interested in what was going on in his heart, I skipped ahead several pages, hoping to avoid intimate details.

April 14th—It happened again last night. Caleb blew his cool. Things have been so good since that first incident. I have walked a fine line between my friends and Caleb, trying to keep the peace, but he simply hates it when I do things with friends when I could do something with him. He doesn't understand that I need diversity. When I say that, he gets so upset and angry that he's not enough. I can't talk to him when he gets like that. I locked myself in the bathroom, waiting for the storm to pass. It did, and he was so sorry when it was over. I felt bad, too, but I wanted to know if he understood. But maybe that is a fight for another day.

I read the passage again and again. Skipping back over a few other pages, I tried to find the other day without success. I flipped forward.

June 23rd—Caleb is at it again. Last night, he got so drunk it was disgusting. He is a cruel man when he's drunk. He said some really hurtful things, which I won't write down because I don't want to remember them forever. He was mad at me because I was working when he wanted to go out. Cripes!! I need to work! I'm not made of money. I think he just hates that I have a job, but The Grill is a great place to work. Sure, the hours are long, but the tips are always good. I made almost $250 on Thursday night. On Saturday, I hope to get even more. That money will buy me clothes. It will help with books and tuition. And he hates that Brenda works there, too. He really hates Brenda. I initially thought

> that if they spent time together, they would become friends, but that didn't happen. The more time they spent together, the more they grew to dislike each other. Mention Brenda's name, and a shroud falls over his face. I can see the steel set into his jaw. I wonder if he's just freaking out because I'm not going back to school in the fall. Instead, I'm taking a year off to get some time to myself—time I'm not getting living here and going to school. But if I leave, then things will end with Caleb, and I don't want that, either. I just don't think that all this togetherness is helping our relationship. We both need time apart to be more than we are together. Caleb doesn't understand that, either. He wants us to spend all our time together. He smothers me. But I love him and am committed to making this work, so I stay and fight. Tomorrow is another day. He'll be contrite tomorrow, sorry for what he said and did. I just wish we didn't have to go through all this to get to those sweet days together. Maybe we need to talk to someone.

I could see that things were falling apart. It was quite early in their relationship, too, considering their first date was in December. They were living together in January—they really didn't know each other. Caleb had never even had a serious girlfriend before Andrea. At least, not one I knew about. Too serious, too fast. Lots of warning signs. I wish I'd been more intrusive, more probing. Maybe I could have counseled Caleb to slow down, breathe, and let things be. I didn't, though. I kept things on the surface. Maybe I didn't really want to know. Maybe I was too busy coping with all I had on my plate as it was without bringing another difficulty into my world. Whatever it was, I didn't, and now it was too late to intervene, too late for so many things.

I put Andrea's journal down. I read enough to know that Caleb was a lot like his father, but Andrea was not Joan. She didn't compromise or agree to her mate's demands. Caleb was playing the man of the house, using the only example he had—Joe. Only times had changed, and women today had minds of their own. They made their own choices and decisions. They didn't follow their husbands, blindly doing their bidding because that was their lot. Caleb would have been better off with a woman who had no spunk, not someone like Andrea. She was like Leah in some ways, which was probably the draw. Her spunkiness probably reminded him of his sister. It was charming and easy to be around. Caleb didn't stand a chance.

I crawled into bed, my thoughts swirling through the details of their lives together. I fell into a troubled sleep, living the stories I read. Joe and Caleb interchanging, Andrea and I appeasing, challenging, and confronting their narrow-minded thinking. I awoke panting, my heart hammering in my chest. I reminded myself to breathe deeply, thus calming myself. It took several minutes to remind myself that I was safe before my heart slowed.

As the dream dissipated into wisps of smoke and floated away from memory, I settled into the rhythm of my breath, in and out, in and out. Glancing at the clock, I saw it was nearing the time to get up. I was going to go back to church today. Maybe this time, I would get there.

CHAPTER SEVENTY-SIX

I didn't make it to church. As the time steadily marched forward into the day, I found it impossible to find motivation. Looking outside, the snow continued to fall, spiraling downward in a dance of a thousand years. I wondered if they heard music as they flitted and fluttered on the wind, a song incapable of being heard by a human ear. How intricate and amazing was the world we lived in?

I spent the day in my pajamas, listening to music, alternating between knitting and reading. Tucking Andrea's journal back inside the box, I thought perhaps I should read one of Caleb's journals. In the end, I just wanted some time to not think, to get lost in an ordinary day. For the first time, I missed television, and I wondered about getting one for days like this—days when I wanted to think about nothing. Days when I could laugh at stupid storylines.

In the late afternoon, I thought about Maxine. Needing a friend, I wanted desperately to believe her. I decided I would wait to see her on Tuesday. In the meantime, I would ask Beckie about her, maybe buy the paper, and read her column. That might tell me more.

I was doing the supper dishes when my phone rang. It shattered the silence of the day, and I jumped at the loud, unexpected sound. Drying my hands on the towel, I hurried into the living room to answer it. It caught me off guard to find out that Joe was calling, as shown on the caller ID. I answered with a great deal of hesitation.

"Hello?"

Not bothering with the formalities of telephone etiquette, Joe got right to the point. "I hear you want your vehicle back."

"Yes, I don't care about anything else. I just want to go out and visit Leah's grave."

"You could have visited it every day, but you left. So, I don't see why you think you should get to visit Leah's grave since you abandoned your family."

His words hit their mark. I trembled. "I didn't abandon you. You forced me out of the house. I had no choice!"

"Had no choice? You had choices. What I did was show you that you can't just decide what rules to follow and those you get to thumb your nose at. A family can't work when one of its members is doing their own thing."

"What are you talking about? I was just doing something for our son, Joe. Our son. What I did didn't deserve punishment. It should have received applause. He was ours, and we failed him."

"What kind of talk is that? Failed him? He let us down! He failed us!" Joe shouted, his voice rising in pitch as his anger took over. I sat at the other end of the conversation, stunned again that Joe was taking what happened as a slight against him, not the cry of desperation that it was.

There was a moment of silence as Joe collected himself.

"I didn't want to get into an argument with you. I just called to tell you that if you want your vehicle back, you can have it on one condition."

"What condition is that?"

"You need to move back home where you belong."

I sat there, stunned. What Joe proposed was insane. For me, there was no going back. Our family unit lay shattered. Destroyed by a lack of grace and mercy. Going back wouldn't improve the situation. I tried to imagine going back to making Joe's meals, doing his laundry, and keeping his house. Comparing that to working hard at Jack's, where some days I was so exhausted at the end of the shift, I wasn't sure I had the energy to walk home, to going back to being a doormat—the answer was painfully obvious.

"I can't come back, Joe. There is nothing for me there anymore." I whispered these words with as much compassion as I could muster.

"Then you will never get your Jeep back. It's as simple as that." He hung up the phone.

I sat there, going over and over the conversation, trying to calm myself and decide if I made the right choice. In the end, I was more frightened of going back to Joe and his oppression than anything else I had to face going forward. Still, doubt swirled. I needed assurance that I made the right decision.

I opened my phone and called my mother. The call went to voicemail. I left a breezy message, telling her not to call me back tonight and that tomorrow would be fine. I set the phone on the charger and walked down the hall to my bedroom. The call from Joe exhausted me. Ready for bed, I was about to pull back the covers when I decided. I went back to my phone and dialed Maxine.

"Hello?"

"Hi, Maxine, it's Joan."

"Hi Joan, I'm glad you called."

I had intended to ask her to take me to Leah's grave on Saturday. But hearing her voice, I lost my nerve. We didn't know each other well enough, so asking for a huge favor seemed like overstepping the bounds of our burgeoning friendship. I quickly thought of an alternative. "I just called to tell you that maybe Tuesday night, after knitting, I'd like to go for coffee with the group. But I'd need a ride if that's okay."

"That's perfect, Joan. We won't keep you up late. I know you have early mornings."

After I hung up the phone and went back to bed, my mind chattered on, keeping me awake. I stopped myself from going down dark and lonely roads, pulling my thoughts back repeatedly. Still, my mind wouldn't settle. I changed positions. Concentrating on my breathing, I eventually fell asleep.

I don't know how long I'd been asleep, but in the night, I awoke with a start. In my relaxed state, I remembered that Constable Harrison had offered to take me to Leah's grave. I wondered if I should take him up on his kind offer. He had always been pleasant and helpful, but I was concerned about his motive for volunteering. Then, I contemplated whether that mattered. He offered, after all. It was just a short drive, and I would offer to pay for the gas or buy him lunch for this trouble. I snuggled back into the pillow, pulled the covers up tightly, and went back to sleep.

CHAPTER SEVENTY-SEVEN

Monday passed uneventfully. During my break, I called Brad to tell him about my conversation with Joe. I railed a little, frustrated that I was asking for so little, and even that concession didn't seem to matter to Joe. Brad assured me that, eventually, Joe would have to comply with the courts or face consequences. His words soothed me, but only slightly. Joe was wily and, more than likely, three steps ahead of us.

After supper, I called my mom again. This time, she answered.

With the formalities out of the way, I asked her how the Christmas plans were coming.

"Well, Wally grumbled a bit, wanting to be south where it's warm, but he'll come for Christmas if we can be in Arizona for the New Year's bash. It's a big night down there, so I agreed. I hope that's okay?"

"Sure, Mom. I can't believe it's so close to Christmas already—slightly over three weeks now. I guess I'd better get shopping."

"Please, don't get me anything, Joan. I need nothing. I know that money must be tight with all your other expenses. So, maybe a little can of mixed nuts or some of those licorice treats I like. I can eat those on the plane to Arizona."

"Oh, Mom!" I cried.

"What? What did I say?"

"Nothing, Mom, nothing. I'm just being sensitive. I received a call from Joe last night. He said I could have my Jeep back if I were prepared to come home and behave myself."

"I hope you told him he could go jump off a bridge!"

"Ha!" I bleated, allowing that one sound to gather momentum until I was laughing. With tears streaming down my face, I caught the wave and laughed, like I hadn't in a long time, right from the depths of my belly. I laughed with abandon until it twisted, and I was crying earnestly, loud guttural sobs that threatened to spill my insides out onto the floor. I sobbed, all the while trying desperately to get the reins on my runaway emotions.

"Joan!" my mother called into my ear. "Get a hold of yourself. Joan!"

I seemed incapable of responding. My mouth opened and closed, but no words came out.

"I'm coming over there." She hung up the phone.

Knowing how inconvenient that would be for her, I went down the hall to the bathroom, gulping large mouthfuls of air as I went. I turned the cold water tap on, bent over the sink, and splashed cold water onto my face. I took a fresh cloth from the drawer and held it under the tap. Wringing it out, I ran it over my face once, twice, three times. Then, I wet it again to refresh the coldness of the material. I returned to the living room. I dialed my mom's number again. She picked up on the first ring.

"I'm just about out the door. I'm on my way," she said instead of answering hello.

"Mom, there's no need, I'm okay."

"Are you really?" She picked at the wound.

"Well, honestly, Mom, no, I'm not okay. I may never be okay. But there is no need for you to rush over here. I think I'm just tired, and I haven't been sleeping well."

"Okay, if you're sure, because I don't mind coming over."

"Yes, you would. It's cold outside."

"Let me call you back. I'm going to cancel the taxi."

"Okay." We hung up.

A few minutes later, the phone rang again. "Okay, they weren't happy, but I canceled the taxi. Now, make yourself a nice cup of chamomile tea and go to bed early. You won't solve all this drama with tears."

"I know, Mom, but sometimes it just gets on top of me, you know."

"Well, actually, I don't know Joan, but I can

imagine. I still think I should have taught you and your sister to treat yourselves better. You wouldn't be living this if I had been a better mother."

"I had a dream the other night, Mom, which scared me. I dreamed that Joe and Caleb were alike, but then there was something about a gun. I guess my mind is drawing parallels between Andrea and me, too. I don't think Joe would shoot me, but his anger is overwhelming, and my dreams are often full of fear."

"Oh. Well … they are just dreams, Joan." She said this softly as if imagining that it wasn't.

"Dreams have meanings. I think I see the parallel between them, between Joe and Caleb. I think that if I'd been more like Leah or Andrea, Joe might have shot me, just like Caleb shot Andrea."

"No. Joan, you can't think that. Whatever put that thought into your head?"

I told her about the journals. "I thought it would be okay, but I'm not so sure. It left me feeling unsettled. I don't know what was going through Caleb's head, but Andrea was upbeat and bubbly in the beginning, and you could see six months in that she was struggling to keep her head above water. The flaws in the relationship were consuming her, driving her to try harder. She blamed herself while trying to figure out how to keep Caleb happy without losing who she was. It was sad to see it in black and white."

My mom was silent. Thinking of Andrea's struggle, I let the words sit between us. "I don't know if it would have happened with Joe and me, but it could have."

"I don't think so, Joan, and really, you don't know that, either. You are borrowing trouble, trying to create drama where there is none. So, nip it in the bud. Put those journals in the trash barrel where they belong. You can't undo what happened, even by reading those private thoughts. It's done. There is no going back."

"I know, Mom, but I feel I need to know."

She huffed. "Why? Why do you need to know?"

That was a good question. I wasn't sure I had a suitable answer. "I just do."

"That's not an answer, Joan. That's a cop-out." Her words stung, and my anger rose. Then, more calmly, she offered me a compromise. "Okay, if you must read them, then wait. Wait until you're more settled. Wait until the wounds you're trying to live with are no longer gaping and raw. Give it six months or a year. Like I said, you can't change it, anyway. If you must read them, don't do it until you're stronger."

I nodded in agreement. "You're right. I'm just torturing myself, sure they will give me answers I can't find inside me. But I agree that there is no undoing what has been done. I'll wait."

"And, for heaven's sake, don't read Andrea's again. She isn't part of the problem. Her stories are private. Read Caleb's if you must, but leave hers alone."

Again, I nodded in agreement, although someday, I would open that book again and read more. It was the only way to see both sides. Then, I changed the subject back to the Christmas plans.

"Okay, back to Christmas. I have ordered Jonathon and Debbie's gifts from the catalog. The nice thing about that is they will deliver them to the Freyden outlet. Without my vehicle, I have no way of getting their presents out there. I was so tempted to get Joe something, too."

"What? Why would you buy him something?"

"I know, Mom, I know. When I saw it, though, it was perfect for him. It took a lot of willpower not to buy it."

"Well, thank God for willpower!"

"Yes, thank God for willpower." I sighed.

"When you come for Christmas, do you want to spend the night?"

I thought of her little, tiny condo with her small second bedroom filled with an excess of everything. "No, it's not that far from here to there. I can even walk if I'm not carrying anything. So, can you come by on Christmas Eve and get my contribution? Getting a taxi early on Christmas morning might not be possible. Are they even running? Do they charge more because it's Christmas?" Not having called to get answers, I hoped my mother would think they charged double. It would make this plan agreeable. I was a little worried that I would struggle with my emotions, and a long walk would help me settle my mind.

We formalized our plans, and then she mentioned that she'd already set up the jigsaw puzzle.

Tears welled up in my eyes again. Caleb loved jigsaws, too. Many a Christmas passed with the two of us bent over a card table, working on a puzzle.

"Oh, Mom, thanks!"

"Okay, enough with the tears." She paused. "It's time for my show. I'll call you soon. Good night."

"Good night, Mom." The phone disconnected. "I love you," I said, putting the phone down.

A rush of affection for my mother poured over me, which was something I hadn't felt in years. She was a tough old bird, but I was finding the softie underneath.

CHAPTER SEVENTY-EIGHT

Tuesday evening, I headed off to the knitting shop. I was a little nervous, hoping that Thelma wasn't there. Linda greeted me affectionately and squeezed my arm before turning away to greet the next group coming in. I continued into the craft room. There were several people already there, mostly chatting. The talk stopped when I entered. Uncomfortable, I kept moving into the room as everyone focused on me. I chose the same chair from the previous week. The ladies spoke again after I took my seat.

"Welcome back, Joan."

I turned—startled. A short, plump woman with blond hair approached me from across the room, her hand extended.

"We," she gestured to the group of women on the

other side of the room, "are glad you had the courage to come back after the debacle that happened last week." The group applauded, and my face flushed a deep crimson as I stood in the center of attention.

"Thank you." It came out as a whisper, so I cleared my throat and tried again. "Thank you all, I appreciate your support."

"I'm Alice, in case you forgot. I'm not good at remembering names, so I thought you could use a refresher." Then, she reintroduced the rest of the women. There was Margie, who was knitting a complicated, bulky sweater for her husband for Christmas—Edna, who was knitting hats and toques for the charity shop at the hospital—Pamela, who was knitting a small blue blanket for a grandchild and Louise, who was knitting a mauve pullover for herself. The women nodded as Alice introduced them. I smiled in return. I tried to repeat their names in my head, attaching them to their project.

The atmosphere warmed. More people came into the room, chatting and laughing with companions, greeting the group enthusiastically. Maxine came in and took the seat beside me again. She shed her long winter jacket, gloves, and scarf before settling into the chair beside mine.

I noted her clothes: a collarless white blouse under a violet cardigan and pleated black slacks. With every hair in place and perfectly applied makeup, she oozed style, even if it was casual. No wonder she wrote a fashion column. She knew how to present herself. I wondered if she would help me update my wardrobe.

She cast on with a bulky cream thread before she finally spoke. "How is your week going?"

"It's going well, actually. How about you?"

"Same old. I've been working hard on the paper's New Year's fashion spread. It is the most extensive look at what's coming in the New Year and what's going out. Thank God, it's only once a year!"

"Oh, I thought they unveiled the new looks in the spring."

"They do. This is the industry tattle-talk. *The Crawford Sentinel* isn't *The New York Times*. It's a small paper, and we're not trendy, but we provide some good information."

I nodded. "So, you're working over Christmas?"

"A little, I suppose, but Sam's family is big on Christmas. Sam's my husband—by the way. Anyway, his brother John, his sister Elaine, Sam, and I will go over to his mom's house for a big dinner. Our kids, of course, will come, too, and the grandkids. Elaine and John's wife are excellent cooks, and they'll have put together a meal that will rival the gods. Sam helps, too. He's a superb cook, far better than me. He loves it, and I don't, so he doesn't mind helping."

"I see." I think of Joe and his disdain for anything he deems woman's work. I thought about him surviving on sandwiches and cereal, supplemented by toast. Then I realized Debbie was most likely obliged to be the meal maker. Poor Debbie. I sighed.

"We go to our son's house on Christmas Eve, and the grandkids open our presents to them that night, then to our daughter's on Christmas morning, and then it's over to Mom's. It's a busy time for sure, but it's also lovely. I do like Christmas. It's so festive."

I nodded in understanding. I didn't want to let her know I was dreading the day. Not because I would be with my mom—that was the only part that would help me get through it. I was dreading it because I wouldn't see any of my kids. Of course, I would try to call Jonathon, but so far, he still has not responded to my phone calls. I highly doubted he would pick up the phone, just because it was Christmas.

Shaking my head, I tried to dislodge the thoughts that would take me down the rabbit hole. I was there to enjoy myself, not dwell on things I couldn't change. I moved the conversation back to a less volatile topic.

"So, can you tell me what's going to be new in fashion, or do I have to wait to read the spread?"

Maxine laughed. "Well, I can't divulge the secrets. Otherwise, no one would buy the paper, and I'd lose my job. But I can tell you that turtlenecks are out, and mock turtlenecks are in. Or are they both out? Or maybe they're both in."

"Thanks! I get the picture." I laughed.

Maxine smiled.

"Okay, so you can't talk about what's coming, so tell me how you came to do what you do."

For the next hour, prompted by the odd question, Maxine told me about her love of fashion and how she found her job at the *Crawford Sentinel.*

"I was still raising teenagers. The letter writing added no stress, so I worried at first. I couldn't handle the commitment and the stress of it and still be there for my family."

I nodded. "I get that."

"Anyway, Sam was so supportive. He took over some of the cooking, and I wrote for the paper. At first, it was only once a month—a Saturday spread on the last Saturday of the month. Once the kids had completed high school, I met with the people in charge. They assigned me a weekly column, including the arts, after that brief interview. It's a hectic portfolio but really rewarding when it comes off."

We continued to knit silently for several minutes. I was thinking about how lucky Maxine was to have a husband like Sam, who encouraged her to be who she was. And I was thinking about Joe and wondering why he couldn't do that.

Linda stood up and clapped her hands to get our attention. As I looked down the room at her, I noticed that Thelma's chair was empty. I wondered if she would return or if she was plotting something. I couldn't borrow trouble.

"Ladies, I just want to remind you that next week is the last meeting before Christmas. We'll wrap up early and have a little eggnog and snacks. Don't forget to bring something for the table. I can't believe that it's almost Christmas again. The year has breezed by, hasn't it? If you can't make it next week, a reminder that we will begin meeting again in the new year. I think the first Tuesday would be the seventh?" There were nods around the room. "Okay, ladies, thanks for coming. See you next week."

Maxine was waiting for me by the door. I hurried to put my things together, not wanting to make her wait. Linda was standing at the door, saying her goodbyes. I stopped beside her. She turned to me, a broad smile lighting her face.

"I hope tonight made up for last week."

"It was a lovely night. Thank you."

"Well, thank you for giving us a second chance. Will we see you next week at the party?"

"I wouldn't miss it for the world."

"Good night, Joan." She smiled and patted my shoulder as I left the store. Outside, the crisp, cold air hit me. Maxine was sauntering down the street. I caught up with her, and we walked to her vehicle in silence.

CHAPTER SEVENTY-NINE

"Are you still up for coffee?" she asked as she started her vehicle. Looking over at me, she waited for my response.

"I think so. I'm feeling great about the group, you know. Without Thelma, I feel more comfortable, that's for sure."

"Okay. If you're sure."

She grabbed her scraper and climbed out to clear the windows. I sat inside, shivering as the cold air blasted out of the heating vents. I watched as the other cars left the parking lot behind the store, a few tooting their horns in farewell. Maxine climbed back inside, tossing the scraper into the back.

"Away we go," she said as she put the car in gear and pulled out of the parking lot into the street.

"I wonder if Thelma will come back for the party." I said it as a statement, not a question.

"If I know Thelma, I think she will eventually come back. Right now, she's feeling slighted, but she'll be back when she figures out how she's going to handle you."

"Handle me? I did nothing to her."

Maxine laughed in sympathy. "I know, but it was your fault Linda asked her to leave. When she figures out how to get down off her prideful broom, she'll be back and either ignore you because you aren't worthy of her attention, or she'll try to befriend you in a gesture of solidarity."

"Solidarity? You're kidding, right?"

"Nope. She's not dumb. She'll want to know which is more to her advantage. When she sees the group has welcomed you, I think she'll offer an olive branch—however, don't forget it's a ruse. She will never be your friend. She will always look for the weak spot, no matter what happens. Be on guard around her."

I nodded. Thelma made me nervous—I couldn't trust her no matter what she did. It was nice to have my feelings confirmed.

We pulled into the parking lot at the coffee shop. I noticed Alice and Louise crossing toward the door. They were both taking baby steps on the icy path. Maxine and I followed close behind. We ordered and paid for our coffees at the long counter. Most of the group had decaf. I had tea, and Maxine ordered hot chocolate. Alice also ordered a piece of pie. No wonder she had an ample figure. I smiled.

The conversations revolved around Christmas plans and a few for New Year's. I kept silent mostly, offering only that I would not be alone.

"Any plans for New Year's Eve?" Louise asked.

"I need to get through Christmas before I can think about what I will do on New Year's Eve. What are you doing?"

"Oh, Bill and I always go to the Top Hat. There's a large group of us who've been friends forever. For some of us, this is the only night we ever see each other, and you know how busy life gets. But it's a good time, and we enjoy it."

"We always have a house party," Alice piped in. "Have the neighbors over, play board games or charades. Then we have a midnight buffet with some of my favorite foods: Lasagna, garlic bread, and a hundred dollars' worth of baking from Jack's Diner, including a pan of those cinnamon buns."

"Jeff and I usually go to an early movie and a late supper," Margie added. "This year, we've considered just staying home. We're going to go by the weather. Nice night, we go. Nasty night, we will stay in and rent a movie on Pay Per View. I'm getting too old for this nighttime winter stuff."

Everyone around the table nodded in agreement.

"So, who's thinking about wintering in Arizona? I know it'll be a few years for me yet, but I'm seriously considering going somewhere warm and missing all this." Alice gestured to the window. We all looked outside as if we didn't know what we'd see.

I finished my tea, saying little but liking the camaraderie of being there with these women. No one asked me about my life. They didn't want to pick the scabs and see what lay underneath. Maybe they did, but they knew asking wouldn't get them answers. Maybe one day, I could talk about it, but I was still raw and hurting—trying to find my way through the minefield that Caleb had left behind.

"You ready to go? I know you have an early morning." Maxine placed her hand on my arm.

I nodded, pushing my chair back from the table.

"Good night, ladies. Thank you so much for inviting me to come out tonight. I have enjoyed myself." I looked around the table into each face as I spoke.

Everyone smiled back. "You're welcome. We will see you next week at the party?" Alice asked, and I nodded.

Maxine wished everyone a Merry Christmas and a Happy New Year, then we headed out. I was feeling mellow and content. Within minutes, she was pulling up to the curb in front of my building. Slipping off my seat belt, I sat there for a moment, trying to gather my thoughts. I wanted to say exactly the right thing.

"Following our conversation on Saturday, I want you to know I'm very glad you stood up for me and that for whatever reason, you've come into my life when I needed a friend."

Maxine turned to me, smiling. "Joan, I won't be at the party next week, and I'm glad you will be going. I have a work commitment that I can't get out of. So, I'm going to say this now. I truly hope you have an amazing Christmas. You've had a rough couple of years and now it's time for you to reap good things. The reality is—this might just be a hard Christmas. I pray you find the strength to get through the day. If you need me, you have my number. Whatever happens, I can at least talk and if possible, I can try to skip out if you need someone."

Tears stung my eyes. I couldn't believe this woman would sacrifice anything for me, a virtual stranger. I tried to say something, but the moment I opened my mouth, I feared I would bawl like a baby. Instead, with tears glistening, I nodded, opened the car door, and climbed out. I walked to the foyer, pulled open the door, and turned back to wave to Maxine. She waited there until I'd gone into the building.

Riding the elevator to my apartment, my emotions roiled like the ocean waves in a storm. I didn't want to let them out. I needed to get into bed and to sleep. The alarm was going to ring too early as it was. Climbing into bed after washing up and brushing my teeth, I purposefully thought about the women and our coffee meeting, keeping my mind from Maxine's offer. I thought about Louise and her friends sitting at an enormous banquet table, laughing and telling stories, remembering old times, and sharing thoughts and events that had occurred since last they met.

I thought about going to the movies or staying home and inviting people in for a night of games. Smiling, I imagined this could be me in the future. Yes, I could do any of those things. Ben's face popped into my head then. Pushing him out of my thoughts, he sprang back. I stopped struggling and let him be the person on my right, the man who sat with me at the movie theater. When I imagined him playing charades, I burst out laughing. My thoughts were now upbeat.

I smiled, curled under the covers, and slept.

CHAPTER EIGHTY

Wednesday, I screwed up the courage to call Constable Harrison to take him up on his offer to take me to Leah's grave. When I heard his voice, a shiver ran down my spine. We went through the formalities, and I regretted calling, feeling unable to ask him for such an immense favor.

Maybe he understood my dilemma because he asked, "So, what can I do for you?"

"Well, I was wondering if your offer to take me to Leah's grave was still open, and I was wondering if this coming weekend would work for you. I apologize for the short notice and would understand …"

He cut me off with a chuckle. "I work Saturday until three. It will probably be too late by the time I get done to get you back to the cemetery before the sun sets. But

Sunday, I'm off. We could go whenever it suits."

"Sunday will be fine, let's say about ten?"

"Ten would work."

"Then I can buy you lunch to thank you for taking me."

"Buying me lunch is unnecessary, but we can have lunch."

"Thank you, Constable Harrison. I appreciate this." I smiled, feeling quite shy.

"You're welcome. And didn't we decide you would call me, Ben?"

Embarrassed, I blushed, glad we weren't face to face. "Yes, I'm sorry."

"No need to apologize." He laughed to ease the tension. "Now, where do I pick you up?"

Having settled the details, I thanked him before hanging up. Using his first name seemed foreign on my lips and added a sense of intimacy and friendship that wasn't there before.

The week passed quickly. I did a bit of shopping after work, but mostly I baked. I put together little bundles of baked goods to give to the people who had made my transition easier. At the dollar store, I picked up some nice Christmas tins for a dollar each. They had different sizes, which was perfect as some of the baked goods took more room than others. I stretched some plastic wrap over the top before pushing the lids into place. This would keep them fresh for the few days before Christmas.

I made lemon squares for Beckie because they were something new—I didn't make them at work. For Jack, I made brownies—he was a chocolate lover. Brad's package contained several types of cookies, and for Maxine, I put together a little of everything.

As Sunday approached, I thought about Ben and our upcoming trip to the cemetery. I was hoping for nice weather—I didn't want to stand there with the wind blowing from the north or snow blowing in my face. A calm day, please God.

On Saturday night, I put a few squares and cookies into a small tin for Ben. I had debated with myself all week. I didn't know if I was being forward or overstepping the boundaries, but I wanted to give him something to say thank you. It wasn't only this trip to the cemetery, all along Ben had been supportive. The other side of the argument was that I did not want to give him false hope that there was anything more. I couldn't promise anything. I wasn't ready to engage in a relationship, nor did I know if I wanted to.

Sunday morning was clear and sunny. We were off to a good start. The temperature was decent, minus fifteen, but with no wind—being at the cemetery would be manageable. Ben showed up right on time, and soon, we made our way down the highway toward Freyden. I glanced over at him from time to time. He kept his eyes on the road.

I could smell his aftershave. It was alluring, and I liked it. I looked at his freshly shaved profile and my stomach contracted pleasantly. I looked out the window, feeling nervous. There was little conversation, at first. I needed to change that, or I'd be a basket case.

We did the formalities when he picked me up. The trite "how are you" was behind us. So, what should we talk about? I picked a trendy topic.

"What are your plans for Christmas?"

"Oh." He seemed startled that I was talking as if I'd woken him from his thoughts.

"Being one of the single guys at the detachment, I am working a double that day. Of course, I will have Christmas dinner, but I'll be on duty. Shane and Nancy Radisson live in Freyden. He's a young constable on the force. I'll go there for my dinner break. It's not a terrible shift. Not much happens on Christmas Day, but you can't leave the post empty." He looked across at me. The intensity of his gaze made me blush. I looked away. "What are your plans?"

"I'm going to my mother's. Her friend from Regina arrives this week. I'll get to meet him, which will be interesting. I can't believe my mother has a boyfriend. It's a little weird." I chuckled softly.

"Why is it weird?"

"Well, I suppose I just never saw my mother as the type of person who needed anyone. She was always aloof and self-sufficient. When Dad died, she seemed relieved and glad to be alone." I hesitated, not sure what I wanted to share. "We haven't been close. She and Joe didn't get along. So we spent little time together over the years. She hasn't spent Christmas in Canada in years, and she's only staying because of me."

Tears flooded my eyes. Why was I talking? I silently berated myself. I should just keep my mouth shut. Damn, damn, damn, damn, damn!

Ben reached over and placed his hand on mine—giving it a quick squeeze. That gesture wrenched my heart even further. Joe would have stiffened, and I would have bucked up. Now I was desperate to get hold of my emotions. Why did he have to be so caring?

"I'm sorry," I blubbered, digging around in my purse for a tissue. "It's been a rough ride."

Ben didn't respond. We were approaching Freyden. He turned off the highway, following Main Street for several blocks before turning left toward the cemetery. Looking out the side window, I saw the familiar houses of my hometown pass by. A few minutes later, Ben turned into the parking area near the small cemetery. He turned off the car. We sat there listening to the ticking of the engine as it cooled.

I grabbed a handful of tissues and stuffed them into my jacket pocket. Dropping my purse onto the floor, I reached for the door handle. Looking back across the car, I noticed Ben watching me. I smiled. My eyes were still moist.

"Thank you, Ben, I appreciate this. I'll be twenty minutes, maybe half an hour if I don't get too cold. You can come back if you don't want to wait."

"I'll wait."

Nodding, I pulled the door open. Carrying a tiny bundle of flowers, a small bunch of pink rosebuds, with some red carnations and baby's breath, I left the car. When you think flowers are a waste of money and I was throwing them onto the winter snow, my purchase seemed extravagant. I needed to show something. I also carried a small plaid blanket.

Before I closed the door, Ben leaned across the seat, handing me the tin of baking I brought to give to him. "You forgot this."

"No, I didn't. That's for you. A thank you and a Merry Christmas rolled into one." He looked surprised. I smiled and closed the car door.

CHAPTER EIGHTY-ONE

I walked down the pathway toward the family plots. As I approached, I noticed that someone had been there recently. There was a ravaged bunch of flowers pushed up against the headstone. I dug them out. There was no card or sign of where they came from. I laid the new flowers in the same place. Then kicking away the snow, I made a place on her grave where I could sit. I lay the blanket down and sat, legs tucked under my body.

"Hi, Leah. It's Mom. Sorry I haven't been here in a while. Life has gone completely chaotic."

For the next twenty minutes, I talked to my daughter's headstone, as if she were sitting across the table from me. Emptying my sorrows into the ground between us, I shared everything with her. I cried, I laughed, but mostly, I talked.

"I miss you, sweetheart, especially at this time of year. Christmas will be different—I'm spending the day with Grandma." I laughed, imagining her response. "I know, it's an unusual year. She has a boyfriend who might be a magician. He's given her back her heart."

Smiling sadly, I wished again—that my mother and daughter could know one another.

"I'll try to get back to see you soon, but I don't have a vehicle, so I need to rely on strangers. Speaking of strangers …" I told her about Ben. After I finished, I patted the ground. The cold was seeping into my bones. "I just miss you, sweetheart. Have a Merry Christmas. I love you."

I stood for a moment staring at the headstone. Then I pulled the blanket off the ground and shook the snow off it before folding it. When I was done, I blew a kiss, turned, and walked back toward the car park.

Ben saw me coming. He started the car before getting out to open the door for me. I was grateful for the warmth inside the car. The heater was going full blast. Removing my gloves, I cupped my hands over the heat vent.

Ben pulled out a thermos and asked if I wanted some hot coffee. The aroma was tantalizing, and I wondered if I should just try a cup. "I put cream and sugar in it because that's how I drink it. Is that okay?"

I told him I didn't normally drink coffee but would try a cup. He poured some into the lid and handed it to me. I took a sip. It certainly wasn't tea, but it was good.

The warmth hit me—I groaned a little. Ben opened the tin of baked goods I'd given him and offered it to me. "But not the chocolate cookies," he teased. I took a peanut butter cookie instead.

"I was just kidding." He apologized. "Have one."

"No, you were not kidding." I laughed. "I know you want them for yourself, and since I can make them anytime, I'll give you these." He laughed too.

Without another word, he reversed out of the parking stall, and we headed back to the highway.

Earlier, I had wondered about asking Ben to take me to the farm. I wanted to see Jonathon. I was going to take him and Debbie some baking. But Jonathon had yet to return any of my phone calls and I was afraid of what Joe might do or say. It was his home, and I didn't need to drag Ben into a war that wasn't his to fight.

Almost as if he could read my thoughts, Ben asked, "Do you want to go to the farm while we're here?"

I shook my head. "I would, but I don't think it's a good idea."

"Are you sure?" He pulled up to the stop sign and waited. If he turned left, we'd be on the road to the farm. Turning right would take us to the highway and back to Crawford.

Torn, I didn't know what to do. Missing Jonathon and wanting to see him was important, but I didn't want an altercation with Joe. I also didn't want to be rejected by Jonathon, not outright and not right before Christmas. My heart contracted painfully. I winced.

"Let me call first."

I pulled out my cell phone and called Jonathon's number. The phone rang several times before going to voicemail. Waiting for the beep, I said, "Hi, Jonathon. It's Mom. I'm out here in Freyden—I've just been to Leah's grave. I wanted to stop by and see if you were at home—maybe you've gone to church? I miss you and I'll call again. Love you." I hung up.

"Let's go to lunch," I said, turning to Ben.

He nodded and turned right. We hit the highway. There was no conversation aside from my agreeing to go to Venetian Velvet, which suited me for lunch. Thoughts of Leah, Caleb, and Jonathon consumed my mind. I pulled myself back every time I got close to falling into the black abyss of despair. I refused to break down in front of Ben. Back in Crawford, we pulled into the restaurant parking lot.

CHAPTER EIGHTY-TWO

It seemed to be good timing, as the waitress took us to a table as we arrived. Ten minutes later, people lined up in the foyer, waiting for a table.

"So, tell me about yourself," Ben said once he ordered his full lasagna with meatballs, and I ordered a salad.

I laughed. "You make this sound like a date!" He had good manners to blush at that.

"I think it's more my police background. I'm always curious about people."

"So, tell me about yourself then," I said, turning the tables on him.

He grinned, his eyes twinkling with amusement. "I guess I deserved that."

"No, I'm serious. Tell me about yourself. You know

a lot more about me than I know about you."

A serious look fell over his face, and he cleared his throat. "Okay. Well, I was born … Do you want me to go that far back?"

I smiled. "Start wherever you want."

"Okay, I was born in Maple Creek, Saskatchewan. My parents were wheat farmers. My older brother still runs the farm. I moved to Crawford to attend college. That's where I met my wife."

My heart skipped. He has a wife! Wait. Hadn't he said he was one of the single guys at the detachment?

"Jane and I married shortly after I graduated. I trained in law enforcement and was working in Crawford by then. Jane was a nurse. We didn't have any children, though. She was busy with her career, and we had lots of time, or so I thought."

He paused, lost in his memories or his regrets. "Then she got sick, and it turned out to be cancer. Pancreatic cancer. She fought valiantly, but it was a losing battle in the end. She's been gone for six years now."

"That's so sad." I stared across the table at him.

He was looking down—but lifted his head to meet my gaze. "I don't know why I told you that. I was going to tell you about growing up in farm country."

Smiling back, I reassured him it was okay. "So, you've been single since she passed away?"

"Well, I had a rough time of it, at first. I took a leave of absence and went back to the farm. They were harvesting, so I ran a combine and put my head back on straight. When I returned, I went back to work, but I hated the stress of the city. I finally transferred, wanting to serve where I would know the people I worked for. I transferred to Freyden three years ago. It's been wonderful. The community is home—walking down the street, I talk to my neighbors. I volunteer with Big Brothers to help young boys who don't have dads. It's been a brilliant move for me."

The food arrived, and we tucked into our meals, both of us lost in our thoughts. I was thankful for the reprieve. Thinking about his wife, I wondered what she was like. My draw to him was now clear—he knew death as intimately as I did. We both lost people too soon.

He ate with gusto, a man who loved food. I picked at my salad. I forgot to ask them to keep the black olives out.

As my pile of black olives mounted, Ben looked over. "You don't like black olives?"

"No, and I forgot to request it without them." I looked up and smiled. "You want them?"

"No, thanks, I don't like them either."

"A man after my heart."

Those words hung there between us. Now it was my turn to blush, and I did it brilliantly. Ben chuckled softly, admitting to the awkwardness of my statement.

"So, tell me about you."

"There's not much to tell really. I married Joe right

out of high school. My mother was against it from the beginning. I didn't care because I was in love. Of course, you know I had three kids: Jonathon, Caleb, and Leah. You must know the story of Leah's death."

He nodded. "When Caleb died, the topic came up at the detachment."

"Well, you know the rest."

"I think you're selling yourself short—however, that's probably enough for today." We finished our meal. The waitress came to see if we wanted dessert. I passed, and so did Ben.

"Just the bill, please."

She was back in a moment with the bill. I gathered my coat and stood. Ben grabbed my jacket and helped me get into it. That seemed foreign, but delicious. Joe had never helped me get into my jacket.

"Thank you."

He nodded, pulling his jacket on as we headed out. I pulled out my wallet to pay for the dinner, but Ben refused my money. He paid the bill, and we left. I was indebted.

"Thank you for lunch, Ben. You didn't have to pay."

"I know—I'm old-fashioned, I guess. I just can't let a woman pay for me. My mother raised me to be a gentleman."

"She did a good job." I blushed again. Why was I allowing my mouth to speak thoughts I needed to keep to myself?

Ben laughed as he opened the car door for me. Again, in the car, we were quiet. I was still biting my tongue. I didn't know what Ben was thinking. He pulled up to the entrance of the apartment building and put the car in park. I opened my door and looked across the seat. Ben was smiling.

"Thank you for today. I needed a visit with Leah. I can never repay you for your kindness in giving me that time."

"You're welcome, Joan. Anytime."

I nodded, grabbed my purse, and exited the car. He waited at the curb until I disappeared into the building. I felt light and heavy at the same time.

I found his attention intriguing, but the history I hadn't let go of—burdened me. It was too much too soon, yet part of me looked forward to the next time—and there would be a next time.

CHAPTER EIGHTY-THREE

The next two weeks were busier than I could have imagined. Special orders for parties mounted on top of my usual busy schedule, and I worked most nights until four. One night, I didn't get home until after five. I was glad I had done much of my baking the week before. Christmas was rapidly approaching, and I had little time to dwell on it.

The night of the knitting party arrived, and I debated whether to go. Aware of my schedule, I needed to get my rest, or I would be exhausted. My promise to Linda made me feel like I was obligated, so I headed out just before seven. I brought some lemon squares for the table and sat closer to Alice, Louise, and the others because Maxine would be away.

Moments before Linda locked the door, Thelma

breezed in. She looked like she had been in a fight. A large bruise had yellowed just over her left cheekbone, and there were remnants of a few scratches on her other cheek. I stiffened as she settled on her usual perch. I kept my eyes on my work as I prayed—she would leave me alone. She did.

At eight, Linda clapped her hands and announced that the party was underway. I could smell the freshly perked coffee.

"Do you smell that, girls?" Louise asked, flapping her hands to draw the aroma closer. "That is one smell that wafts directly from heaven. Fresh coffee. There is nothing like it."

We chuckled as we stuffed our knitting into bags and headed to the table. Linda had placed everything on paper plates, and the selection varied. There were several kinds of squares, and I chose those I always enjoyed when I attended functions: Nanaimo Bars and Matrimonial Squares. Neither measured up to mine, but they were edible. I washed them down with tea in a foam cup, which was one sin of the modern world.

Thelma and I continued to avoid one another as much as we could in the confined space of the knitting room. At one point, we reached for the same napkin from the opposite sides of the table. I looked up into her face and almost asked about her injury. She gave me a defiant look and snapped up the napkin with such force she sent several others to the floor. Her embarrassment was obvious.

At that moment, I glimpsed the vulnerable young girl she must have been. She was a damaged soul who used anger and animosity to keep people away. What was she afraid of? She had everything she ever wanted and more. Then I remembered something Maxine said. "Thelma's father sold her into marriage to Bobby Graham. He didn't believe anyone would marry her without his money. He made a deal with the devil to ensure he had grandchildren."

I doubted that she ever felt loved. Was her mother equally callous? Again, compelled to ask her about her injuries, I paused. Thelma, perhaps sensing my intentions, spun away from the table before I could. I shrugged. That moment of vulnerability was gone, and I doubted if what I witnessed was real or whether it was only what I wanted to see.

I didn't stay long because of work. At eight-thirty, I announced my departure. There were hugs and calls of "Merry Christmas" as I pulled on my jacket. Alice came over—her winter jacket zipped over her ample abdomen.

"Merry Christmas, Joan. I hope to see you in the New Year."

"Thanks, Alice. Merry Christmas to you, too." I hugged her quickly.

Linda came over. "I'll walk you out."

We moved from the room to the door. Before I left, I turned back. "Thank you, Linda, for everything. Have a Merry Christmas."

"Merry Christmas to you, Joan, and may you have abundant joys in the New Year."

Tears stung my eyes at the exuberant kindness she laid on my shoulders.

"Thank you!" Inadequate to say more, I turned and walked the short distance home.

CHAPTER EIGHTY-FOUR

By the end of the week, I had my Christmas parcels wrapped and ready. The festive tins were an excellent find—all I needed was to pop on a colorful bow and my wrapping was done. I had spoken to Maxine on Sunday afternoon, telling her of my visit to Leah's grave and my conversation with Ben. She showed the exact amount of encouragement and enthusiasm I needed to feel like I was on track. I smiled at my luck.

During our conversation, I asked her to pop by before Christmas and she made a brief stop on the evening of the twenty-third. I gave her the package, and she gave me one in return.

"Now do not open this until Christmas," she instructed me. We hugged and wished each other a Merry Christmas again. Then she left. Her schedule was busy, but I was thankful she took the time to stop by, however briefly.

I hadn't decorated my apartment, and it was hard to feel like it was Christmas without some sort of reminder. I didn't have the excess cash to get a tree and decorations, anyway, so I just played Christmas carols, trying to give myself some Christmas spirit.

Christmas Eve was a flurry of morning activity at the diner, but we closed just after lunch. The atmosphere was festive, with many people dropping by with cards and good wishes. A few cards even included my name. The regulars appreciated they hadn't lost their baked goods when Marta retired.

I went home to my empty apartment, feeling a little anticlimactic. I expected to find some of the season's joy seeping into my bones. Instead, being alone felt like a letdown. I shook off that feeling as I placed the package from Beckie and Jack next to the pile of gifts on the dining room table. There was the present for my mom—a lovely scarf I found on sale at Sears, a travel mug with some hot chocolate mix for Wally, the present from Maxine, and the last present I had to deliver—the cookies for Brad.

Shortly after supper, Mom and Wally rang the buzzer. They came to collect the presents and packages so my walk over in the morning would be unencumbered. Wally was not at all what I expected—he was nothing like my father, as I guess I expected him to be. Wally was tall and broad, a big man, his face not quite handsome, but full of character. He had sparkling blue eyes, a sincere smile, and a head full of silver hair.

Shaking my hand firmly, he walked into my apartment with authority and confidence. His good humor was clear in his manners and his speech. He was the reason my mother lost her bitter edge. And it was clear he loved her by how he looked at her. I was happy for my mom.

They stayed for a cup of tea. I helped them down to the car with all the presents and food and stood there in the foyer, my heart full, as Wally tucked my mom into the vehicle before closing her door. Trying to remember the last time Joe had been gallant, I had no memory of a time, even during our dating years, when he helped me into or out of the vehicle. No, Joe would have been putting the vehicle in gear, as I was still half in, always in a hurry to get where we were going. I smiled at the thought, but it was a sad smile. I sold myself cheap to the first bidder, didn't I?

Before I went up to my apartment, I stopped on the fifth floor. Walking down to Brad's apartment, I knocked on the door. I heard the stereo playing classical music. The volume lowered just before he pulled open the door. Handing him the little package, I wished him a Merry Christmas.

"This is unexpected." He smiled, taking the brightly wrapped package. "Come in." He stepped back to allow me entry.

Protesting, I said, "I can't stay long." Stepping

inside, I continued, "I just wanted to give you the gift." When Beckie appeared around the corner of the living room, carrying a glass of red wine, my awkwardness increased.

"Hi, Joan." Beckie smiled.

"Oh. I'm sorry. I'm interrupting." Reaching for the doorknob, intending to make my escape, Beckie grabbed my arm.

"No, you don't. Come right in here and sit down. You're not interrupting anything. Brad and I were just listening to some music and drinking a glass of wine."

Embarrassed and feeling like I was in the way, I stayed regardless of what they said.

I accepted a glass of ginger ale and then settled on the fat, dark leather chair when Beckie chose the loveseat. My bones turned to rubber. I was certain there was a picture of this chair beside the word comfortable. There would be no springs biting into my bottom. I almost sighed.

Then I looked around the room, noting everything was expensive and I wondered, not for the first time, why Brad was living here and not up in some ritzy neighborhood. I didn't realize I had spoken aloud until Brad laughed.

Embarrassed, there was a strong desire to crawl under something and melt into the floor. What was wrong with me? Brad, taking a seat next to Beckie, dismissed my apology and told me that his house had burned to the ground when his neighbor's house caught fire in a windstorm. The entire cul-de-sac where he lived was gone before the firefighters had things under control. I remembered hearing something about a huge fire back in September.

Then he surprised me by telling me he owned the building. I did not know he was my landlord and my lawyer. He confessed that a vacancy here seemed like the most practical solution to his sudden housing problem. He moved in while he rebuilt.

"The house will be ready before the end of January," he said. "In the meantime, I am enjoying living close to the office and not having to drive on icy roads."

We fell silent momentarily, then Brad picked up his glass and turned to Beckie. "Let's make a toast, shall we?" He waited for Beckie to retrieve her glass. "Here's to good friends, lovers, and new beginnings." He gently tapped his glass on Beckie's before reaching it toward me. I gently bumped my glass against his. Then together we sipped. Beckie was beaming as she set her glass down again.

"So, are you ready for tomorrow?" She looked over at me.

I nodded. "Yes, Mom and Wally were here and picked up the baking and the presents. You?"

"Yes, we're ready. Jack is puttering around the kitchen and I'm going home in a little while to help him finish up. I came over to help Brad move his presents over. His tree is a little small." She pointed to the two-foot tree sitting on the side table in the corner. It was barely visible behind a stack of wrapped packages sitting in front. "We also have to make a few stops on the way."

"I'm Santa Claus! Ho, Ho, Ho!" Brad grabbed his flat belly and tried to shake it. Beckie and I laughed at his antics. My heart soared with gladness for these people—people who made these past months bearable.

"Well, Santa, I won't keep you long." I was already edging toward the door.

"You'll sit there and breathe," Beckie commanded. "You've had a busy week, and we aren't in a rush, so I don't want you to feel you are in the way. Please, just chill."

Feeling nicely put in my place, I took a deep breath and sat back in the overstuffed chair. The conversation rambled on, Beckie and Brad jesting with one another like an old married couple. It did my heart good to see them together. I was very pleased to have been a part of seeing them making progress in their relationship. Next week, when I put the year behind me and turned over the blank page for the new year, I would remember this as one highlight.

Nearly an hour later, I was finally back in my apartment, alone. I found my cell phone and checked for messages. There was a missed call. I looked at the number, hoping it was Jonathon. The call was not from him—it was Ben's number. I called him back. He answered on the first ring.

"Merry Christmas, Joan."

"Merry Christmas, Ben."

"I just called to say that. Have a good night." He hung up.

Smiling, I set my phone down.

CHAPTER EIGHTY-FIVE

Christmas morning dawned. The weather had brightened significantly over the past week, but lots of snow remained on the ground. The temperature was going to be mild, a balmy minus ten Celsius. I climbed out of bed, showered, and prepared for my day. Then I sat down for a light breakfast: a cup of tea and a bagel with cream cheese. I turned on the radio and listened to nonstop Christmas music.

I always loved Christmas carols. Singing or humming along with the music, my spirits rose. I purposely kept my thoughts away from what had been or what might have been and focused only on what was. For the first time in years, I was going to have Christmas with my mother, and I was looking forward to it.

When the sun was up and the chill dissipated, I

pulled on my winter boots, grabbed my coat, scarf, and mittens, and headed out. I bundled up in the foyer and stepped out into a bright winter morning. The streets were quiet, and I walked along, my thoughts going back over the time I spent with Ben a couple of Sundays before. It seemed almost a lifetime ago, yet it was only just less than two weeks.

The day was so pleasant that I meandered my way to my mom's condo. I wandered down streets I hadn't seen before, enjoying the feeling that I was passing homes where small children had only hours before squealing with delight as they ripped open brightly wrapped packages. Try as I might, melancholy swept over me when I thought of those long-ago Christmases when the kids were small. Their excited faces on Christmas morning tugged at my heart. Why hadn't I cherished those moments more? Then I grew angry with myself because I promised to stay away from this line of thinking and enjoy the day.

I turned onto the next street, trying to force my thoughts in a different direction. There was a realtor's sign on the front lawn of that white bungalow with green shutters. My stomach flipped with excitement before I tamped it down. My reality was that a house was unaffordable, even as quaint as this one.

Studying the house from the boulevard, it looked forlorn. Was this perfect little house empty? Where were the owners? Were they snowbirds like my mom? Were they on vacation to some sunny destination or skiing at some mountain resort? Or were they gone, leaving the house bereft of love and joy on such a special day?

The house tugged at my heart as I compared it to my situation. I assigned feelings to the inanimate object, and it made me sad this structure was all alone without the people to love it. Stop it! This isn't getting you anywhere. I straightened my shoulders and moved on.

Then I remembered Brad's comment the first day we met. "What about living arrangements? Do you want to live in an apartment building? You don't want to get a house?"

Yes, I wanted a house. I wanted this house. I could not rationalize my feelings, but there was a connection to that dwelling. If it had a garden or at least room for one in the back, it would be perfect. I lifted a prayer to heaven. A prayer of want. In a moment of spontaneity, I pulled out my cell phone and took a picture of the sign, thus recording the realtor's name and contact information.

I walked away, stopping at the corner and looking back up the street. There was a canopy of large trees sheltering the pavement. The residents maintained the neighborhood well. And best of all, it was only a few more blocks from the diner, so walking to work was still possible.

I sighed. Unless Joe played fair, I would never see this desire realized. Joe would have to find his heart, and I didn't know if he was humble enough. That thought added to my feelings of despondency.

I walked on until I arrived at my mother's street and continued south for several more blocks. Arriving at her condo, I rang the bell and waited. Wally opened the door with a flourish.

"Come in, my dear. Come in out of the cold."

He reached out and pulled me into the warm entryway. He opened the closet and grabbed a free hanger. When I'd shrugged off my coat, he took it and hung it up before ushering me down the hallway into the kitchen. My mother was at the stove.

"Merry Christmas, Joan." She set the spoon down, came across the room, and hugged me lightly. It felt good and foreign. We hadn't been a hugging family. I hugged her back, feeling a tremendous wave of affection overtake me. Tears stung my eyes. I took a deep breath and stepped back.

"Okay, what needs to be done?"

"Wally and I have everything under control. The kettle just boiled, so if you want to make a pot of tea … that would be helpful. Then we can go into the living room and open presents."

The teapot was sitting on the counter, so I made tea. I found the cups and saucers on the sideboard. Mom's china. Using the tray they were sitting on, I took the teapot and the cups into the living room and set them on the coffee table.

The small tree was lit up, the tiny little lights blinking sequentially. It reminded me of my mom and dad's arguments regarding Christmas lighting. He hated the blinking lights, but Mom loved them. I remembered sadly that we never had blinking lights growing up. Mom was like me in more ways than we cared to admit. It was bittersweet that the real Beulah emerged, only after Dad died.

Underneath the tree sat only a few tiny boxes. Most of them were the ones I wrapped and sent over. Well, what did I expect? Did I think that Joe or Jonathon would have a miraculous change of heart just because it was Christmas? I realized sadly that I had hoped something would break, and obviously, nothing had.

Wally came in with a tray of my baked treats. He sat them beside the tea and stood there waiting for my mother. She wasn't long, but she came in empty-handed.

Mom sat on the couch and Wally gestured I should take the chair. He waited until I sat down before he lowered himself down next to Mom.

"Okay, presents!" Mom said. "Joan, please do the honors?"

I arose, went to the tree, and picked up the packages. I delivered them handily. There were three packages for me—one from Maxine and two envelopes. Mom had only one present, the one from me, and Wally had two. I wondered why Wally didn't give Mom a present.

CHAPTER EIGHTY-SIX

"You go first, Mom," I said.

She looked perplexed and passed the buck to Wally. He chuckled and opened his present from Mom. She gave him a beautifully handcrafted leather wallet. He expressed his admiration for it as if it were a crown jewels. Inside, he found a five-dollar bill. He leaned over and kissed my mom on the cheek.

"Thank you, love."

"You're welcome. I bought it from a native fellow in the mall. It's good quality."

Wally pulled out his old wallet and moved his cards and cash into this new treasure. His old wallet was thin and tattered. I saw why my mother wanted him to have a new one. We sat there watching him, no one thinking about opening the next gift. When Mom finally noticed, she pointed at me.

"Okay Joan, your turn. Open the green one first."

Obediently, I slipped my finger under the lip of the envelope and pulled it open. I slid out the card. On the front was a Santa with a large sack on his back. He was standing on the edge of a snow-covered chimney. It read "Ho Ho Ho." I opened the card. Inside was a gift card to the local mall. The amount on the top read $250.00. It was from Wally. I looked at the amount and shook my head. Tears stung my eyes.

"This is too much."

"No, my dear," Wally said. "It's just the right amount. It's good at any store. You can shop anywhere in the mall. You can get yourself some new clothes, or a new book. Treat yourself. You've had a rough go this past year, and if you can't treat yourself well, then who can?"

Tears were flowing down my cheeks. They landed on the card, leaving blotchy stains. Mom tutted. She left the room, coming back with a box of tissues. She placed it gently in my lap and rubbed her hand across my shoulders.

"Come on now, this is supposed to be a happy day."

"I know!" I blubbered.

Wally looked a little shell-shocked and squirmed in his seat. He didn't know how his generous offer caused so much hullabaloo.

"Okay," Mom said as she returned to her seat. "My turn." She grabbed the box I wrapped. She plucked at the ribbon before tearing off the paper. Opening the box, she gasped. "Oh my." She pulled out the scarf gracefully, wrapped it around her neck, and tied it with stylish precision. She looked gorgeous.

Watching her through my teary eyes, I smiled. "You look beautiful, Mom."

She smiled back. "Thank you, dear."

It was my turn again, and Mom advised me to leave the other envelope to last. Obediently, I lifted the package from Maxine. I picked at the edge, not wanting to destroy the beautiful wrapping. Inside the narrow box was another gift card envelope. This one had a poinsettia on the front cover and the words, "Just for you." The gift card was for the Wool Shop. I was gobsmacked at her generosity.

"What is it?" Mom asked, curiously.

"It's from Maxine. It's a gift card for $50 from the Wool Shop. I guess she wants me to keep coming to the knitting group." I smiled happily.

"She's very generous. What are you going to get with it?"

"I don't know yet, but I'll think of something."

"Okay Wally, you have one left, too." My mom pointed to the gift I brought for him. He ripped off the paper with gusto to reveal the travel mug and hot chocolate.

"Wow, hot chocolate! How did you know I wasn't a coffee drinker?"

"Mom told me about your love of hot chocolate.

That's a special blend of flavors, too. I hope you like them."

"If it's chocolate, I'll love it. Thank you, Joan."

I thought there was only one present left, the red envelope from Mom. I was about to open it when Wally stood and moved toward the tree. He rustled among the branches and finally withdrew a long velvet box. He handed it to Mom. "I had to hide this in the tree. Leaving it out would have revealed what it was and spoiled the surprise of the day. Merry Christmas, Beulah."

She looked at him with such love that my heart melted. Tears pricked my eyes. She opened the box like it might explode, tenderly. She didn't gasp—but broke into a wide grin. "You old dog," she whispered to Wally. "You saw me admiring this in the jewelry store in the mall and you went back to get it. It is beautiful and I love it." She pulled the diamond bracelet out of the box. Wally took it from her, wrapping it around her wrist. She dipped her hand to give me a good view of the stunning adornment.

CHAPTER EIGHTY-SEVEN

A few minutes of adulation passed before my mom spoke. "Do you have any more surprises, or can Joan open her last gift now?"

Wally chuckled. "Nope, I am done … for now." Mom swatted him lovingly.

On cue, I slid my finger under the envelope flap and pulled out the Christmas card. The flowery verse appeared on the front and continued inside. I skimmed through it, not absorbing the entire gist. Taped to the inside of the other flap was another gift card. This one was for the furniture store. I read her inscription.

"Joan, I wish you a Merry Christmas. It's been a rough ride for you, and I am sorry I wasn't there to lean on. Take this card and get yourself some decent furniture for your new home. You deserve much more than someone's cast-offs. Love, Mom. PS The card is worth five thousand dollars. Go crazy!"

Five thousand dollars! I read those words again, my eyes tearing up. I looked up at her. She was beaming. I tried to smile, but my face wasn't cooperating. My chin wobbled, and I burst into tears again.

"Thanks, Mom!" It came out as more of a squawk than words. This time, I was up and crossing the room. Mom stood, and we embraced.

"Don't you dare say a word to your sister. She's not getting any money—her delinquent husband would pour it straight down his neck." I nodded, still blubbering.

"Okay, now there's the jigsaw puzzle. You and Wally can get busy. I will call your sister and then you can talk when I'm done." She padded off toward the kitchen.

Wally stood and moved the card table into the room. He passed me the lid of the jigsaw puzzle. It was a beautiful street, probably Paris, in the rain, so the lights reflected off the street. A lovely picture, but it's difficult to assemble. I opened the box and picked out the edge pieces. I put all my thoughts on hold as I picked away, tossing the body of the puzzle into the other half of the box.

"Yes, Merry Christmas, Susan," my mother said, passing me the cordless phone. "Here's Joan."

I took the phone. "Merry Christmas, Susan."

"Merry Christmas, Joan." She slurred her greeting. Oh, wonderful. She had already been drinking.

"So, are you having a good day so far? What did you get for Christmas?"

"I got a bottle of Jack Daniels. Best dang gift ever." Her laugh was hollow, her bitterness as ripe as a black banana. "What did you get?"

"Mom gave me a jigsaw puzzle. It's a rainy street in Paris. Wally and I are just getting into it."

"That all you got?"

"No, Wally gave me a gift certificate for the mall."

"How much?" Her voice rose an octave—I sensed her anger.

"It was for twenty dollars." Her scalding tone caused me to diminish my good fortune to prevent her from becoming even more ill-tempered.

"Well, that's pretty much worthless. What can you buy with that?"

"A book or two, depending on the price. Or something on sale, maybe some bath soaps."

"I guess. Did you get anything else?"

"No." My heart was now beating in my stomach. I didn't like where this was going.

"What! Nothing from that useless jerk?"

"Do you mean Joe?"

"Yeah, the guy that threw you out of the house."

"Please, Susan, don't talk like that. Joe didn't throw me out. I left."

"Same difference. Men are all similar—useless bastards, the whole lot of them. Ignorant fools. All they want is someone to warm the sheets. They care nothing about you. Oh, they say they love you, but they cheat on you, and then they throw you away when you have nothing left to give."

I heard a loud voice in the background, but the words were unclear. "Get lost, jackass!" She yelled back, although she was still holding the phone, so the brunt of her shriek pierced my ear.

There was more noise. This time, the odd word was intelligible. The shouter was drunk, too.

"Okay, Susan. I need to go. Mom needs help in the kitchen."

"Sure, you go. Be the dutiful daughter." She hung up.

"Merry Christmas, Susan," I said into the disconnected receiver. "Merry Christmas."

CHAPTER EIGHTY-EIGHT

Mom appeared and took the phone out of my hand. I looked into her concerned face. "Now you know why I cannot send any money. I have tried talking to her. I have asked her to come home too many times to remember. She simply refuses to see that she needs help, which breaks my heart."

I did not know that things for Susan had deteriorated so far. When was the last time I spoke to her? Not since I called her to tell her about Caleb. We had never been close, and when she married and moved across the country, the geographical distance kept us that way. It possibly made it even easier to forget I had a sister most of the time. It was unfortunate she was living such a life.

Mom looked at me with tears in her eyes. I took hold of her arm and squeezed it. There was an understanding, a knowing between us as we silently shared the guilt of motherhood. Why is it that mothers bear such a burden? We feel that every failure our children experience is our fault. What we did and said was not right or enough. There was a moment of connection where we both understood the other's pain. She patted my hand and went back to the kitchen, the phone in hand.

I started working on the puzzle again, ignoring the turmoil swirling in my stomach. I can't imagine living with someone who drank. Joe was against alcohol, and for that, I lifted a prayer of thanksgiving. I sat there sorting puzzle pieces and thinking about Joe. Was Debbie hosting Christmas? Did they like the presents I sent? I thought about last Christmas. It was the first one without Leah and the last one as a family.

This morning, I promised myself I wouldn't take this walk today, but the call was strong. Unable to fight the yearning to go back, I stopped fighting and walked down memory lane. The morning came back as clear as if it was yesterday. I had been numb for months, just going through the motions of living. It was like someone had climbed into my heart, closed all the doors, shuttered the windows, and turned off the lights. Shut in and silent. There were no feelings, good or bad.

During December, I shopped with no enthusiasm, picking up presents with little thought for the receiving person. Joe decided—he made the list, and I obeyed. He wanted to get Jonathon a tablet—a little laptop that operated programs to help him around the farm. It needed to have hot spot capabilities so access to the internet would be possible outside of the house.

Jonathon suggested we get Debbie an e-reader. I had done as I was told. Of course, there was no mention of Caleb. He faded away into his college life, hardly coming home. I called him weekly to touch base, but he hadn't been home since Thanksgiving. I was out of touch and tired of chasing him. Had I known it would be his last Christmas, I might have made more of an effort. Really. I might have made a bigger effort.

The guilt, my guilt, brewed. I kept sorting puzzle pieces.

I did not know what to get Caleb. He had a laptop for his schooling. He had a smartphone. I didn't know what he needed. I was out of touch with him. He was elusive, not coming out to the farm often, and he didn't always pick up or return phone calls. He was distancing himself from us, and I was powerless to stop him.

Walking through the stores, trying to see anything that might appeal to him, I spent hours at the mall, going in and out of the stores, even. At the computer stores, the slick salesman would begin his spiel. My eyes would glaze over. I didn't understand RAM, ROM, gigahertz, or bytes. They would talk to me as if I was supposed to know, so I just nodded as they rambled along, then I thanked them for their time and left. It was overwhelming.

At my wit's end, I finally settled on getting Caleb some clothes. That's the worst thing you can do to your kids at Christmas. I gave electronics and gadgets to Jonathon and Debbie and clothes to Caleb. When he opened the boxes on Christmas morning, I saw his disappointment. Sure, he was gracious. He thanked me and kissed my cheek, but I had failed him.

I spent the day in the kitchen. Joe, Jonathon, and Debbie sat in the living room watching sports. Caleb was in his room. I went up just before dinner to talk. He was elusive again, not giving me satisfactory answers about his feelings. Maybe he didn't know how he felt, or maybe talking about them would release the dam holding back years of resentment and anger. I didn't push, fearing his wrath.

When Caleb left to go back to school, I was relieved. Can you imagine? I was happy to see him leave, his presence making me aware of the pain we were harboring and feeling that I didn't want to pick the scab off emotions. That scared me.

And there I sat, on a fold-up chair, in my mother's living room, tossing puzzle pieces, my thoughts swirling violently. I took a deep breath. I saw Caleb's face as he opened that box of T-shirts and pants, his smile as he pulled them out, forced and tight. Joe's comment was banal and ignorant. Jonathon watched silently—Debbie complimented this design or that, trying to mask the tense and uncertain feelings wafting through the room. My heart broke—shattered into a million pieces. Tears welled up, spilling down my cheeks unabated.

The dam finally broke for the sorrow I harbored in

my heart.

Wally looked up. I saw him rise through my blurry, watery gaze. He left the room, and a moment later, my mom rushed in.

"Joan, take a deep breath now. It's going to be okay."

"No, Mom. It's not! It's never going to be okay ever again."

I pushed back from the table and bent double to ease the pain that grew in my belly. It radiated outward at amazing speed, covering me with feelings that were intense and frightening. The sobs came then. They formed deep clumps, rising from my toes, bunching into huge, black, oily masses as they crawled upward. The blackness spread, growing tentacles that wrapped around my heart, spreading into my lungs, making it hard to breathe. My flesh was now black and dry—arid from the heat of the pain. The depth of my sadness left my heart scorched. With my sorrow unleashed, it threatened to consume me.

I envisioned crawling across the broken glass to feel anything other than these raging emotions. The desire to run and scream and beat my chest overwhelmed me. Relief would come if I punched a hole in the wall, broke a window, or destroyed the house. Aching to hurt someone, to see the blood pour from their wounds, to assuage my guilt was powerful. But I did none of those things. I sat there, hugging my knees. Sobs, low, guttural grunts, and barks poured out of me. A fire raged in my veins. Inside my body, itchiness grew, but I didn't know how to stop these raging emotions.

My mother stood stoically beside my chair, rubbing my back in circular motions, telling me to let it out. This soothed and angered me. I wanted her to stop, and I wanted her to pull me into a hug and tell me that everything was going to be okay. The grief was so intense as it made its passage through my body that I rocked under its force. Maybe I would shatter into a thousand pieces and fall like fragments onto the floor. In a moment of sheer madness, I tried to grab the reins on the beast that was driving me into the abyss, but I was powerless against the momentum. It was too late to save myself. I was going in.

CHAPTER EIGHTY-NINE

I slipped to the floor, curled into a tight ball, and wept like it was the end of the world. Weeping for Leah and Caleb—weeping for Joe and me—weeping for Jonathon, too. Every dark stain, every black and sad memory, I squeezed them all out in my tears and sobs. I emptied the pot of bitterness that had surrounded my heart for years.

The sobs eventually subsided, leaving me exhausted. My mother helped me to my feet and led me into the spare room. She steered me to bed. I crawled into it, falling asleep before my body even settled. Hours later, I awoke. My eyes were sore and puffy. A hollowness echoed inside as if I had poured out everything and nothing was left.

In the bathroom, I ran some cold water onto a

washcloth. The cool cloth was soothing as I wiped my face. Rinsing the cloth, I repeated the ritual several times, paying close attention to my aching eyes by laying the cold cloth on each eye for a minute before rinsing again in cold water and doing the other eye. Finally, I was ready to face the world.

The aroma of roasting turkey hugged me as I walked into the living room. Mom and Wally were watching a Christmas movie. They sat cuddled up together. The tears flowed again. My mother noticed me and moved away from Wally. I smiled through my tears.

"How are you? Can I get you a cup of tea?"

"Thanks, Mom. I can get one."

"No, you sit. You've had quite a day. I'll make a pot of tea. The turkey is nearly done. We'll eat in a little while."

Obediently, I sat in the chair. Wally turned off the television. "Oh, don't turn it off on my account."

"I was watching it for your mother. It's one of those sappy movies on the women's network," he whispered, winking at me.

I smiled at his benevolence. How did my mother find this prince?

"You're a good man, Wally."

He smiled at me. "Your mom is a good woman."

We smiled at each other, nodding in agreement. I chuckled. Wally joined in. My laugh grew louder and more intense. Wally smiled more broadly, keeping up with me. I kept going, unable to stop. My laughter grew in intensity, building to near hysteria.

"Here's the tea!"

Mom came in with a tray of tea and cups. Her presence and calm demeanor helped me rein in the runaway that threatened to take me back into the abyss.

"Thanks, Mom." I took a deep breath, and my emotions settled.

The cup of tea, a spicy apple blend, was just what I needed to feel refreshed. Mom poured herself a cup—but took it back into the kitchen.

"Do you need help, Mom?"

"No, you sit and enjoy your tea. I just want to get the vegetables going."

Twenty minutes later, I joined her in the kitchen. The half turkey was resting on the counter, the skin golden brown, perfectly roasted. Two pots sat steaming on the stovetop. A bowl of yams sat on the counter, and Mom was mashing the potatoes.

"Set the table, please," she said without turning from her task.

I gathered three of everything, setting it out on the small round table. Mom had already adorned the table with her best lace tablecloth. The festive napkins added some color to the scene.

"Thank you, Joan. Now we can set the food out. I'll get a bowl for the Brussels sprouts." She handed me the potatoes, now settled into a nice crystal bowl. "Wally, dinner is ready."

Wally appeared in the doorway as I set the bowls

down. Mom followed, carrying the carrots and a small basket of miniature dinner buns. My stomach growled.

"Wally, would you carve the turkey? Then bring it to the table, please." She turned back, opened the oven, and withdrew the bowl of stuffing she put there to keep warm. Christmas dinner was now complete. Mom gestured for me to sit on the right side of the table. She took the one on the left, leaving Wally in the chair between us.

Wally carved the turkey at the counter and then brought a platter of white and dark meat to the table. He sat down and smiled at us.

"Looks like we have a feast here. We've much to be thankful for." He reached over and took my mother's hand before extending his right hand toward me. I took it.

"Let's pray."

We bowed our heads. "Father, we have much to be thankful for this Christmas. I have these two wonderful women beside me, a meal to delight the gods, my health, and the many blessings you bestow upon me daily. You are an awesome God, full of goodness and mercy. Bless this food, Lord. Bless our conversation, and I ask for special blessings for Joan. You know the circumstances, and I ask for your grace and mercy to surround her and keep her as she walks the path you've laid before her. In Jesus' name, we pray."

In unison, we uttered, "Amen."

I looked up, tears watering from my eyes. Wally and

Mom were looking at me. I smiled, my chin quivering. I cleared my throat.

"Okay, let's dish up this delicious meal."

I grabbed the stuffing and heaped a spoonful onto my plate.

CHAPTER NINETY

There was no conversation as we passed the bowls around, each of us taking a serving of everything. I tucked into my first bite, closed my eyes, and groaned. Mom's stuffing always tasted like heaven. It wasn't over-spiced, not under-spiced, but perfect.

"This is a delicious meal, Mom, thank you."

Mom looked over at me, her eyes glistening. "I will always regret staying away at Christmas because of your husband and not getting to know my grandchildren." Mom said, her eyes glistening. "I blamed you because accepting I was a coward was not possible."

Tears rose in my eyes. "It's okay, Mom, really it is. I played my part. Joe made it hard for me to have everything I wanted. He thought all I needed was him and our kids—no one else. He wouldn't have accepted you at our house, but I never even tried. I'm just as guilty."

A few tears ran down our cheeks as we stared at each other. A flood of love rose inside me.

"Okay." Mom cleared her throat. "Now, we can leave it."

I took a deep breath, and we moved on. The conversation turned to plans for New Year's. Wally regaled us with tales of New Year's parties in Saskatchewan.

"There was this one woman, Mrs. Garner. She dressed demurely. I thought she was one of the most strait-laced women I knew. Then, one New Year's Eve, she brazenly kissed me open-mouthed. I was so shocked."

We laughed at his expression of surprise as he relived this experience. He laughed openly before continuing. "I blushed, shocked that she would try it in a crowded room like that. My wife wasn't far away, and her husband, too. Yet, there she was trying to …" He stopped and cleared his throat. "Humiliated, I told no one about what she had done, especially my wife! After that first year, she never did it again, to me anyway. At the next New Year's Eve party, I was quite nervous when she approached me. She reached up and pecked me demurely on the lips, wished me a Happy New Year, and moved on. I put it down that she must have had too much to drink the year before, and I let it go."

"Funny enough," he continued. "Years later, she ran

off with her son's football coach. That's when the stories circulated. Apparently, she'd kissed most of the men in the district over the years. No one ever talked about it. I mean, my next-door neighbor had experienced her advances, and he never spoke of it to me, thinking like me—he was the only one she did this to and was too embarrassed to admit that he was afraid of her. After she left, though, there wasn't a man in the county who hadn't kissed old Ruby, even if they hadn't, I suppose." He laughed. "Some men bragged they took advantage of her invitation and visited her when her husband wasn't home. Poor George. I think he fell into the bottle after she left. He was ashamed that he wasn't aware of what his wife had been up to. Took his kids a little while to shake him back to normal." He shook his head sadly. "So, I guess all I can say is that none of us knows what goes on inside another's head or heart. We just have to take it as it comes and thank God for his grace when we slip."

"You're a wise man, Wally Stevens." My mom smiled at him, her eyes filled with love and laughter.

My heart flipped over. When was the last time I saw my mother this happy? I thought back to the Christmas dinners at home—Dad would sit where Wally sat, Mom on his left—Susan and I to his right. We would say a terse and perfunctory blessing before consuming the dinner in silence. All of us stared at our plates, waiting for the moment to escape from the tension that surrounded every family meal.

My mother deserved this … she deserved to be happy. Tears welled up, but these were tears of gratitude. My mother looked up, caught my eye, and smiled. She knew what I was thinking.

"Okay, let's clear this up. I'll make some tea, and we can dig into some of that lovely baking Joan has provided."

Mom stood and cleared the table. I stood with her, and soon, we had the dishes loaded in the dishwasher and the food in containers for me to take home as they were leaving the next day for Arizona.

Mom kept enough turkey for a sandwich for her and Wally, but the rest of the bird and the half carcass were mine. I thought about a nice turkey and rice soup, remembering it was one of Caleb's favorites. This memory didn't bring tears, just a wave of sadness for what was gone and a small amount of anger that he'd been so foolish. That was new. Anger. Surely Caleb was not to blame—was he? I shook off those thoughts.

The kettle was boiling, so I made the tea. Mom put some of the baking on a platter. I took the teapot to the table before I grabbed the teacups and took them over. I sat down as Mom placed the platter of goodies down. Wally came in from the garage carrying a cardboard box. He set it on the counter and loaded all the food inside it. Then he moved it back to the unheated garage before joining us at the table. Mom poured the tea. We took our cups and a treat and settled back in our chairs.

It had been a wonderful day. Even the breakdown

had been cathartic. Life was going to get better, having crossed over the huge barrier of grief and sadness. The monsoon had not broken me. No illusions that I was over my losses—but the depth lessened.

I finished my tea, setting my empty cup back into the saucer. At that moment, it was as if someone had flipped a switch. I was so exhausted. I didn't even know if I was going to get home.

Mom looked at Wally, and a silent message passed between them. He arose from the table and gathered my gifts from the living room. He put those into the box in the garage, then grabbed his coat and mine.

"Time to get you home, little girl," he said with a chuckle.

CHAPTER NINETY-ONE

It must have been exhaustion speaking, but suddenly, I didn't want to go home. If I left there, Christmas was over, and my mom would leave for Arizona. I didn't want her to go, just when I'd finally found her.

Sensing my fear, my mother came over with my coat. "Now Joan, everything is going to be okay. I'm only a phone call away. You are going to be fine."

She helped me into my jacket, and then, just as she'd done for years when I was a little girl, she zipped it up, smoothing the shoulders before she slid her hands down to take mine. We stood there, looking into each other's eyes, hand in hand. Then she hugged me tightly. I hugged her back. Embarrassed by this flood of emotion, she was the first to break.

"Okay, you get to bed. You've had a full day. I'll call you in the morning before we head out."

She steered me toward the door to the garage. I stepped into my boots, wrapped my scarf around my neck, and slipped on my gloves. Wally was in the SUV, waiting patiently. The engine was running, the door to the garage wide open, and letting in the Arctic air. I kissed Mom on the cheek.

"Good night, Mom. I love you." Then I turned quickly and scrambled in beside Wally.

Mom stood on the step, hugging herself against the cold. She waved as the door to the garage descended. When she was out of sight, a slight pain flared in my heart. I resigned myself to the fact that she was leaving and took comfort that she would be back in the spring and we would have a summer together.

Wally offered to help me upstairs with the box of food, but it wasn't heavy, so I declined. "Thanks, Wally, I can manage."

"Only if you're sure." He seemed reluctant to take my word for it.

"I'm sure." I turned to leave—but swung back. "Wally?"

He stopped his hand on the door handle, looking at me expectantly.

"Thanks for all you've given my mom. She is happy, and I love you for that."

"She's a wonderful lady, your mom. I am the lucky one."

We stood there and smiled at each other, unwilling to break the ambiance that settled around us.

"Merry Christmas and Happy New Year, Wally."

"Merry Christmas, Joan, and God's blessing for the New Year." He winked at me.

I smiled and turned away, tears pricking my eyes again.

I rode the elevator to my floor, eager for my bed. Inside the apartment, I put the food in the fridge and tucked the gift certificates in the cupboard beside the glasses. Then I washed my face and went to bed.

As I drifted off, I realized Jonathon hadn't returned my call. I heard nothing from him again. A bead of anger bounced inside my heart. It hurt me that he had so little regard for me that he wouldn't even call me on Christmas Day. Taking a page from Wally's playbook, I lifted him up in prayer.

"God, I am angry with Jonathon for being heartless. I don't understand why he is doing what he is doing, but I ask for your protection for him and me. Help me not be bitter toward him. Help me forgive him. Thank you."

Sighing, I turned onto my side and slipped off to sleep.

Later, I would think about what I'd done. Something inside me broke that afternoon as I sobbed out all the pain I was carrying. It seemed natural to pray to God. That was the first prayer I uttered since Leah's death.

I was healing.

CHAPTER NINETY-TWO

In the days following Christmas, I kept busy. Everyone wanted something sweet on their tables at this time of year, but many people had no time to bake themselves. Now, cupcake stores and donut shops abounded. Every grocery store had a bakery section filled with cookies, cakes, and pastries to satisfy a multitude of appetites.

Marta had warned me, but it still amazed me how much baking we sent out every day. It was good to keep busy. Homesickness burned inside me. I missed Leah, Caleb, Jonathon, and the life I used to live. So, coming home exhausted or working an extra hour kept me from dwelling on what was gone.

Maxine agreed to go with me to the furniture store in the new year. She was going to help me decorate my home. I had been in touch with the thrift store, and they agreed to come and get all the old stuff. I willingly donated it back, and they were grateful to be allowed to resell it.

New Year's Eve arrived. I was at a loose end. Maxine was spending the night with her family. Beckie and Brad were going dancing. I didn't know what I wanted to do. Wanting to stay home, I found I didn't want to be alone, either.

The café closed early, so I arrived home earlier than normal. As I picked up my knitting, my focus waned. Shortly afterward, having not stitched anything, I put it down. I was fidgeting and unsettled.

At six o'clock, I went for a walk. It was a mild night for mid-winter. Already, the nights were growing shorter again—the promise of spring lay well ahead in the coming year. I was mostly content with the future, as it was in my mind, although there was a squiggle of promise for more. What I wasn't content with was Jonathon's silence. I called him earlier that day. Again, the call went to voicemail. It was like he was never home, and if he was—he wasn't talking to me. I hated to imagine what the conversation was like when the phone rang. No, I didn't want to know.

I was in the foyer a few minutes later, and as I crossed the floor, my cell phone, neatly tucked inside an upper pocket, rang. It took me a moment to remove my gloves and get the phone out. Fearing the call would go to voicemail, I answered without checking the caller ID.

"Hello?"

"Hello, Joan. It's Ben. Happy New Year."

Ben! My heart flipped over. "Oh, hi, Ben. Happy New Year to you, too!"

"Did you have a good Christmas?"

"It was wonderful. You?"

"It was a decent day. No trouble calls, so work was easy. I ate a sumptuous turkey dinner. It was all good." He paused, perhaps waiting for me to comment. When I didn't—he continued. "Why I was calling—I was wondering if you wanted to go to the cemetery tomorrow. I have the day off, so you have a ride if you are interested."

Since my transformation on Christmas Day, I wanted to go to the cemetery. Feeling optimistic for the first time in years, I wanted to tell Leah that things were now going to go forward. My life was finally changing for the better. But I also was reluctant to call Ben again so quickly, not wanting to take advantage of his kindness. Now, here he was, offering to give me what I seemed incapable of asking for.

"Thank you, Ben. That would be nice. I am truly grateful."

"No problem, Joan. Glad to be of service. So does ten a.m. work?"

"It's perfect, thank you."

"Okay, see you then. Have a pleasant night, Joan. Happy New Year."

"Happy New Year, Ben. See you tomorrow."

I hung up. The unsettled feeling in my heart dissipated, but I still headed out for a walk. I walked until I finally arrived at the little white clapboard house with the green shutters. The house seemed more abandoned on this frosty night. It tugged on my heart, and I sent up another wish.

I walked around the block and took the back alley to get another look at the house from the back. They replaced the tiny hedge that framed the yard in the front with a white picket fence that contained the large backyard. There was an immense tree shading a patio table and chairs covered under a layer of snow. Uncertain of the reality, I imagined a large garden on one side, a place for vegetable plants and maybe some raspberry canes and strawberry runners.

I was being silly, planning on buying an unaffordable property, but I was in love with this house … it was calling me. My feelings about this house were unexplainable, but I felt this house was perfect for me.

Walking for a few more blocks, I wound my way through the neighborhood. What a lovely part of the city this was. Mature, but not run down. Large vintage houses with verandas and upper balconies. It made me wish I had been born in the era when these houses were new, when life was less complex and more secure. Realizing I was romanticizing history, an existence I had no way of understanding, I shook my head and smiled.

I headed home, feeling more content with my life. Whatever happened in the future, I was going to rise to it. My thoughts turned toward my children. I arrived back at the apartment and decided I would have to hunt Jonathon down. If Ben were willing, tomorrow, I'd have him take me to the farm. Speaking to Jonathon was worth the hazard of running into Joe—a risk I was willing to take.

CHAPTER NINETY-THREE

The next morning, true to his word, Ben rang the buzzer a few minutes before ten a.m. I told him I'd be right there, grabbed my coat and gear, and headed down to the elevator. I rode down in silence, thinking it was rare to share it with another tenant or guest. For all the months I lived there, I counted less than a handful of times I rode the elevator with someone. For a large building, it wasn't particularly busy. At least, the elevator wasn't.

Ben was waiting patiently. I climbed into the vehicle beside him.

After exchanging pleasantries, he pulled out of the parking lot as I buckled my seat belt. The traffic was light, and we were soon out of the city, heading south toward Freyden.

Like a teenager on her first date, I was tongue-tied. In the silence between us, I compared Ben and Joe, recognizing that Ben's compassion toward me—his gracious understanding—and his willingness to give … were qualities I did not experience in my marriage.

Joe was decent in his own way, but his world revolved around him. He silently demanded things, and the consequences were emotional. We all learned to tiptoe around his temper. I had sailed the course, but when I needed a safe harbor for my feelings and grief, I found only a squalling tempest. Joe was not a port in the storm.

Ben offered me stability in his quiet strength. I imagined he would hold me steady as I railed against the unfairness of life while not taking it personally. Maybe I was reading him wrong, but I didn't think so. He exuded a confidence I hadn't experienced.

Joe liked his world to be orderly because, in disarray, he felt out of control. Ben appeared to stand like a sturdy oak in the storm, letting it rage around him but not letting it affect his confidence that things would be okay once the wind dissipated.

I smiled. I was romanticizing again, allowing my wishes to create a reality that I didn't know was real or not.

"What are you smiling about?"

I laughed aloud. "You don't want to know." Then I blushed deeply, embarrassed at my thoughts, at the idea of sharing them.

"Sure, I do." He smiled as he glanced over at me.

Shaking my head, I said, "I was just thinking about Joe." It wasn't a lie, though it wasn't the truth, either. "Would you mind dropping me at the farm for a minute after the graveyard. I'd like to see Jonathon if he's in. I miss him and he won't return my calls."

"Whatever you want." He nodded in agreement.

"Thanks."

There was no more conversation after that. We rode the rest of the way in silence. A minute or two later, Ben navigated into Freyden and soon after, he parked at the cemetery. I hadn't time to get flowers, so I had nothing to set on her grave today. At first, I was frantic about that, but then I realized it was okay. Just being here was enough.

"I won't be long Ben, thanks again." I pulled open the door.

"Take as long as you need. I'll be right here."

I nodded and climbed out of the car.

It was a beautiful winter day. The sun was shining, reflecting light off the crisp, sparkling snow. I walked along the cleared paths through the graveyard until I had to turn. There were footprints in the snow—a set of large footprints and a smaller set. Jonathon and Debbie.

Stepping toward the gravestone, I saw a tiny brown teddy bear, with a heart necklace, sitting half-buried in the snow. The tag pinned to his chest read, "Merry Christmas, Leah." My heart burst and tears flowed. How beautiful. My son's heart was still beating. I needed to know that. It meant that he hadn't completely lost himself in Joe's world. He was still feeling. He was still reachable.

Staying for half an hour, I told Leah about Christmas, about my breakdown, and the subsequent recovery of my sanity. I told her about her grandmother and how lucky I was she found Wally because he softened her heart and made her human again. Leah's forgiveness for my mother's absence and the judgments that kept her outside our family for years seemed to infiltrate the air. She heard me.

CHAPTER NINETY-FOUR

I was shivering by the time I slid back into the car. The warmth hit me immediately. It was wonderful. Pulling off my gloves, I stuck my hands over the vents. Ben laughed as he put the car in reverse.

"Buckle up, please."

I obeyed, and soon we were cruising back through town. On the road to the farm, my nerves jangled over my decision to see Jonathon. Why was he not returning my calls? Was I doing this for myself? What if he refused to see me? Was I prepared for that? What if he was openly hostile?

I thought back to the day he helped his father burn Caleb's belongings and move me out of the marital bedroom. What I remembered wasn't hostility. He had been quiet, but he'd smiled at me. He didn't hate me. But then I left. I moved out and that might have tipped the scales against me. Maybe I was going to get an earful of disdain. Maybe he would tell me some ugly truths as he saw them.

We turned into the lane, and a moment later, the house came into view. The house looked no different from when I left. That surprised me. It should have, shouldn't it? The house was no longer a home, no longer holding a family within its walls. It should look different.

We passed by the main house and Ben parked outside Jonathon's tidy home. He turned off the car and looked at me. "You want me to come with you?"

"No, thanks. I think I need to do this on my own."

"Okay, I'm right here if you need me."

I exited the car and climbed the wooden steps. Knocking on the door, I listened intently for some movement. Knocking again, I looked left. I thought I saw the curtain move, but I wasn't sure. Calling Jonathon's name. I knocked again. Trying the door, I found it to be locked. Funny, we never locked our doors. I looked back at the car and knocked one last time.

An enormous cloud descended over me as I turned away from the door. Although I wasn't certain, I thought someone was at home. But no one answered, which spoke volumes. I stepped back down the wooden stairs and saw the tractor coming from the barn. With hope rising, I thought Jonathon was coming, but it turned out to be Joe.

I tensed as he pulled up behind the car, blocking Ben's vehicle from retreating. This would not be pretty. My stomach lurched. My heart raced as he opened the cab door and climbed down from his lofty perch.

Ben stepped out of the car. Glancing his way, I let him know I was grateful for his presence but didn't need him to interfere.

Over the loud sputtering of the tractor, Joe yelled. His tone was mocking. "Brought a bodyguard, I see."

"No. Ben was kind enough to take me to Leah's grave."

"Ben, is it?" He stared hard at Ben. "Are you sleeping with him?"

"Not that it is any of your business, but no." My face warmed.

He looked at me like I was lying, and he would prove it. "So, what are you doing here?"

"What does it look like? I'm here to visit my son."

"Well, he's not home. Not that he'd have answered if he were. He wants nothing more to do with you. You are not welcome around here, so I suggest you get back into that car and get off my property."

Unsure how to refute what he was saying about Jonathon, I wanted to prove him wrong. Unfortunately, Jonathon wasn't there to tell me differently. I played the only card I had.

"How can I leave when you've purposely blocked in the car?"

"Not my problem, sweetheart. You're a smart girl.

You know how to get away, you've done it before."

The woman I was before I left would have lowered her head and turned her attention to her task without another word. Since leaving Joe, I discovered I really wasn't that person, and maybe I'd never been. Maybe I spent my entire married life playacting. Whatever was inside me now wasn't timid, and she certainly had a mind of her own.

I walked over to Joe. I stood close enough for him to reach out and hit me if he wanted. A part of me was itching for him to do just that. Out of the corner of my eye, I saw Ben move closer, too.

"You know something, Joe, I am no longer scared of your temper. You are a coward and a bully. And since I am no longer afraid of you, I suggest you get back into your tractor and back the hell up."

A flash of anger crossed Joe's face. He turned red, his eyes widened, and his body stiffened. Curling his hand into a fist, I realized he was thinking about hitting me. Then he forced it to open wide. I waited for it as I stared into his face. I refused to show him I was terrified. He needed to know I was an adversary now.

He leaned close to me, so close his breath caressed my cheeks. "May you rot in hell, Joan." He looked into my eyes, and I crossed another line, but I didn't care.

"Right back at you, Joe. Not a day goes by that I don't thank God that I'm free of you. You're evil and arrogant and a hideous human being." The hair on the back of my neck stood up. I was tingling with fear and the anticipation of something vile.

CHAPTER NINETY-FIVE

It was a surprise to me that Joe straightened up, spun on his heel, and retreated to the tractor. He climbed back in, revved the engine, and drove away without looking back. The air rushed out of my body. Before I dropped to the ground, Ben was beside me, guiding me back to the car. I was ashamed that he had witnessed the interaction between us. I stooped to Joe's level, and it didn't feel good.

Ben put the car in gear without saying a word, and we were soon back in Freyden. Neither of us spoke about what had transpired at the farm. I was trying to understand my feelings. Ben was allowing me to do what I needed to do without interruption. He navigated the car down the quiet street and, minutes later, we were on the highway again.

The ride back to Crawford continued to be a quiet one. We were only a few miles away from the outskirts of the city when Ben finally spoke.

"Are you interested in having lunch with me?"

Part of me wanted to, just to feel normal for a little while. Part of me wanted to go home, crawl under the covers and weep for what I went through that day.

"I don't think so, not today," I said, quietly. My heart wrenched as I spoke those words. My heart wanted to go, even while my head was trying to go somewhere else.

"Okay, I understand."

"Thank you."

The conversation died again. My thoughts were swirling. Ben seemed disappointed, which was heavy and too cumbersome for me to manage in my fragile state. I had to ease things. As Ben pulled to a stop in front of my building, I released my seat belt but didn't open the car door. Sitting there, trying to plan what I wanted to say to clear the air. I didn't want to sever our connection, so I had to choose my words wisely. Before I communicated my thoughts, Ben opened the conversation, and when he spoke, it was as if he was reading my thoughts.

"I know you're probably ashamed about what happened back at the farm. I want to assure you that you have nothing to be embarrassed about. You, maybe for the first time in your life, gave your husband a helping of what he gave you over the years. By the look on his face, I would say he expected you to cower and whimper when he said what he did, or at the very least, snivel and beg for mercy. Standing up to a bully is an admirable thing and you nailed it. I am proud of you."

I was too shocked to speak. More thoughts swirled until there was a maelstrom spinning behind my eyes. But he wasn't done.

"I accept that you have a lot on your plate, many things to sort through. I am not asking you to set it aside and come to me. All I am offering is a helping hand and the shoulder of someone who can take it. I would be a liar to say that I don't hope something develops between us. But I know you are not ready, so I am doing my best to be patient."

"Thank you," I muttered. It was all I seemed able to say.

"So, yes, I am disappointed about lunch, but I know there will be other days. In the meantime, I think you should go upstairs, take a nice hot bath and relax. Tomorrow is back to routine, bringing a certain normalcy back into your world. The holidays shake people's lives up. January brings it back into balance again."

I nodded in agreement. "Thanks for understanding, Ben."

"No need to thank me. I am a friend. If I add to your problems, then I am not a very good one."

Tears sprang to my eyes, and I ducked my head, hoping Ben wouldn't see. He opened the console, pulled out a small travel package of tissues, and handed it to me. He'd seen. I smiled as I opened the plastic tab and pulled one out. I dabbed my eyes.

"Would you like to come up for tea or something?" I looked over at his handsome face.

His blue eyes twinkled, happy that I made the offer. "Not today, Joan. I think you need some downtime, to sort yourself out. My stopping for tea would only prolong that." He patted my arm. "You do like I said. Hot bath, hot cup of tea, maybe watch TV—listen to music. Relax."

CHAPTER NINETY-SIX

Ben waited until I was inside the building before pulling away. The moment I lost sight of his car, his absence appeared significant. Part of me wanted more. Most of me was afraid of it. As I rode the elevator up, with a couple from the seventh floor this time, I let all thoughts of Ben go. I needed to focus on Jonathon and Debbie.

As I ran myself a hot bath, sprinkling a generous amount of bubble bath into the water, I placed a call to Jonathon. Once again, the call went to voicemail. I left a brief message, explaining I'd been out to see him and wished him and Debbie a Happy New Year.

Then I stripped off my clothes and climbed into the hot bath. I leaned back against the cold porcelain, tensing for the moment of impact, then relaxing as the cold disappeared under my shoulders. I lay there in the warmth, picking through the bones of the day again. Picking and picking until there was nothing of value left to look at.

I realized returning to Joe was out of the question. I shuddered, remembering his offer that I would get my vehicle back if I came home. I had refused him then because it was a ploy to gain control. Today I understood the farm was no longer my home. I had tolerated Joe's abuse for years—being away from it made me see it differently. It disgusted me how I had tolerated his behavior. I didn't want to return to the role of peacemaker and comfort giver in our unbalanced relationship, where I received only shallow and conditional responses.

Joe was the father of my children and a huge part of my past. I didn't want things to continue as they were. We would never be best friends, but I wanted to get to a place of civility. Coming out to visit Jonathon and Debbie and fearing an altercation with him was imminent was not appealing. Would Joe ever be amenable to this future?

Eating an early supper, I waited for the clock to roll around to seven—taking the chance that I would find Joe at home. He'd have finished the evening chores, had his supper, and he'd be resting in the chair reading the newspaper or watching TV. I dialed his number.

The phone rang four times. I was just about ready to hang up when he answered.

"What do you want, Joan?"

Funny how I once welcomed the call display, so I didn't have to answer calls I didn't want to. Now it left me feeling exposed. Ignoring a phone call can give the impression that it is from an unwelcome caller.

"Hello, Joe." I paused. He didn't respond. "Joe, I just wanted to apologize for this morning. I shouldn't have said what I did, and I'm sorry."

"So, you should be."

His ungracious response irked me, but I took a deep breath and plowed on. "Look Joe, I don't want to fight with you."

"Well, you sure fooled me," he snapped back.

Another deep breath. "I'm sorry, Joe, if I've hurt you. That wasn't my intention. I …"

"Well, you didn't hurt me, Joan, because you didn't win."

"This isn't a contest. I'm not trying to win anything."

"Really? It's me, Joan. Be honest."

"Joe, please …"

"No, Joan. I don't know why you called. You've made your bed. You walked away from here, and this place is no longer where you are welcome. I trust you will stay away in the future."

"What about Jonathon? Am I no longer allowed to visit my son?"

"He wants nothing to do with you. When you walked out, he closed the door on you, too."

"Did you encourage him to do that, Joe?"

"He didn't need any encouragement from me. He thinks as I do. You abandoned your family. You walked out on us, forfeiting any claim on anything to do with us. He's been a willing participant—he's legally the owner of this farm and all its holdings. I signed it all over to him before I started divorce proceedings. He owns it all—therefore, there is nothing for you to claim. I own nothing but the clothes on my back. Everything is in Jonathon's name."

The open confession of his ruthless maneuvering took me aback. I did not know Jonathon was so angry with me.

"But …"

"And guess who drove your Jeep out of that city parking lot. Jonathon did that. He was a willing participant. He wants nothing to do with you."

Discouraged, this conversation wasn't going anywhere. I had wanted to build a bridge between us. Instead, Joe was burning it down.

"That junk you sent him for Christmas went directly to goodwill. None of us want your crap. He was going to send it back to you until I helped him realize you'd get your money back if he returned it. This way, you still pay, but he gets the recognition from the charity. Win-win in my books." He paused for a moment. "So, if there's nothing else, I'm hanging up now."

"No, I guess not." I sighed in defeat.

"Oh, and Joan?"

"Yes?"

"Don't you ever bring that goon back here again, either. He is less welcome here than you are. Just stay the hell away from us from here on in. We'll all be happier for it."

I heard the click as he hung up, but I held the receiver against my ear for a few more beats. Here I was, thinking we might bury the hatchet. Unfortunately for me, that hatchet lay buried deep in my chest. Just when I thought life was going in one direction, I was ducking curve balls and not too successfully, either.

CHAPTER NINETY-SEVEN

I put the phone on the table in front of me. Emotions hung heavily in the air around my head. Tendrils of despair drilled their way under my skin. I was too tired to care, too tired to push them away. Too tired to think about fighting. So, I leaned against the back of the couch and let them do their worst.

The phone rang. I jumped. Looking down at the caller ID, I chastised myself for doing to the caller what Joe had done to me minutes earlier. Before I read the information, I pushed to answer. It was Ben.

"Hi, Joan. I'm just checking in to see that you're doing okay." His voice was strong and sincere. I burst into tears.

"Joan, what happened? Talk to me," Ben urged.

I tried to tell him, but the words came out garbled

and unintelligible. "Joan, take a deep breath, calm down. Breathe, breathe."

I listened to his words, feeling the rolling seas calm under his direction. I gulped in deep breaths, doing my best to control the rudder.

"Just breathe Joan, just breathe. You can do it. That's a good girl, slow and steady now. Keep it up." His calm and assured voice gave me something to cling to. I tossed out my rope and secured myself to his steadiness.

When I finally found my voice, I told him what had happened and shared with him what Joe had said. He didn't offer advice, nor did he pass judgment. He just listened. With my sad tale of woe spread out between us, he offered me comfort.

"It's unfortunate that Joe can't let go of his anger. Maybe he's not ready, maybe he'll never be. But if he gets there, he'll know that you'll accept his apology. I hope he does, for both of your sakes. Unforgiveness is the cancer that will eat you alive if you let it."

His words were unexpected. Joe would have chastised me for expecting a positive outcome, adding insult to injury. I never walked away from Joe feeling soothed. Ben's comments added a layer of salve to the gaping wound, a healing balm allowing me to reflect again one day without pain. Again, I compared the two men, conscious of their differences.

After a few more minutes of inane conversation, we hung up. I was relieved because several times I had nearly asked him to come over. Yearning for some human comfort, I wanted him to take me in his arms, to feel the comfort of his body on mine. I wanted to give myself to him, to nestle under his arm after we had exhausted our passions. I wanted to curl my fingers through his dark hair and run my thumb over his perpetual five o'clock shadow. Blushing at the ache that coursed through my veins, I groaned.

I never experienced this with Joe. Our lovemaking was adequate, but not passionate. It was functional and purposeful, but not intimate and unifying.

I laughed, thinking about how I needed a cold shower. I wondered what my mother would say. Then I laughed aloud. She would tell me to get him into my bed as soon as possible. She was a wise woman, although I had no intention of doing that. Not yet. I wanted to be ready for that—I didn't want to jump into something with both feet too soon. If my life was going in that direction, I wanted to meet him on an equal footing, not drag him down to my level, so he had to lift me up. My experience with Joe taught me that he didn't elevate me—he held me back.

I was looking for love when I rushed into marriage with Joe. I didn't know who I was, so I let Joe tell me. He defined me and I became that person. I was never equal, never a partner. I was his maid, his cook, and his housekeeper. Despite being a servant and bearing his children, he never expressed his satisfaction or pride in me.

Even though Ben was different, I still wanted to ensure we built our relationship on a sturdy foundation. If—we were going there. For now, I just had to keep my raging hormones from pushing me faster than I wanted to go.

My lust-filled dreams were satisfying. I consummated my relationship without involving Ben at all, just his dream presence. Or who I imagined he was since I never saw a face.

CHAPTER NINETY-EIGHT

January passed in a blur of snow and wind, separated by days of sunshine and blue skies. The temperature fell deep into the basement and walking to work was brutal. I bundled up with hats, scarves, and layers of mittens. I was glad that the long coat kept the wind from biting my legs too much.

It was winter. As the month wound down and February popped up, the snow and cold gave way to warmer days. The groundhog saw his shadow, so we were in for six more weeks of winter, but the storms were less severe. Winter lost its grip, and we were rushing headlong toward spring.

Ben took me out to Leah's grave on Valentine's Day. We hadn't seen each other since New Year's Day, even though we spoke a half dozen times on the phone.

Ben usually called to check on me, and I called him once, too. I think it made him happy that I finally reached back.

Mom phoned me from Arizona the day after her birthday on February twenty-sixth. Wally had proposed marriage, and she had accepted on the condition that he wouldn't make her live in Regina. He had no issues with that, so he put his house on the market.

I was over the moon for her. They hadn't set the date and wouldn't until they came back to Canada. All she knew was that she wanted a summer wedding, exchanging vows in the sunshine of a beautiful city park.

My divorce settlement was still a long way from being complete. It was slow going. I was eager to have it finished.

I continued to walk past that little house. It stayed on the market well into the spring. Even though I often looked at the photo of the realtor's signpost, I somehow never found the courage to inquire about the asking price. I wondered about the circumstances of the little house as the weeks passed and it stood stoically empty—still up for sale. Discussing it with others, they suggested the owners were asking too much for the property. Or maybe there was something wrong with it. Something no one wanted to deal with.

It was all speculation, but as the days warmed, I seriously considered making the call. I found it sad that it seemed to be empty—devoid of life whenever I walked past. The house needed to be loved, and I was the right person to do that. By the time I returned to the apartment, though, I had convinced myself I wasn't ready for that sort of commitment. Buying a house was an unaffordable decision.

Then one day in mid-April, I saw the SOLD sign. I had not predicted the amount of disappointment I felt. Part of me thought the house would wait for me and stay on the market until I was ready. That was silly of me and highly romantic. But then, I romanticized a lot of things.

With the house lost, I stopped walking down that street. I didn't want to see the people who purchased my house—or make friendly conversation with them if I saw them out in the yard. It was easier just to think of it as outside of my life. Yet, I thought of that house still. Whenever I planned something for the future, I thought of the garden I would have planted, the curtains I would have sewn for the kitchen, and the welcome people would feel when they walked into my perfect little home.

My apartment was pleasant, especially with the new furniture Maxine helped me to pick out. It was warm and friendly, but it wasn't home, and had never really felt like one. It was a shelter, and it was safe, but it was utilitarian, too. The wall color was bland, and the carpets were a swirl of brown on brown. Rentals don't offer you personality, they offer you neutrality in spades. I promised myself I would have a few planters on the balcony for flowers and vegetables. A few tomatoes, maybe some carrots and onions. These simple vegetables required little space.

Maxine suggested I get into one of the community garden spots, but I still didn't have transportation. I didn't want to have to rely on the goodness of someone to get to another out-of-the-way place. I had enough of that and hoped the court would soon make Joe comply with the court order to return my vehicle. So far, he had ignored the requests.

CHAPTER NINETY-NINE

I hadn't heard from Jonathon. My weekly calls to him still went unanswered, but I kept calling. It was getting tiring. Despite my frustration with him, I chose not to lash out, even though I think I had every reason to do so. I just put on my cheery voice and left him message after message after message.

Work continued to go well. We successfully removed the jelly roll from our menu, replacing it with the lemon square I gave Beckie for Christmas. She enjoyed them so much that she insisted on adding them to the menu, and I agreed to do so on the condition that we phase out the jelly roll. I still had trouble with them. Marta had a delicate hand with them. Me. Not so much. It always stressed me out the days I had to put one of them together, so it was an appreciable change for me to get them off the menu.

Brad asked Beckie to marry him on Good Friday. They both waited a long time for each other, and I was pleased to see them making a future. They were getting married in the summer. Beckie immediately asked me to make the wedding cake. With Mom and Wally's wedding also taking place in the summer, it was shaping up to be a busy one. I was looking forward to the weddings, to seeing people I loved and cared about moving forward in their lives.

Wally sold his house in Regina—mere weeks after it went on the market. He and Mom flew there for a week to clear the house. They shipped a few of his more treasured belongings to Crawford, where, with Ben's help, we rented a small storage place for them. They disposed of most of Wally's possessions by selling or giving them away. Then he flew back to Arizona and Mom flew to the East Coast.

My sister, diagnosed with stage four stomach cancer, was dying. Her husband had left her, and she was on her own.

Mom moved her into a palliative care unit. She also arranged for Susan's children to step up with visits. Susan's family, fractured because of the drinking and abuse, stayed away. Somehow, Mom convinced them to set aside the bitterness so she could fly back to Arizona for a few weeks to spend time with Wally. She returned to be with Susan at the end.

When Susan died, Mom sent me a plane ticket for

the funeral. Mom's old, fragile, and worn appearance shocked me. It broke my heart to see how this tragedy had aged her.

The funeral turned out to be a quiet memorial. Susan had few friends left, so the service was mostly family. It wasn't a celebration of life, because she had little to celebrate. Dick hadn't even bothered to show up, which was probably for the best. As I was hugging Janice, her eldest daughter, goodbye the morning I was flying back to Alberta, I asked for a bit of her ashes. I told her I wanted to scatter them where we grew up, to bring a part of her home to where she was born. Janice graciously complied, and I tucked the small plastic bag inside my suitcase.

Now that spring was here, I planned to scatter Caleb's ashes at the site of Leah's accident. I wanted to put him at the place where he died, the first time and the last time. I came to believe that the end for Caleb began with his sister's death, and it spiraled until he finally did the unthinkable.

Leaving the East Coast, Mom and I flew to Toronto together. Then she changed planes, going south to Arizona. I flew on to Calgary alone. I took the bus to Calgary to catch the plane a week ago and intended to take the bus back again. As I debarked from the plane, Ben's presence completely caught me by surprise. A jolt of pleasure zinged me upon seeing him.

"How did you know I would be on this plane?" I asked, hugging him in greeting.

"Well, I've been meeting every plane coming from the east since yesterday." He spoke earnestly, but there was a spark of humor in his eyes.

"No, you haven't! Have you?"

He laughed. "No, your mom called me last night. She told me when you'd be arriving."

"But how did she get your number?"

"You shouldn't leave your phone unattended."

"That sneaky old woman." I laughed, secretly pleased.

We walked over to the luggage carousel and waited for my suitcase to slide down. It took several minutes. I stood beside Ben, sneaking glances occasionally. He, too, was sneaking glances at me. I finally bit the bullet and slipped my hand into his. He squeezed my hand and smiled at me. I liked this man.

We stopped for dinner before making the long drive home. When I arrived at the apartment, Ben helped me inside, carrying my suitcase. I stopped in the foyer to pick up my mail. Inside were the usual bills and junk mail items, but there was also a card from my mother. I nearly forgot that my birthday was coming. It was two days away—April 27th.

On the back of the card, in bold block letters, she had written, "CALL ME BEFORE YOU OPEN THIS. DO NOT OPEN UNTIL APRIL 27th!" I laughed as I showed it to Ben in the elevator.

"She really is a bossy old lady."

He nodded in agreement. "She certainly knows

what she wants. But she is also adorable."

Then I laughed. "Really? You think my mother is adorable?"

He laughed and then grew serious as the elevator stopped on my floor. "I think she's a lot like her daughter."

My heart skipped. It beat double time, and my face flushed. I ducked my head as I stepped out of the elevator. Oh God, I wasn't ready for this.

My hands shook as I tried to put my key into the lock. Ben finally took the key from me and slid it easily into the cylinder. He opened the door and stepped back to allow me to enter first. I stepped inside—the stillness of the empty apartment hit me. It was so devoid of life. Ben stepped in behind me and closed the door. I turned toward him, unsure of myself, uncertain of our future. If we had one. He was so decent. But I hadn't completed the divorce process yet. I had so much baggage. I wanted him, but I was terrified at the same time.

I looked up into his face and tried to smile, but I faltered as tears sprang to my eyes. Funny, I hadn't shed one tear for my sister, yet I stood there, weeping for a future that balanced precariously in front of me.

With swift confidence, Ben wrapped me in his arms and kissed me. He was gentle, and the stirrings of longing fluttered deep inside. I kissed him back, my tears making our kiss salty. Then he broke away, hugged me tightly, and stood back. Standing there, separated by inches, the absence of his warmth left me abandoned and empty.

"I understand, Joan, that things are a bit upside down for you. I am not trying to force you to do anything you don't want to do. I will be patient like I said. And I will wait until you are ready to move forward. Joan, I know you have the same desire as I do, but I respect that your life is still uncertain."

Looking into those deep blue eyes, my body ripe for his touch, I did what I promised myself I wouldn't do.

I took his hand and led him down the hallway to my bedroom. I'm not sure who was more surprised, but it was luscious. Later, as I lay nestled under his arm, my head on his chest, I had made the right decision for me. Whether the relationship went forward—or never went beyond this night—our lovemaking fractured Joe's hold on my life. It was the last frontier for the demise of our marriage. I abandoned my feelings for Joe, but my body still belonged to the only man I ever experienced. Ben removed that forever.

Laying there for a long time, unable to sleep, I listened to Ben's gentle rhythm. I ran my hand across his furry chest. He stirred. I stopped for a few seconds, and then I moved lower. He came fully awake. He rolled over and looked deeply into my eyes. I smiled back, reaching toward him. He kissed me, gently, tenderly, then more passionately.

I let myself get lost in the dance.

CHAPTER ONE HUNDRED

Marta was there the morning I came back from the funeral. My body ached from a night with Ben, but it was a delicious ache. One I hadn't experienced since early in my marriage, long before my children were born. Back then, I thought we were still madly in love with each other, before the pressures of family life dropped on top of us.

Marta filled in for me during my absence. I was so grateful to her. She met me at the café with my keys. We entered the storeroom together, just as we had all those months ago. She hung her jacket on the peg next to mine, chatting the whole while about how things had gone. When the dough was rising, she made us a cup of tea. As we settled on the stools in the lunchroom, she reached over to pat my arm.

"So, you are looking well this morning. The time off was good for you, no? You look radiant, like a bride after the honeymoon, no?"

I blushed. "Oh god, is it that obvious?"

She chuckled. "To those who don't know you, it isn't. But to those of us who love you, you cannot hide it."

"I am so embarrassed. This is a novel experience for me. Good grief! I was a virgin on my wedding night, and I've never been with another man until last night."

"It's the cop, no? He is a good man."

"I know, Marta. I'm just not ready for all this, yet the opportunity presented itself and like a cat in heat, I leaped on him."

She laughed. "You are a woman, Liebchen, with needs, physical needs. He is a man. It is natural that you want to take things there. You have feelings for him, no?"

"Of course, he's been a good friend to me. He has been there for a long time, silently waiting for me to get myself together. He didn't pressure me, not one little bit. Then Mom arranged, behind my back, mind you, for him to meet my plane. I was so glad to see him. Then he kissed me for the first time and I just …"

"Jumped his bones." She leaned back and laughed again.

She was enjoying my misery.

"My dear girl, you are in love with him. He is in love with you. There is nothing wrong with what you did. It is natural. Making love is beautiful. My George and I were active in the bedroom right until his passing. We loved one another and we showed it."

"But do I love him, Marta? I don't know. Maybe it's just gratitude. I might not love him the way he loves me. Oh God, what am I going to do?" I laid my head in my hands.

"You are going to stop this. Answer me this, can you see the two of you together across the breakfast table tomorrow?"

I nodded.

"How about next year or the year after?"

I thought about her question.

"How about in five years' time, or ten or twenty? Can you still see him there when you're old and gray, and he's old and bald? How about when you're a doddering senior? Can you imagine him being there? Can you imagine your life without him at any of those stages? You think about it, Liebchen. You think and when you know that your life would be empty if he weren't there, you have your answer."

We went back to work then. Marta helped me settle back into the rhythm of routine. She left before lunchtime, giving me a quick hug, and telling me to call her if I needed her.

"Thank you, Marta. You are a wise woman. Thanks, too, for being here for me while I was gone. You are such a blessing."

She beamed at me. "You are going to be all right,

Liebchen. Be kind to yourself." Then she was gone.

The baking kept me busy. Beckie asked about the trip, offering condolences for my loss again. It was nice to get back into the routine. After work, I walked into my apartment, feeling the emptiness more powerfully than I ever had before. I made myself a cup of tea and wondered if I would feel as empty if I were living in that lovely little house. I had to admit that I would. That little house might be more like a home to me, but it also needed a family. That's probably why I never made an offer. I wasn't a family, all on my own.

Stripping the bed, I washed the sheets and remade the bed before I made supper. I must have picked up my phone half a dozen times, preparing to dial Ben, but each time I put the phone down, the call never made. Finally, just before bedtime, I screwed up my courage and placed the call. It went to voicemail. He must be working. I left a message.

"Hi, Ben, it's Joan. I just wanted to thank you for last night. I hope you're having a good day. Talk soon, okay?"

Hanging up the phone before I blurted out, "I love you," I considered my feelings. Was I. That man scrambled my feelings, making me uncertain what was in my heart. Later, as I crawled into bed, the phone rang. It was Ben.

"Hello?"

"Hi, Joan. I received your message. Is it too late to call?"

"No, I'm not asleep yet."

"Good. I wanted to thank you for last night, too. It was perfect. I know it took a lot for you to take that step."

Blushing, I thought about his chest, arms, and lips on mine. I closed my eyes and took a deep breath. What animal did I unleash yesterday?

"It was nice, wasn't it …" It was a statement, not a question. His voice took me right back to that night, to the feelings, the pleasure, the longing. "I wish you were here."

He chuckled, low and deep. "Me, too," he whispered. "I'll let you go to sleep now. I just wanted to tell you to have sweet dreams."

"Good night, Ben." Again, the words "I love you" hung unspoken in the air.

"Good night, sweet Joan."

I hung up the phone, turned onto my side, and closed my eyes. Breathing deeply, I thought about last night as I drifted off.

CHAPTER ONE HUNDRED ONE

My birthday fell on a Saturday. I made lunch plans with Maxine, and my supper date was with Ben. We hadn't seen each other since the night we slept together. As I prepared for my day, my insides contracted about seeing him. Wanting it to be a perfect day, I reminded myself often that I had nothing to be nervous or anxious about.

The plans for my birthday also included putting Caleb to rest. Leaving a message on Jonathon's phone, I let him know I was going to scatter Caleb's ashes in the late afternoon. I encouraged him to invite his dad, too. If he wanted to be there, he should be. But I cautioned I didn't want trouble. It was simply time to let Caleb go. Placing the box of ashes in a canvas tote made it easy to carry them as I walked to my lunch date. I slipped the tiny bag containing Susan's ashes into it as well.

I forgot about the card my mother sent me until it was too late to open it. Sleeping late, I scrambled to get ready to meet Maxine. The card was bulky. It wasn't just a card inside. I tucked it into my purse as I rushed out the door. I would open it at supper with Ben.

Meeting Maxine at our usual restaurant, The Emerald Tea House, I slipped into my chair, apologizing for being late. She smiled and handed me a card.

"Happy Birthday, Joan." As I took the card, the room grew slightly noisier. A few more members of the knitting group came in. Calls of "Happy Birthday" rang out. Several cameras captured the shocked expression registered on my face.

"You guys!" I beamed happily. "This is so unexpected!"

"We surprised you, didn't we?" Alice smiled at me.

"You sure did!" I looked around at the smiling faces. "I've never had a surprise party before!"

"Never?"

"Nope, never."

"Well, then it's about time you had one."

The waitress came with menus. We each took one and, because I had little time, we ordered quickly. After we took care of that, we relaxed and enjoyed our time. They passed me wrapped packages and cards, and I took my time opening the gifts, thankful for all my many blessings.

The presents were thoughtful—a gift card for the

knitting shop, a recent bestseller, and a necklace with an angel pendant. It was overwhelming. Lunch came and the chatter around the table was light and joyous. We laughed and enjoyed our time together, and it all ended too soon. Ben showed up to collect me for my trip to Freyden. The girls "oohed and aahed" as Ben crossed from the door to our table. I blushed deeply.

Making my goodbyes, I handed some packages to Ben while I hugged everyone, promising I would see them all on Tuesday night at the knitting club. I left, feeling blessed with the new life I had created for myself.

Once inside the vehicle with Ben, an awkwardness overcame me. Breaking the tension, he leaned over and kissed me quickly on the lips before starting the car. I blushed again, certain all the girls saw that kiss because he parked right outside the window. Those girls were going to give me some ribbing about that.

Then we were off. I held the canvas tote on my lap, cradling the ashes like precious cargo. I suppose they were. This was all I had left of my sister and my son. I planned to spread Susan's on my dad's grave. Our first stop was the graveyard.

We had done this so many times now that Ben was surprised when I asked him to join me at the graveside. He exited the car, locked the doors, and followed me down the path. As we walked along, I reached over, took his hand, and walked the last bit together. There was a level of awkwardness introducing him to my daughter, or my daughter to him, I suppose. Talking to a deceased loved one seemed normal, when on your own. Talking to them in the presence of another felt stiff and unnatural. But I did it anyway. I told Leah it was my birthday and shared my plans with her. I told her I hoped her brother Jonathon would be there and maybe even her dad would have finally let down his anger enough to make his peace with what had happened. Ben stood silently off to the side, letting me do what I needed to do.

I took some of Caleb's ashes and poured them near the headstone. Then I walked several rows over and spilled all of Susan's ashes on my dad's grave with a handful of Caleb's. When I finished, I stood, and Ben and I walked back to the car together.

We arrived at the bridge minutes later. I hadn't been there since Leah's death. I saw the white crosses standing with their ragged decorations still visible. This was where Caleb had ended his life. A deep sadness dropped onto my shoulders. No one else was there. Ben parked, and I exited the car, bringing the box of Caleb's ashes with me. I handed my bag to Ben, then walked over to the crosses and thought about how there really ought to be four. But Joe put these crosses there, so asking for another two was probably expecting too much.

I stood for a minute, letting thoughts of Caleb surround me. Glancing at my watch, I noted the time. In my message, I told Jonathon four o'clock. It was nearly four now. The disappointment rose. I just didn't know how to get through to him. Then I heard a vehicle coming. I looked up.

What I saw was surprising.

My red Jeep was coming down the road toward me. Unable to see who was driving, I also didn't understand what that meant.

Another vehicle followed behind.

Joe's truck.

Not Jonathon's truck—Joe's truck.

CHAPTER ONE HUNDRED TWO

Both vehicles pulled up and parked on the opposite side of the road. Joe walked around to the front of my jeep to join Jonathon and Debbie. Jonathon walked to the back door and opened it. When he turned around, he was holding a tiny bundle. A baby! Tears sprang to my eyes, and my vision blurred. I blinked, but the tears kept coming.

Jonathon crossed the road, carrying the tiny bundle in his arms. My heart ached. New life. It had happened while I was in exile. They kept this tiny miracle from me, and I wanted to rage at its unfairness. I wanted to yell at Jonathon for being so cruel to me. I stiffened under the weight of my emotions.

"Hi, Mom," Jonathon said quietly and with a great deal of humbleness in his voice. "Before we get started,

I want to tell you how sorry I am for what has happened since Caleb's death. I have been wrong in how I treated you." He paused and looked at Debbie.

She nodded, silently encouraging him to continue.

He looked back at me. "I was so angry at Caleb for what he did. I couldn't believe he acted so cowardly. It made me sick to think we were brothers." He gulped, struggling with his emotions. "Because of that, I took Dad's side against you. It made little sense to me—you forgave him so quickly and gave him a funeral he didn't deserve. Because you spent good money on him. I was angry with you, too."

I stared at him, amazed that he felt that way.

He continued. "Debbie kept urging me to make peace with you, but you know how stubborn I can be. She worked hard to get me to see things differently and I can tell you that this caused a great deal of grief in our home, too. Debbie never gave up on me. She made me listen to every one of your messages. That's why she never answered the phone. She wanted me to hear your words for myself."

I looked over at my daughter-in-law—she had tears in her eyes. "I'm so sorry, Joan. It was the most difficult thing to do. You do not know how often I wanted to pick up and tell you how sorry I was about how things were going, but I could not."

I should have been grateful for her confession, but I was angry. I saw her silence as a betrayal. If she answered just once—picked up the phone and told me I had an ally—it would have made my struggle easier. Instead, she left me swinging in the wind for months. Now she was confessing her compassion. I wanted to slap her.

"Mom, Debbie told me every single day since you left to call you. I refused. You had chosen Caleb over me. And, not Caleb, my brother, but Caleb, the murderer. I was incapable of wrapping my mind around what you were doing."

Unable to speak, I stood there staring at him. I was struggling with my emotions. I didn't want this day to be about Jonathon or me. It was supposed to be about Caleb, but that seemed impossible now.

"We were going to tell everyone about the baby in November, you know, have a family dinner and a big announcement. We wanted to ensure she was far along before we told anyone. But we didn't get the chance. And since I was angry with you, how could I tell you? I didn't want to talk to you because I didn't understand. As Debbie's pregnancy progressed, her pleas that I call you became insistent. I remained resolute, until this little bundle came into the world. The moment I held her in my arms, I understood that what you did all those months ago was normal and was what having a child is all about. It came to me, and totally broke me. I bawled like a baby that day. I was in Crawford, so I stopped by your apartment, but you weren't home. Then I stopped by Jack's Diner and learned you were out east. It seemed like a sign then to wait and tell you on your birthday, to bring you the best present we had … your granddaughter."

I looked at the sleeping baby. I stepped closer and pulled back the blanket partially covering her face. She was so beautiful.

"Would you like to hold her?"

I nodded. Ben stepped forward and took the box from my hands. Then Jonathon laid the little angel in my arms. I cuddled her close, moving away from her parents, cooing into her ear, taking in her smell, the preciousness of having her in my arms. I had taken several steps away when I turned back and spoke for the first time.

"What's her name?"

Jonathon looked at Debbie. "We named her Leah Joan."

I wept then.

I let go of my anger and resentment and clung to the tiny bundle in my arms. She was the future, the new beginning. Several minutes later, she stirred. I returned to my son, who stood with his arm around his wife. I handed the baby back to her mother. Then I stepped in front of my son and hugged him.

He hugged me back, whispering, "I'm sorry, Mom. I'm so, so sorry," over and over in my ear. We rocked and hugged for a long time. When we parted, we were both wiping our faces. Debbie, too, was crying as she rocked her baby.

CHAPTER ONE HUNDRED THREE

I had forgotten Joe was even there until that moment. Looking around, I saw Ben leaning against the hood of his vehicle. His expression was unreadable. One of those police tactics—I thought. Then I spotted Joe standing awkwardly off to the left, away from us, but near the crosses. He had on a clean cream-colored shirt and jeans. He was wearing a bollard tie. This was his casual "dress-up outfit." He looked uncomfortable, but he was there. In his hand, he carried his Bible.

I turned away from Jonathon and stepped toward him. "Joe?"

He cleared his throat. "Hi, Joan."

I couldn't believe he was so cordial. He'd been so nasty to me the last time we spoke—the same day I last saw him. He looked smaller than I remembered him.

Smaller and less threatening.

"Thank you for inviting me. I want to apologize for everything. It was not right—what I did."

"Why, Joe? Why did you do that to me? All I wanted was to give Caleb something, to take care of him."

"I know." He raked his hands through his thick hair. The gesture made me notice how many grays had sneaked in since we lived as man and wife.

My anger rose again. "You know?" I hissed. "Then, why, Joe, tell me why you treated me with such disdain and hatred? Why did you make me feel like my feelings didn't matter? Oh God, you are such an asshole."

Joe looked at me—his eyebrows raised high. I never raised my voice in anger toward him nor swore. I was immediately remorseful.

"I'm sorry, I shouldn't have said that." There was a pause as we stared at each other. "You still haven't answered me, Joe. Why?"

"Well," he replied. "I guess I was angry. Caleb did an unthinkable thing. It wasn't right. At first, that's all I saw, but after you left, I remembered how I never gave him a break, how I tried so hard to make a man of him. That made me angry. I wanted him to be a man like his brother. I couldn't accept him for who he was before this happened. In a way—I was responsible for what he did, and I took that out on you. I didn't want to admit it to myself."

Joe was pacing now, moving back and forth. He

took a deep breath.

“When you left—that annoyed me. I thought for sure that you’d be back. But you didn’t come back, and I felt helpless. My pride wouldn’t let me tell you I needed you. My anger wanted to punish you for leaving me, so I took back your vehicle, hoping that would make you see sense. It didn’t work, either. I sent divorce papers. Nothing I did worked.”

I couldn’t believe this was the man I married all those years ago. He never spoke about his feelings like this.

He continued. “After you stopped at the house that day, New Year’s Day, I was going to explode with all the turmoil going on in my head, so I called Pastor Mark. I’ve been seeing him for counseling since then. He helped me see what was going on, sort out my feelings, and forgive the unforgivable. He’s been good at helping me see I needed to make things right. But I didn’t know how.” He turned back to face me.

“Then Jonathon told me about today. And I had to come. Wait here.” He moved back across the road and stood on the bumper. From the bed of the truck, he pulled up a white cross. He set it on the ground. Then reached in and pulled out a second one. Tears welled up again.

Joe picked up the two crosses and moved back with a cross in each hand to where I stood. Decorations festooning the crosses represented both Caleb and Andrea.

"This is six months past time," Joe said. "But better late than never. Jonathon?"

Jonathon left Debbie's side, ran to Joe's truck, and picked up a post pounder. He brought it back to where we stood and together the two of them planted both crosses where Caleb had taken a life and lost his own. Debbie and the baby joined us as the crosses entered the ground.

I had forgotten about Ben by this point. Reeling from the many surprises that came my way, I focused on the crosses. I was still in shock, still trying to come to grips with the words that contradicted the actions I experienced. It was like living in the Twilight Zone.

When the crosses were in place, I said, "I guess it's time to spread the ashes."

I had a moment of panic then, not sure what I had done with them. Turning around, I saw Ben leaning against his vehicle, looking away from us, trying to give us privacy. A huge pang of guilt hit me for what he must be going through. He probably felt unwanted and forgotten. I walked over to him.

"Sorry, Ben, I did not know …" I gestured to the vehicles across the road from us.

"I gathered that. I was going to leave, but I wanted to make sure you were okay before I did that. Is he trying to talk you into coming home? Is that what this is all about?"

Taken aback at his suggestion, it had never crossed my mind that Joe was asking for a second chance.

"He had mentioned nothing to me." My stomach flipped over. What did this mean? I looked back over my shoulder at where my family stood. Joe was watching intently, his expression unreadable but hard.

I looked back at Ben—he was holding the box of ashes. He handed them to me without my asking. They were heavier than expected.

"Do you want me to wait here?"

Again, I looked over my shoulder. "Do you mind?" I asked when I turned back to him.

"Do what you need to do, Joan. I'm not going anywhere. We have a date when this is over."

CHAPTER ONE HUNDRED FOUR

My heart pounded—it thumped in my belly. I was terrified and unsure, knowing I wanted my family back, but I was not sure that included Joe. Could I have my son and granddaughter if I brought Ben into the equation? I had been apprehensive about moving on right from the start. Now I understood why. I should have listened to myself. I said nothing in response. Taking the ashes, I moved back to the crosses—to my family, my heart heavy and forlorn.

I opened the box and removed the bag of ashes.

"How do you want to proceed?" Jonathon asked.

"Oh, well, I don't know. I thought I was going to be on my own." All three of them looked humbled by my comment. "So, maybe we each take a handful and then share a memory of Caleb, a good one, and scatter the ashes around his cross?"

"That sounds good," Joe agreed. "And I'd like to read a passage from the Bible, too."

I nodded.

"I'll go first since I had the least time with him," Debbie offered. She handed baby Leah to Jonathon before reaching into the bag and taking a handful.

"So, my favorite memory was the night of our wedding. The day had been busy, and I was feeling a little stressed with it all." She looked over at Jonathon and smiled. "The wedding had gone off without a hitch, but there was still a lot of stuff to get through. The reception, the dance. I wanted it all to be so perfect." She smiled at all of us then.

"Do you remember the toasts? Caleb and Leah had jointly welcomed me to the family?" We nodded in unison.

"Well, what you don't know is that shortly before he gave the speech, he came to me and gave me a very different version."

"Really? What did he say?" Her story piqued Jonathon's curiosity as if this was the first time he had heard this story.

"Well, what he said aloud to the crowd was quite touching. You know, telling me I was welcome and that you were lucky. What he didn't say were the more personal sentiments."

We stood there, waiting. No one spoke—we simply waited for her to share her memory.

"Now, I'll probably paraphrase because it's been a long time since I heard these words, so here I go. He said—that all his life, he had wanted to grow up to be like Jonathon, that he'd never quite achieved that. He expressed his pride in his brother and emphasized that above all, he desired our marriage to be blessed and happy.

"Then he said that when I first dated Jonathon, he'd watched me closely. He said he did that because he wanted to ensure I was the right woman. I knew that I had what Jonathon needed in a wife. He said his observations gave him insight and wanted me to know only one thing. I was perfect in every way, except I had to learn to be equal with my husband, and that being equally yoked was more than believing the same. We had to pull together to get through things. I hadn't taken those words well, believe me. But when he died, and we struggled with the test God placed before us, I saw he was right. I think it strengthened our marriage, and I will always be grateful for that."

She paused and sighed before continuing. "Comparing those words to how his life ended, though, I have a hard time believing it was the same kid, you know?" She looked at me for confirmation.

I didn't tell her that the Caleb of the night of her marriage differed from the Caleb in the car that night several months ago. He'd lost his sister, and, in my heart, I know he blamed himself for not stopping Leah from leaving the dance. I know I had told him he was not at fault more than once, but the shadow over his head never lifted. Even though he sometimes seemed like his old self, I recognize that in some ways he was not. But I stayed silent. Maybe one day I might tell her, but not today.

Looking up to the sky, she added, "Thank you, Caleb, wherever you are, for your wisdom back then. I miss you." Taking her handful of ashes, she sprinkled them liberally around the base of the cross Joe made for Caleb.

We stood then, for a moment, no one moving—as we lost ourselves in our private thoughts.

Jonathon passed the baby back to Debbie before he stepped forward. He scooped up a handful of ashes and then stood back. He dropped his head forward, took a deep breath, and spoke.

"My favorite memory was when Caleb started school. He was so little, and I was a giant next to him. I was four years older, of course, already in grade five. He was nervous as we waited for the bus. Then he did something he didn't do very often. He reached up and he took my hand." Tears flowed then, rolling in rivers down his cheeks. Holding baby Leah, Debbie laid her hand on his back, between his shoulder blades.

"My first instinct was to pull away and tell him he was a baby. I looked down into his eyes, and I saw his fear. So, I just squeezed his hand and held on."

A sob escaped, and I cried along with my son. I never heard the story before.

"There were so many times when we were growing up, fighting and at odds with each other. How many times since he died have I wished for those times back and done them differently? But the guys at school gave me so much grief that I never let him in again. I treated him like a baby. I pushed him away, letting the opinion of my peers keep my brother at arm's length."

Jonathon looked around the group then, tears still streaming down his face. "He deserved a better brother than the one he had. And that is my most cherished memory. When I close my eyes, I can still see his perfect little face looking at me. It makes me sad and happy at the same time."

He stepped over to the cross. "Caleb, forgive me for not being the brother you needed. I love you still and miss you, too. Be at peace."

CHAPTER ONE HUNDRED FIVE

Again, we stood silently, letting Jonathon's message sink into our hearts.

Then I held the bag out to Joe. He looked at me but didn't move to take a handful.

"Are you not ready? Do you want me to go first?"

He gulped. "I don't know if I can do this at all. I wasn't …" He broke off.

"Of course, you can do it," I encouraged. "But I'll go first and give you some time to think."

I reached into the bag and took a handful. Holding the plastic bag in my left hand and the handful of ashes in my right, I moved away to the cross.

"Caleb, first off, I love you. I've always loved you, and I will always love you. You were a treasure I adored and cherished from the moment I realized your presence.

I had such hopes and dreams for your future, and I'm sorry they will never come true.

"My most cherished memory? I have so many, but if I had to choose one, it would be the Christmas you were in grade two. Do you remember that Christmas? It was the year that you made me a Popsicle stick picture frame. It was spray-painted gold, and inside, you put a picture of the two of us, taken at the fair the summer before you started school. You and I were riding the carousel. You were aboard the fierce-looking gray horse, and you were laughing. That was an awesome day, too.

"But the picture was the best because it told me that nearly two years later, that day was still special to you as well. I loved that present, and I loved you to bits." I looked around the group. Only Joe wasn't crying. "I wish you were here, Caleb, that you'd never done this terrible thing. That you were still part of us. But I know that's impossible, so I release you to find peace wherever and however you can." I poured my handful of ashes around the base of the cross. Then I poured a second handful around Leah's cross, and finally, I poured a third around Andrea's. When I was done, I stepped back and held the bag out to Joe.

This time, Joe took a handful. He stepped over to the cross and bowed his head. Instead of sharing a memory, though, he prayed. "Lord, thank you for giving us Caleb, and I ask your forgiveness for not cherishing him as I should have. As his father, I thought I was doing the right thing by trying to change him. He needed to be strong, not sensitive. His gifts were not my idea of manly, but I didn't seek your will. I made my decisions based on my beliefs and drove a deep wedge between us. He never came to me for advice. He avoided me, and I mocked his accomplishments. I ask your forgiveness for that, Lord."

There was a long pause, and I wondered if he would say anything more. He finally looked at me. Then he bowed his head again. "This is my favorite memory of you, Caleb. You were fifteen or sixteen. Jonathon had gone on a church mission to build that orphanage in Mexico. While he was away, I reluctantly made you my right-hand man and constantly nagged you because you didn't match up to your brother's performance. Sure, you were thorough, and there were no complaints, but I did anyway."

I knew the story. I cried.

"So, it was early March, maybe late February. Calving season, anyway. There was the young heifer, a first-time calver. You were out there on a chilly night, watching her, and it was taking too long. Then, you noticed the calf was breaching. I'd shown you a hundred times how to use the calf pullers, but you seemed unable to get them to work, so you just grabbed those hooves and pulled. That heifer dragged you around the pen, but you refused to let go. The calf finally came free—you fell to the ground, and the calf dropped right on top of you, breaking your nose. But you didn't let that stop you.

You cleaned out the calf's mouth and nose and rubbed him until he was up and moving, and his mom took over."

Joe cleared his throat. "So, I gave you that calf because I was proud of you. Then, come the fall, you refused to sell him, so when you went to school, I loaded him up with the other calves. You came home, and, well, you weren't happy."

Looking around at us, Joe smiled sadly. "You're wondering why this is my favorite memory, aren't you? It was not a merry time, for sure. But when I look back at all I put you through and how often I stepped on you—that day, you didn't back down. You told me off. Okay, I was quite angry with you then, but in retrospect, I realized you were the man I wanted you to be. I'm just sorry it took your leaving to make me see what you were."

Bending low, Joe poured his handful of ashes around the cross. I still had lots of ashes left, so when he was done, I took the bag and poured out the rest of them around both crosses. Then, I shook the bag to make sure there was nothing left. When it was over, Joe put his hand on my shoulder and moved in for a hug. Then Jonathon joined us, and the three of us stood there, wrapped in one another's arms, crying for what we lost.

I finally broke away and stepped back, gulping for cold air. My eyes were puffy—my nose was stuffy. I looked at Jonathon and Joe. Joe smiled at me, a sad smile. The reading from the Bible no longer mattered.

"Thanks again, Joan. I appreciate you letting me be here, especially since I didn't deserve it. Will you walk with me for a bit? I have some things I want to tell you."

CHAPTER ONE HUNDRED SIX

I nodded, and we moved down the road across the bridge. Joe had his hands in his back pockets. We hadn't gone far when he spoke.

"I like your hair."

I reached up and touched it, then blushed. "Thank you."

We walked a little farther in silence.

"First off, I want to apologize again. Jonathon drove your Jeep here. It's yours to take. I'm sorry that I took it from you. It was juvenile and selfish of me. I was just trying to get you to come home. It didn't work, though. You're one tough cookie."

He chuckled and then glanced over at me. "You're not laughing."

"No, I'm not laughing, Joe. You were so

disrespectful. I've had to rely on the kindness of friends to get to Leah's grave. Thankfully, I lived close to the café, so walking to work was an option, but taking my vehicle was cruel."

"I know, I know." He raised his hands in surrender. "I'm saying sorry now, but I can't go back and undo it."

Nodding, I said nothing else.

"I know you didn't want the divorce, and again, I'm the one to blame here. I also know that you have asked for nothing in the settlement, but Jonathon thinks you deserve something." He stopped and took my hand. We stood there facing each other. "I am struggling with this because I'd rather stop the divorce altogether. I want you to come home where you belong, Joan."

What he said was a surprise, given all that had happened since I left. I stood there looking at the man I spent twenty-seven years with. He was a man who had been tough as nails but whom I had promised to love, honor, and cherish until death do us part. Looking back down the road to where we started, I saw Ben standing there, leaning against his vehicle, watching us intently. I saw my son moving the baby seat from the Jeep, securing it in Joe's truck. Debbie was sitting in the truck, the door open. She was probably feeding the baby, but I couldn't see that from there.

I longed to be part of that world, to be only a few hundred feet from that darling baby. To hold her every day, to watch her grow up. That would mean forgiving Joe and dealing with my mother, who wouldn't be happy with that decision, although maybe she and Joe could work out their differences now that Joe seemed to repent for his sins.

What about my job, my new friends, and the knitting group? I thought about Ben and our night together.

"Say something, Joan, please."

"I'm sorry, Joe. This hit me right out of left field. Part of me wants to take you up on your offer because of baby Leah. But a lot of water has gone under the bridge. I don't know if what we had is still there."

"It is, Joan, at least for me."

"Well, I'm confused, Joe. With everything I've had to deal with these past months, not to mention I have a relationship with my mom again, I don't know if I can come back. There's my job, which I love, by the way, and new friends. I've built a life in the city, and I don't know if I can be happy going back to being just a wife."

"You could get a job in Freyden," Joe suggested.

"I suppose I could. Can I think about it?"

I saw a flicker of anger cross his face. "Sure, think about it. I'll wait to talk to the lawyer about the divorce and settlement."

"Joe, I don't want your money. I know it will all go to Jonathon. If I decide not to come back … let's just wait to see, okay?"

"Okay." I heard the disappointment in his voice. "You know, I am really sorry."

"I know, Joe. I promised I would think about it.

Please give me some time. I deserve that much, don't I?"

"I'm just worried that you won't, though. You'll go back to the city and forget."

"Forget?" I snapped. "Forget? How could I ever forget? You and I had twenty-seven years together. We have …" I longed to say three children but choked on those words. "We have a son and a perfect little grandchild. I can't forget. But like I said, I need time. I have a lot to think about."

"It's him, isn't it?" Joe said, nodding toward Ben, his expression hard and unfathomable.

"Don't go there, Joe. He is a friend. He's been good to me and helped me a lot. Do not make this about him."

"I'm sorry. I'm sorry," he said, his voice challenging and not remorseful. He ran a hand through his hair again. His eyes reflected his desperation for me to jump back into his world. His animosity toward Ben allowed me to see he wasn't a changed man. How long would it be before he would argue about my going to work? Or be angry with my friends.

We walked back. I went to Ben. "Joe is giving me back my vehicle. So, I guess I will follow you to the restaurant."

"What changed his mind?"

"Well, he's remorseful, I guess."

"Did he ask you to come back?"

"Yes, he did."

"What did you say?"

"I told him I need some time because I have a new

life, and I'm not sure I'm ready to go back. I need to think."

"Okay. So, we're meeting at the usual place then?"

"Yes, if you go now, I'll be right behind you."

CHAPTER ONE HUNDRED SEVEN

Ben climbed into his vehicle and navigated to the road, disappearing across the bridge. He left a cloud of dust in his wake. I stood watching him go, feeling sadness wrap itself around me. So many options, and my fear that someone was going to get hurt, shivered through my thoughts.

Walking back across the road, I found Jonathon and Joe standing outside the truck. Debbie was still sitting inside. Baby Leah was in her carrier, fast asleep. Disappointed that I could not hold her one more time, I sighed.

Jonathon held the keys out to me. "Here you go. Dad made sure it had a full tank of gas. We renewed the tags and the insurance, so you're good to go."

"You can always come back to the farm, Joan." Joe

watched me from the side. "If I picked up a cake and some ice cream at the grocers, we could celebrate your birthday."

"Thanks, Joe, but I have plans."

"With the cop?"

"Yes, with Ben."

"So, he is your boyfriend." Joe sputtered—his voice hard.

I shivered as the familiar tone washed over me. "No, he's just a friend. He's the one who's helped me to get to Leah's grave regularly. He's shown a great deal of compassion for me, so please don't disrespect him."

Joe said nothing, but I saw his jaw clench. He wasn't happy and was struggling to keep his peace. He might have softened, but I worried he would revert to his old ways should I return for good. Glad for today—because there would never be more.

"I will be in touch, Joe, as soon as I decide." Walking over to Jonathon, I kissed his cheek, hugged him briefly, and then stepped back. "Take care, Jonathon, and don't be a stranger, okay? Call me."

"I will, Mom." He stepped toward me and hugged me again. "I will ensure you get your settlement if you decide not to come home. After all, I've got the money," he whispered conspiratorially.

Stepping back, I looked into his face, understanding that all this generosity was not Joe's doing. It all came from Jonathon. He was the one I had to thank for any settlement funds coming my way and possibly for my vehicle being given back to me.

I moved to the truck. Debbie slipped out and hugged me tightly. I was still angry with her, but she did what she did because she loved Jonathon. I needed to work through my feelings and let them go, but it would take some time. In the meantime, I hugged her.

"Take care of my granddaughter and my son."

She stepped back and nodded at me. Tears swam in her eyes. I hugged her again. Then I looked into the tiny little face, sleeping soundly in the back of the truck. I ran my finger down her cheek, across her pouty lips, and under her chin. She squirmed a little but didn't wake up. I exhaled. New life, new beginnings. It was all going the right way.

I left them then, climbed into my Jeep, and started the engine. I looked around, thankful to have my wheels back again. Joe pulled out ahead of me, honking once as he drove past. I turned the other way, taking the same road Ben had traveled several minutes ago. Driving again after all these months seemed weird, but it didn't take long to feel as if I had never stopped. I hit the highway, cranking the radio up but didn't sing along.

It wasn't the day to sing. At least, not yet.

CHAPTER ONE HUNDRED EIGHT

I was nearly back in the city when my cell phone went off. I answered the call—it was my mom.

"Hold on, Mom, I'm driving. I need to pull over."

"You're driving?" she asked as soon as I parked at a historical marker pull-out along the highway.

"Yes. It's been quite a day so far." I ran my free hand through my hair. "I don't even know where to start."

"Well, start at the beginning. That's always a good place."

She was aware of the plan to scatter Caleb's ashes. We had talked about it on the plane to Toronto. Mom encouraged me to do it on my birthday instead of Mother's Day, which had been my plan. I told her about Jonathon, Debbie, and Joe coming and breaking down when I mentioned the baby, Leah Joan.

"You have a grandchild?"

"I know. They kept it a secret. Apparently, Jonathon came by while I was with you in Newfoundland. Then they showed up to surprise me on my birthday."

"Well, I'll be damned!" There was some silence as we both grew pensive. "So why has he not talked to you all these months?"

"The usual reasons—guilt, anger, resentment. Jonathon says that when he held his daughter for the first time, he understood why I did the things I did and that he had to forgive me and ask for my forgiveness. The part of this that bothers me the most is Debbie, and maybe she's a convenient scapegoat. But all these months, she never once picked up the phone, even though she knew it was me. She says she wanted Jonathon to hear my messages firsthand, but her actions seem unforgivable."

"Well, it's callous and mean-spirited at best but not unforgivable, surely?"

I laughed. "You're right, Mom. It's not unforgivable, but I am furious at her."

"So, how was Joe during the ceremony? Did he take part, or was he an angry bystander?"

"That's the most confusing part of this whole thing. He was decent and nice, bringing handmade crosses for Caleb and Andrea. He acted repentant. When we had finished the ceremony, he wanted to talk to me, and we went for a little walk. He told me he wanted to stop the divorce. He wanted me to come home again."

"You didn't agree to that, did you?"

"No, I didn't. I told him I needed to think about things. He said that if I still wanted to get a divorce, he wouldn't stand in my way, and he would make sure I got my share. He gave me back my vehicle."

"What's the catch?"

"I don't know if there's a catch. He seemed genuine about everything, but I am concerned that he will revert to form once he has me back under his roof."

"Was Ben there?"

"Oh, Mom, this must have been horrible for him. He stayed apart from us. He stood near his vehicle, and he must have felt like he was unwelcome. I didn't handle his presence very well, forgetting he was there when we were in the thick of things. When Joe gave me back my vehicle, I sent him away. I'm meeting him at the restaurant, but I do not know what I will tell him."

"Do you have to tell him anything?"

"Well, I don't want to lead him on."

"So, you're going back to Joe?"

"No, I never said that. I don't know what I'm going to do."

"Well, if you're not going back to Joe, you don't have to end things with Ben. Do you?"

"I guess not, although technically, things haven't gone too far with us." There was no way I was telling my mother that I already slept with Ben.

"Well, he's a nice man who seems to like you. He

jumped at the chance to meet your plane when I called him."

"Yeah, about that. You could have told me. His presence there surprised me."

"Are you telling me you're angry with me about that?"

"No, Mom, I'm not angry. I was just a little taken aback. It was a pleasant surprise."

"So, you have some big decisions ahead of you, Joan. And I'm afraid I will add to that a little."

"What do you mean?"

"It's obvious you haven't opened your card, so open it already."

I had forgotten about Mom's present. Pulling my purse toward me, I dug into the depths to find the envelope. I tore it open and pulled out the card. The front of the card offered a generic birthday message. Inside was a folded piece of paper. Pulling it out, I read the card. Then I opened the folded sheets. Taped to the sheet were two keys. It took me a minute to understand what I was reading.

"This is a rental form. I don't get it."

"Yes, Joan, it's a rental form. You know that little house you liked so much, the white one with the green shutters?"

"Of course, but it is no longer for sale."

"I know. Wally bought it."

"Wally bought it?" I struggled to understand what was going on.

"Well, you were always talking about that house and no matter how much encouragement I gave you to call the realtor, you never did. So, when Wally sold his house in Regina, he needed to invest that money somewhere. What better way than in another property."

"Okay, but what does this have to do with me?"

"Well, we had someone look at the house, make sure it was sound, and then Wally bought it. Since you were uncertain about your ability to afford a house, he set up the rental idea, but it's rent to own. Wally is the mortgage holder, and you own the house. It's all legal."

I flipped to the second page. Attached was the legal contract.

"What you have are just copies. The real ones are all ready for you at Brad's office. All you need to do is sign them and you can move in."

I sat there, stunned. This was so out of left field. I had never considered that the lovely little house would become mine once I saw the SOLD sign on the realtor's post. I'd let that dream go, and now it was firmly back in my lap.

"So, it would seem, my dear, that you have some big decisions ahead of you."

"What if I don't take the house?"

"Then you don't take the house."

"But won't Wally be angry with me? He's gone to a lot of trouble to set this up for me. He's invested his money and …"

"Wally is a smart man. He will either rent the house

to someone else or sell it."

"It sat on the market so long—he'll never get his money back."

"Well, you let us worry about that. This cannot factor into your decision. You need to figure out what's best for Joan. I cannot tell you that. I know what I want to see happen, but I cannot tell you what to do."

"Please, tell me what to do!"

Mom laughed. "You'd hate me for it, so no. I won't."

"Oh, God." My phone beeped. "Mom, I need to go. My phone is going to die. I'll call you later."

"Happy birthday, Joan. I'm glad you've had a good day."

"Thanks, Mom. I love you. Bye."

CHAPTER ONE HUNDRED NINE

Hanging up, I noticed I was seriously late for my supper date now. Would Ben even be waiting for me when I arrived at the restaurant? I needed to call him, but my phone was dying. I leaned over and popped open the glove compartment, looking for the charger I used to have in the car. It lay curled on top of the owner's manual.

I pulled it out and plugged it into the port. Once connected, I dialed Ben's number. It rang several times before going to voicemail. My heart sank. Rubbing my hands over my face, I struggled to keep it together. I put the vehicle in gear, checked the highway, and pulled into the lane, picking up speed. As I neared the city, my cell phone rang.

I did not look at the caller—hoping it was Ben. It

was.

"Hello?"

"Hi, I see you tried to call me. I was waiting at the restaurant, but you didn't show."

"I'm so, so sorry, Ben."

"Why? What is going on?"

"Lots, that's what. Look, I'm driving, too, so if you still want to meet for supper …" I looked at the clock. It was nearing seven thirty already. "Well, a late supper, I guess. But if you want to meet, then I will tell you all about it."

"Well, we've lost our reservation at Houlihan's. Let's meet at Boston Pizza. The one on the south side?"

"Sure, fine. That works—I'm about ten minutes away."

"Okay, I'll meet you there."

Hanging up, I struggled to rein in my emotions that were all over the place. I did not know what I wanted or where I wanted to go. The tug of my family was strong. But I was also facing a powerful future. I could go any way I wanted, and it wouldn't be wrong.

I just didn't know what I wanted, and I didn't know if I really trusted Joe.

CHAPTER ONE HUNDRED TEN

I made it to the restaurant before Ben. I went in, allowing the hostess to seat me at a table near the back. Ben came in a few minutes later. Watching him walk across the restaurant, my heart beat a little faster. He was a handsome man, tall, fit, and formidable. I saw a few women turn to watch him, and it filled me with pride that he was coming to join me.

He bent down and kissed me on the lips before sitting across from me. I watched him settle in, wondering how he was feeling and what he was thinking.

"So, you've had an amazing day."

I nodded, taking a sip of my ice water. "It's been one for the record books, and there's more you aren't aware of."

"You're talking about the house?"

"You know about that?" I sat back in my chair, staring at Ben as if he was a stranger.

"Yes, I know about the house. Your mother is a very influential woman, isn't she? What she wants, she gets. She had me get the realtor's information for her, and then I checked out the house for them."

"And you never said a word?"

"She swore me to secrecy. It was her surprise, not mine."

"Wow." I sat back in my chair. "Wow."

"Are you upset with me over this?"

"I don't know if I'm upset. Life has thrown me more than one curve ball today, and I'm unsure what to do about it. Joe, Jonathon, the new baby. The house and the fact that you've colluded with my mother to shape my future, well, it is unsettling."

"Look, Joan. I can agree that all that happened today is overwhelming—however, it has nothing to do with me. All I did was help your mother. There was no collusion here. I didn't tell her about the house or influence her to buy it for you. If you need me to be the bad guy because you don't want to upset the new relationship with your mother, then I have broad shoulders. But I'd prefer it if you didn't point your finger at me." He paused, staring at me. "Besides, her buying you a house here in Crawford isn't convenient for me. In case you forgot, I don't live here."

I blew out my breath. He was right. I was taking my

frustration out on him.

"I'm sorry. Let's not talk about this now. Let's just have an enjoyable meal and celebrate my birthday. That's why we're here, after all."

We placed our orders, and both ordered lasagna—Ben with meatballs, me without. We kept the conversation light. The server and her pals came around and sang Happy Birthday to me. Free dessert was the reward for my public humiliation.

When the meal was over, Ben paid the bill and walked me to my vehicle. "I guess this means that our trips to the cemetery are over. You have your vehicle back now."

"I guess it does, although I must tell you again how much I appreciate all you've done for me. Honestly, you've been such a blessing."

"I'd like to be more, Joan."

"I know."

Running my fingers over his bristled cheek, I smiled into his eyes. He grabbed my hand, kissing the palm. Wanting to invite him back to the apartment, I closed my eyes. I wanted to feel his body on mine, but I also had an offer from my husband that needed consideration. Taking this man to bed was only going to cloud the issue. I groaned as Ben pulled me into his arms. He kissed me tenderly. Melting, the flame of desire erupted—my body was on fire. I kissed him back, pushing myself against him, feeling his desire.

I pulled back, pushing Ben away. Stepping away

from his embrace, I patted my hair.

"I can't do this right now. Oh God, how I want to, but I need to figure out what's best for everyone."

"All you need to do, Joan, is to do what is best for you. No one else matters."

"True, and since it may not fall in your favor, I think that making love with you, as much as I want to, won't help me. I need a clear head and a clear heart."

I looked up into his face and saw his sadness. He was uncertain that he would be the victor, and I gave him no assurances. Moving in, I kissed him lightly.

"Thanks so much for supper, Ben. I will be in touch."

Then I opened the Jeep door and climbed inside. Tears sprang to my eyes, and I kept my face averted so that Ben wouldn't see them. I backed out of the parking spot and headed to my apartment.

CHAPTER ONE HUNDRED ELEVEN

At home, I made a cup of tea and sat in the living room, trying to come to terms with my thoughts. I finally pulled out some paper and made a list. The pros and cons of the choices as they lay before me.

Going back to Joe would give me my family back. Well—my fractured family. The best thing about it was the baby. There was no guarantee that I would spend as much time with her as I wanted, even if I lived with Joe. Being with Joe would be familiar and normal. What I seemed incapable of getting over was his reducing me to the role of housekeeper.

Although he was repentant at the ceremony today and admitted he was getting help, my going home might stop that. He'd think he won me back, and life would return to normal. I'd be the maid, the cook, and the housekeeper. What about the changes I've made? Would I have to change back? Would I have to give up who I'd become to live in that house again?

Maybe I was selling Joe short? He'd been my husband and lover for over half my life. He was familiar, and part of me still loved him. I'd always love him regardless of where it went. Was I convinced he changed? Or was he just trying to sell me a bill of goods? For now, I gave him the benefit of the doubt.

Moving on—I thought about Ben …

I liked him a lot. The newness of our relationship was exciting. I liked his concern for me, and my mother liked him, which was a good thing. I know she would support me going back to Joe, but he'd have to prove he changed for her to accept him in totality.

I wanted Ben physically. Just thinking about him sent my blood racing. I took a deep breath and moved on to the next page.

The house. I still couldn't wrap my head around it. Pulling out the card, I looked at the papers my mother had tucked inside. I saw the keys. Before changing my mind, I tossed the list aside, grabbed my purse and keys, and left the apartment. I needed to see inside that house.

It took me only a moment to get there. I parked on the street and sat there looking at the house. I couldn't believe it might be mine. Sliding out of the Jeep, I sauntered up the front walk. I climbed the three steps and pulled open the screen door. The key slipped into the lock, the tumblers aligned, and the door opened with ease.

Inside, the hardwood floor gleamed brightly at me. The drapes on the front window were too heavy for them—they were from another era. Rich brocade was no longer trendy. That needed to be changed. Walking farther into the house, I went into the kitchen. It was clean and bright, though the cabinets were a little dated. Looking around, I tried to imagine my new furniture in this space. If I painted the cabinets crisp white, attached new handles, and hung some bright curtains over the window—it would be perfect.

Going out the second entry to the kitchen, I stood in a hallway. One way led past the arched living room passage to the front door, and the other led to a bathroom and one bedroom. The windows were large and bright, letting in a lot of sunlight. The closet was much like the ones at the farm—it was not large but adequate. Spinning around in the center of the room, I thought about paint colors. So many possibilities. My imagination swirled as I envisioned.

Heading back toward the kitchen, I took the three steps down to the back door. I stepped out onto a deck, one end of it covered against the elements. Standing at the edge, I looked out at the yard. A garden took up a little more than half the space, raspberry canes standing like sentries on the far side close to the fence. The rest was grass, with some flower beds around the outside. I smiled as I walked down the steps, taking the sidewalk toward the back fence. About halfway there, I turned around and looked at the house. I was home.

Walking back into the house, I secured the lock behind me. I strolled through the rooms again, turning on the lights and turning them off. There was a door that opened to the basement. Taking the steps down, I found an unfinished space, except for one bedroom tucked into the back corner. The furnace was relatively new, as was the hot water tank. There was a serviceable laundry room as well. An archaic washer and dryer sat there as evidence of that.

Climbing back up, I took the stairs to the third level. Here, I found two more rooms—the roof slanting up to a peak about three feet from the floor on the north and south walls. Windows on the other walls allowed the space to seem bright and airy. Both rooms had small closets. Inside the smaller bedroom, the chimney claimed about half the space, but it was still usable. Again, the paint choices were questionable, but paint was cheap.

The house was lovely—inside and out.

Back downstairs, I toured the main floor again before leaving by the front door. Stepping onto the front step, I took in the neighborhood. I liked what I saw. Shade would cover the entire street when the trees budded out. I locked the door behind me and took a deep breath before walking back to my vehicle.

I drove back to the apartment, my thoughts swirling. Once inside, I picked up the list and wrote the pros of being in the house, starting with the fact that it felt like home. The joy of having my space, of not having to be the maid, the cook, or the housekeeper for anyone, went on the list, too. I slipped the job into the mix because staying in the house meant keeping my job. I liked my job very much. Sure, it was hard work, and some days, the workload frazzled me, but more often, it gave me feelings of fulfillment and contentedness.

Walking to work, although a little farther, was possible. The house had a second bedroom upstairs, so baby Leah could come to stay when Debbie and Jonathon needed a break. I could have some family time with the newest member of my family.

Would I have chosen this life? I thought about that for several minutes. No, this wasn't my choice. If life hadn't handed me so many twists, if Leah hadn't died, if Caleb hadn't taken his life and others, and if Joe had supported me and not tossed me out … if—if—if.

Had none of these things happened, I would have lived out the rest of my days at the farm. I would have three children who would marry and have many grandbabies. I wouldn't know the difference, and I don't think I would have been truly unhappy.

But life threw me more than a few curve balls, and now I have the chance to live a new life. It would be a life on my terms, where I explored my needs and likes and dislikes without worrying about someone else. Sure, it might be selfish, but it also felt right.

I sat there for hours, going through the scenarios. The decision was huge, and I would not take it lightly.

The wrong choice closed doors I would find locked against me in the future. I needed to maintain what I had while exploring what else was out there.

With that, I made my decision. I would take the house and take it one day at a time. This new life, the one I stepped into months ago, was the right one for me. I hoped Joe would understand, stick to his word, and abide by my decision without repercussions.

As for Ben—well, I liked him. I liked him a lot but didn't know if I was ready to take on a new relationship. I also didn't want to shut him out of my life altogether. He was important to me. I hoped he would accept that I needed to take things slowly. Time was what I needed to fully heal, to reconcile the past and all that I lost and endured.

I was forty-seven years old and had gone from my mother's house to Joe's. I had never been on my own until a few months ago. I was discovering things about myself and liking what I saw. Learning to love myself for the first time had brought me joy, and learning to stand on my own two feet was paramount to keeping that. I was excited about the future and what it held for me.

Having made my decision, peace settled into my bones. I was strong and in control of my future.

Maybe it was time to read the journals again.

Digging out the box, I chose one near the bottom.

A cup of tea beside me, I read …

AFTERWORD

Dear Reader,

News stories of men murdering their wives and girlfriends are epidemic. In Canada, an intimate partner perpetrates sixty-six percent of all murders of women. In the United States, that statistic is only thirty-four percent. This information is from 2021 and even if it may have dropped—it's still too high.

As a reader, writer, and total mystery buff, there is nothing like a good murder. Unless it happens in your family. Then, it becomes something else. Thankfully, murder has never happened to me, but it shaped my fear of intimate relationships.

In my early teens, I stayed up late one night watching *The Ghost and Mr. Chicken* starring Don Knotts. The movie was a comedy, but my vivid imagination forced me to stay curled up on the couch instead of going to bed. I should have gone to bed.

The movie that followed terrified me. I wish I could tell you the title or even who starred in it. I have searched many times to no avail. In my memory, I can picture what the man in this movie looked like, but I cannot find him on a list of the stars from the film noir of that era.

The movie's opening scene showed a man and woman parked at Lover's Leap. He asks her to marry him, and she laughs hysterically. Her impertinence caused him to strangle her in the convertible and throw her off the cliff. As the scene ended, I sprang from the couch and slapped the off switch on the television as I ran to bed.

I slept little that night and for days afterward, a fear grew in my soul. Men are dangerous. Don't trust them … don't be alone with them … don't laugh at them.

There were more situations in my early life where men caused me to fear them. A naked man trying to break into my apartment. The police found and arrested him that night. Inebriated, he was looking for love in all the wrong places.

Another time, I was living on the main floor of a house when a man crawled through my open bedroom window. I got him to leave, but I no longer sleep with an open window.

The scariest one came when I lived on the edge of a wilderness area near the river. The building was a four-plex, so I did not feel isolated. I had good neighbors. One morning, a man ran by my window. When he saw me, he stopped to stare. His attention confused me until I noticed he was naked and aroused. I ran to the phone.

By the time I got back to the window, he was gone. I hung up the phone, relieved. My view changed moments later as he pressed his private area against the window. He had straddled my patio railing and the windowsill. I called the police. They never found him.

I noticed weird things the following week, like the outside light bulb being removed and noises that I could not interpret. I stayed in my apartment with the lights off. Weeks went by and the incidents tapered off as the weather turned colder. This made me less vigilant.

Several weeks later, as I left my apartment at six o'clock on a Sunday evening, this man confronted me. He was naked and threatening to do things to me. Terrified, I unlocked the passenger door of my car with my left hand as he pressed himself to my right side, whispering in my ear. I shoved him away. He laughed. Taller and stronger, I was no match for him.

I walked to the back of the car as he continued to tell me all he was going to do. When I got to the driver's side, he laughed again, telling me I was going in the right direction … toward the wooded area. I screamed, and he laughed as I looked around the neighborhood. No lights were on in any house nearby. I was alone.

I moved back toward the passenger side taillight. He continued to talk and threaten me, standing by the rear bumper on the other side. I knew it was now or never. I lunged for the passenger door, scrambled inside, locking the door behind me. He ran to the other door, finding it locked. He raged, pounding his fists on the car's roof, shouting his frustration and anger at losing his chance.

Furiously shaking, it took me some time to get over the console and into the driver's seat. All the while, the man vented his wrath. He jumped onto the car and was sitting on the windshield, masturbating, screaming in anger. He finished and jumped off the car before I got the key in the ignition.

When I exited the parking spot, I saw him standing on my patio, putting his clothes back on. I raced to a friend's house, falling down the stairs to her door. My demeanor scared her. Inside, I called the police, but again, they didn't find him.

They took my car, fingerprinting me for exclusion. I was thankful I had washed my car that morning, so the evidence was mostly his. Law enforcement did not collect his DNA—it was the early eighties. I never went back to this apartment. I moved to a new town twenty miles away, but I still had nightmares for months.

Years went by and no other incidents occurred. But I never got married and lived on my own terms.

Listening to talk radio, I heard many stories in the news of jilted husbands or lovers refusing to let go, needing to hold onto someone who no longer wants to be there. The results were often deadly, the consequences dire. I wrote short stories trying to understand the mind of someone who perpetrates these felonies. Despite all my years of watching true crime, the offenses of the younger men made no sense to me. I could not understand how any man barely starting his life could do something so heinous. My obsession took me in the direction of writing a novel. What came out was a mom's story. What happened to her? How did the family deal with what happened?

This book is not representative of any family. I know nothing about the perpetrators or anything about the victims' families other than the reports in the newspapers. I chose instead to read books about mothers who had to deal with the aftermath of murder. Sue Klebold's book *A Mother's Reckoning: Living in the Aftermath of Tragedy* was the first. From there, I wrote this book using my imagination and events that happened to friends in relationships.

The towns I placed my story in are fictitious. I avoided setting the book in any specific location because intimate partner murders aren't limited to a single city, province, state, or country. It happens all over the world.

Thank you for coming along on this journey through Joan's healing. I appreciate your time, and I hope you enjoyed meeting her. Andrea and Brenda's mothers have their own books. If you liked this novel, please stay tuned for the release dates of the two standalone books jumping off from the murder/suicide of Brenda, Andrea, and Caleb.

God bless you all. Stay safe.

Leslie Johnson

leslie.johnson2014@gmail.com

ABOUT THE AUTHOR

Leslie Johnson grew up in the shadow of Chief Mountain near the Alberta / Montana border. She loves to read, spending countless hours inside a good book. Many nights, her mother would find her under her covers with a flashlight reading her latest library find, long after she was supposed to be asleep. She still lives in windy southern Alberta where she moderates a writing group. If she's not writing, reading, or gardening, she's working on a jigsaw puzzle, playing with her cat, Milo or taking a walk in one of the many parks in the area.

www.ingramcontent.com/pod-product-compliance
Lightning Source LLC
Chambersburg PA
CBHW020637120726
47906CB00001B/6

* 9 7 8 1 0 6 9 3 5 8 8 8 2 *